Valentin Bertsch

AF238969

Uncertainty Handling in Multi-Attribute
Decision Support for Industrial Risk Management

Uncertainty Handling
in Multi-Attribute Decision Support
for Industrial Risk Management

von
Valentin Bertsch

universitätsverlag karlsruhe

Dissertation, Universität Karlsruhe (TH)
Fakultät für Wirtschaftswissenschaften, 2007
Tag der mündlichen Prüfung: 6.12.2007
Referent: Prof. Dr. O. Rentz
Korreferenten: Prof. Dr. U. Werner, Prof. Dr. J. Geldermann, Prof. Dr. S. French

Impressum

Universitätsverlag Karlsruhe
c/o Universitätsbibliothek
Straße am Forum 2
D-76131 Karlsruhe
www.uvka.de

Universitätsverlag Karlsruhe 2008
Print on Demand

ISBN: 978-3-86644-207-8

Uncertainty Handling in Multi-Attribute Decision Support for Industrial Risk Management

D I S S E R T A T I O N

zur Erlangung des akademischen Grades eines
Doktors der Wirtschaftswissenschaften
(Dr. rer. pol.)

eingereicht an der
Fakultät für Wirtschaftswissenschaften
der Universität Fridericiana zu Karlsruhe

von
Dipl.-Math. techn. Valentin Bertsch

Referent:
   Prof. Dr. O. Rentz
Korreferenten:
   Prof. Dr. U. Werner
   Prof. Dr. J. Geldermann
   Prof. Dr. S. French

eingereicht am: 2. Juli 2007
Tag der mündlichen Prüfung: 6. Dezember 2007

In zweifelhaften Fällen entscheide man sich für das Richtige.

Karl Kraus (1874–1936)

Vorwort

Die vorliegende Arbeit entstand während meiner Tätigkeit am Institut für Industriebetriebslehre und Industrielle Produktion (IIP) der Universität Karlsruhe (TH). Die Grundlage der Arbeit lieferte unter anderem ein umfangreiches Forschungsprojekt zum Risiko- und Notfallmanagement, das von der Europäischen Union im 6. Rahmenprogramm gefördert wurde.

Mit Freude nutze ich an dieser Stelle die Gelegenheit, all denen zu danken, die mich bei der Erstellung dieser Arbeit unterstützt haben. Besonderer Dank gilt meinem Doktorvater Prof. Dr. Otto Rentz für die Betreuung der Arbeit. Bei der ehemaligen Leiterin meiner Arbeitsgruppe „Technikbewertung und Risikomanagement" Prof. Dr. Jutta Geldermann (jetzt Universität Göttingen) möchte ich mich ganz herzlich für die Anregung zu dieser Arbeit, die Übernahme des Korreferats und ihre fachliche und persönliche Unterstützung bedanken. Darüber hinaus danke ich Dr. Michael Hiete, der die Leitung der Arbeitsgruppe Anfang 2007 übernommen hat. Des Weiteren gilt mein Dank Prof. Dr. Ute Werner (Lehrstuhl für Versicherungswissenschaft der Universität Karlsruhe (TH)) und Prof. Dr. Simon French (Manchester Business School) für das Übernehmen der Korreferate sowie für viele wertvolle Hinweise und fruchtbare Diskussionen.

Weiterhin haben die sehr gute Arbeitsatmosphäre im Allgemeinen sowie die unzähligen Diskussionen an der Kaffeemaschine im Besonderen zum Gelingen der Arbeit beigetragen. Insbesondere möchte ich mich hier bei meinen ehemaligen Kollegen Dr. Hannes Schollenberger und Dr. Martin Treitz sowie bei meinen Kollegen Jens Ludwig und Mirjam Merz für die freundschaftliche Zusammenarbeit und die konstruktiven Diskussionen auch über diese Arbeit hinaus bedanken. Weiterhin gilt mein Dank allen anderen – auch den ehemaligen – Kolleginnen und Kollegen des Instituts. Außerdem danke ich meinen Diplomanden, die insgesamt einen wichtigen Beitrag geleistet haben.

Im Rahmen des von der EU geförderten Forschungsprojektes EURANOS („European approach to nuclear and radiological emergency management and rehabilitation strategies") sind zahlreiche berufliche aber auch persönliche Kontakte entstanden. Dabei möchte ich besonders dem Projektkoordinator Herrn Wolfgang Raskob (Forschungszentrum Karlsruhe) und Dr. Florian Gering (Bundesamt für Strahlenschutz) für die wertvollen Anregungen und Diskussionen danken.

Nicht zuletzt danke ich meiner Freundin Judith, meinen Eltern und meinen Geschwistern sowie allen Personen, die mich stets unterstützt und mir zur Seite gestanden haben.

Karlsruhe, im Dezember 2007 Valentin Bertsch

Contents

List of Figures   v

List of Tables   ix

1 Introduction   1

  1.1 Decision Support for Industrial Risk Management 2

    1.1.1 Industrial Risks 2

    1.1.2 Multi-Criteria Aspects of Industrial Risk Management 4

    1.1.3 Uncertainties in Decision Processes 5

    1.1.4 Risks in the Energy Sector 6

  1.2 Objectives and Structure of the Thesis 8

2 Multi-Criteria Decision Analysis   11

  2.1 Purpose and Scope of MCDA 12

  2.2 Multi-Attribute Value Theory 14

    2.2.1 Steps in a MAVT Analysis 15

    2.2.2 Interpretation of MAVT as a Weighted Norm 24

  2.3 Multi-Attribute Utility Theory 28

    2.3.1 Steps in a MAUT Analysis 29

    2.3.2 Bayesian Decision Analysis 38

  2.4 Summary 41

3   Simulation-Based Uncertainty Analysis   **43**

   3.1   Classification and Treatment of Uncertainties   44

   3.2   Data Uncertainty   51

      3.2.1   Modelling and Propagation of Data Uncertainties   51

      3.2.2   Visualisation of Data Uncertainties   52

      3.2.3   Principal Component Analysis (PCA)   55

   3.3   Parameter Uncertainty   62

      3.3.1   Multi-Dimensional Inter-Criteria Sensitivity Analysis   65

      3.3.2   Multi-Dimensional Intra-Criteria Sensitivity Analysis   68

      3.3.3   Visualisation of Parameter Uncertainties   71

      3.3.4   Principal Component Analysis (PCA) for Parameter Uncertainties .   74

   3.4   Combined Consideration of Data and Parameter Uncertainties   77

      3.4.1   Integration of the Simulation Based Approaches for Parameter Uncertainties into MAUT   78

      3.4.2   Combined Consideration of Data and Parameter Uncertainties in the PCA Plane   82

   3.5   Summary   83

4   Decision Support for Nuclear Emergency and Remediation Management   **85**

   4.1   Background and General Setting   86

      4.1.1   Events at Nuclear Installations   86

      4.1.2   Moderated Workshops   87

   4.2   RODOS   89

      4.2.1   The Conceptual Structure   90

      4.2.2   Data Assimilation and Uncertainties in RODOS   91

      4.2.3   Economic Consequence Modelling in RODOS   94

      4.2.4   Web-HIPRE   96

| | 4.2.5 | The Explanation Module | 97 |

4.3 A Hypothetical Case Study 100

4.4 A Moderated Workshop 103

    4.4.1 Problem Structuring 105

    4.4.2 Preference Elicitation 107

    4.4.3 Selected Results 110

4.5 Uncertainty Modelling for the Case Study 115

    4.5.1 Data Uncertainty Modelling 115

    4.5.2 Preferential Uncertainty Modelling 118

4.6 Results for the Case Study 120

    4.6.1 Visualisation of Results for Deterministic Values 120

    4.6.2 Results Taking Data Uncertainties into Account 123

    4.6.3 Results Taking Preferential Uncertainties into Account 128

    4.6.4 Combined Analysis of Data and Parameter Uncertainties in the Context of the Case Study 137

4.7 Summarising Discussion of the Case Study 139

5 Conclusions and Outlook   **143**

5.1 Conclusions for Industrial Risk Management 143

5.2 Conclusions Concerning the Multi-Criteria Approach 145

5.3 Outlook 147

    5.3.1 Sequential Decision Making 147

    5.3.2 Indirect Consequence Assessment and Cascading Effects 151

6 Summary   **153**

Bibliography   **157**

A The Explanation Module   **177**

A.1 Content Determination 178

A.2 Discourse Planning 178

A.3 Sentence Generation 180

    A.3.1 Statistical Comparisons 181

    A.3.2 Sensitivity Analysis 182

A.4 A Step Towards Explaining the Results of Multi-Dimensional Sensitivity
Analysis 185

B Additional Data and Statistical Tests for the Case Study   189

B.1 Data Uncertainty Underlying the Calculations of the Case Study 189

B.2 A Statistical Test for the Data of the Case Study 200

    B.2.1 Procedure of the W Test 200

    B.2.2 Application of the W Test to the Data of the Case Study 201

List of Figures

1.1 Framework of Industrial Risk Management 3

1.2 Decision Support in Different Phases of an Emergency 8

2.1 Key Phases of MAVT [adapted from Belton and Stewart, 2002] 15

2.2 Example of an Attribute Tree (Hierarchy of Criteria) 17

2.3 Linear Value Functions 19

2.4 Exponential Value Functions 20

2.5 Performance Scores for the Example Illustrated as a Stacked-Bar Chart . 22

2.6 Sensitivity Analysis Graph for the Considered Example 23

2.7 Spider Diagram for the Considered Example 24

2.8 Illustration of a Spider Diagram Incorporating Weights 25

2.9 Exemplar Illustration of Different Alternatives in $\mathbb{R}^3$ 26

2.10 Exemplar Illustration of the 1-Norm in $\mathbb{R}^3$ 27

2.11 The Relation Between the Shape of a Utility Function and Attitude to Risk 30

2.12 Expected Utilities for the Considered Example Illustrated as a Bar Chart 35

2.13 Weight Sensitivity Analysis in MAUT for the Considered Example 37

2.14 Risk Attitude Sensitivity Analysis in MAUT for the Considered Example . 38

2.15 Process of Bayesian Decision Making [adapted from French, 2003] 41

3.1 Classification of Uncertainties [adapted from Basson, 2004] 48

3.2 Representation of Uncertainties in Results by Showing Results for all Scenarios (Left); Same Results Sorted by Alt_4 (Right) 53

3.3 Representation of Uncertainties in Results by Means of a Stacked-Bar Chart 54

3.4 Alternatives and Attributes Evenly Spread in the PCA Plane 58

3.5 Alternatives and Attributes Unevenly Spread in the PCA Plane 59

3.6 Projections of the Alternatives on the PCA Plane and on the Weighting Vector 60

3.7 Visualisation of an Aggregated Ranking in the PCA Plane 61

3.8 Representation of Data Uncertainty in the PCA Plane: Clearly Distinguishable Scatter Plots 61

3.9 Representation of Data Uncertainty in the PCA Plane: Scatter Plots are not Clearly Distinguishable 62

3.10 Intersection of the Weight Intervals and the (Hyper-)Surface Representing the Valid Weights in 3D 66

3.11 Proposed Procedure to Ensure that the Sum of the Weights is Equal to 1 68

3.12 Value Function Shapes for Different Values of the Parameter ρ_i and Illustrative Visualisation of an Interval $I(\rho_i)$ 70

3.13 Value Function Shapes for Different Values of the Parameter x^i_{max} 71

3.14 Possible Results for the Considered Example when Varying the Quadruple $(w, \rho, x_{min}, x_{max})$ 72

3.15 Possible Results Sorted by Alternative 4 73

3.16 Backwards Calculation 74

3.17 Projected Weight Space Ω in the PCA Plane 75

3.18 A Preference Region within Ω in the PCA Plane 76

3.19 Combined Illustration of all Preferential Uncertainties in the PCA Plane . 77

3.20 Expected Utilities Sorted by Alternative 4 for $\kappa = 0.25$ (left) and $\kappa = 1$ (right) 79

3.21 Uncertainty Factor for Different Values of κ (Left: $\kappa = 0.25$, Right: $\kappa = 1$) 80

3.22 Weight Space Exploration for Uncertainty Factor   80

3.23 Combined Consideration of Data and Parameter Uncertainties in the PCA
     Plane   82

4.1 Steps of a Moderation Cycle and of Multi-Criteria Decision Analysis [adapted
     from Geldermann and Rentz, 2004]   89

4.2 The Conceptual Structure of RODOS [cf. e.g. Ehrhardt and Weiss, 2000;
     French et al., 2000]   90

4.3 Data Assimilation and Uncertainties in the RODOS Model Chain [adapted
     from Rojas-Palma et al., 2003]   93

4.4 Access to Background Information in Web-HIPRE [cf. Bertsch et al., 2006b]   97

4.5 The Process of Preference Elicitation and Evaluation in RODOS and Web-
     HIPRE [adapted from French, 2000; Bertsch et al., 2006b]   99

4.6 Ground Contamination for Iodine I-131 in the Surrounding Area of the
     Nuclear Power Plant   101

4.7 Ground Contamination for Caesium Cs-137 in the Surrounding Area of the
     Nuclear Power Plant   102

4.8 Attribute Tree for the Hypothetical Case Study   107

4.9 Results of Decision Analysis Illustrated as a Stacked-Bar Chart   110

4.10 Sensitivity Analysis on the Weight of "acceptance"   111

4.11 Sensitivity Analysis on the Weight of "impact"   111

4.12 Extract of a Comparative Report   112

4.13 Spider Diagram for the Case Study   121

4.14 PCA Plane for the Case Study   122

4.15 Expected Utilities for $\kappa = 0.5$ Visualised as Bar Chart   124

4.16 Sensitivity of Expected Utilities with Respect to κ 124

4.17 Sensitivity of Expected Utilities with Respect to the Weight of "accep-
     tance" (for $\kappa = 0.5$)   125

4.18 Overall Performance Scores for the Different Scenarios   126

4.19 Visualisation of Uncertainties in Results Using a Stacked-Bar Chart 126

4.20 PCA Visualising the Uncertainty of the Data in the Different Scenarios . . 127

4.21 Impact of Inter-Criteria Preferential Uncertainties on the Results 129

4.22 Impact of Inter-Criteria Preferential Uncertainties on the Results Sorted in
       Ascending Order of "Rmov,T=0" 130

4.23 Backwards Calculation Concerning Inter-Criteria Preference Parameters . 131

4.24 Impact of Intra-Criteria Preferential Uncertainties on the Results 132

4.25 Backwards Calculation Concerning Intra-Criteria Preference Parameters . 133

4.26 Impact of all Preferential Uncertainties on the Results 134

4.27 Impact of all Preferential Uncertainties on the Results Sorted in Ascending
       Order of "Rmov,T=0" 135

4.28 Complete Overview of the Impact of Preferential Uncertainties in the PCA
       Plane 136

4.29 Expected Utilities Versus Cumulative Percentage Sorted by "Rmov,T=0"
       (Left) and "Disp" (Right) 138

4.30 Combined Illustration of the Impact of Data and Parameter Uncertainties
       in the PCA Plane 139

5.1   Influence Diagram for Multiple Time Steps and Multiple Attributes 148

5.2   Decision Tree Corresponding to the Influence Diagram in Figure 5.1 . . . 149

A.1   The General Structure of the Explanation Module 177

A.2   Text Plans for the Comparative Report 179

A.3   Text Plan for the Sensitivity Analysis Report 179

A.4   An Illustrative Comparative Report 182

A.5   Extract of an Illustrative Sensitivity Analysis Report 184

A.6   Proposed Text Plan for a Multi-Dimensional Sensitivity Analysis Report . 185

List of Tables

2.1   Decision Table Corresponding to the Attribute Tree in Figure 2.2 18

4.1   The International Nuclear Event Scale (INES) [cf. IAEA, 1999] 87

4.2   Selected Decision Attributes and their Respective Meanings 106

4.3   Higher Level Criteria and their Respective Meanings 106

4.4   Decision Table – Part 1 – Values Directly Calculated by RODOS 113

4.5   Decision Table – Part 2 – Values Estimated by Experts and Stakeholders (On a Fictitious 0–100 Scale) 114

4.6   Sampled Values for Mean Wind Direction and Source Term Relative to Deterministic Values 116

4.7   Assigned Weight Intervals 119

B.1   Decision Table – Part 1 – Scenario 1 190

B.2   Decision Table – Part 1 – Scenario 2 191

B.3   Decision Table – Part 1 – Scenario 3 192

B.4   Decision Table – Part 1 – Scenario 4 193

B.5   Decision Table – Part 1 – Scenario 5 194

B.6   Decision Table – Part 1 – Scenario 6 195

B.7   Decision Table – Part 1 – Scenario 7 196

B.8   Decision Table – Part 1 – Scenario 8 197

B.9   Decision Table – Part 1 – Scenario 9 198

B.10 Decision Table – Part 1 – Scenario 10 199

B.11 Results for the Test Statistics W_{ij} (All Values in the Table are Dimension-
     less) 202

Chapter 1

Introduction

In modern industrial production networks and their external environment, complex decision situations need to be resolved with respect to their potential impact on the society in a wide variety of circumstances. Usually, various scientific expert groups are involved with heterogeneous technical background knowledge in different disciplines. Know-how from economic, ecological, engineering and natural sciences must be brought together, taking into account political and socio-psychological factors. For instance, political decisions must be justified and communicated to the public. Similarly, the rationale behind entrepreneurial or managerial decisions needs to be explained to the employees but also to the shareholders of a company. Thus, the way in which a decision is communicated is of particular importance. Risk communication and participatory approaches for decision making have gained increasing importance, in particular in societal and political areas such as risk governance or emergency management after extreme events – both man-made and natural [for recent reviews see, e.g. Beierle and Cayford, 2002; Renn, 2004; Geldermann et al., 2007].

The frequency of the occurrence of extreme events has increased considerably in recent years – on a global scale, but also in Germany. However, neither are we well prepared on a civil level nor on an industrial or economic level to cope with the consequences of unexpected emergencies. Because of the global interlacement, the hierarchical structure and the dynamic evolution of industrial supply chain networks, the tracking of consequences of disasters becomes a highly complex issue.

1.1 Decision Support for Industrial Risk Management

The complexity of contemporary production systems and an increased environmental vulnerability indicate that current problems with industrial risk management require a rethinking of safety management [Bernold, 1989; UNISDR, 2002]. In order to handle potential risks to and emanating from the industry and consequently to mankind as well as the environment, an integrated approach to risk management and industrial environmental policy is needed. Consequently, risk management in industry is related to major accident hazards [Seveso II Directive 96/82/EC], to occupational health and safety [ATEX Directive 94/9/EC] and to the environment [IPPC Directive 96/61/EC].

1.1.1 Industrial Risks

A production company, complete industrial production systems or the society in general are exposed to various different types of risk every day. However, when using the term *risk*, it should be noted that there is a wide variety of different definitions of *risk* in literature. The exact meaning depends to a large extent on who defines, i.e. on the discipline in which it is used. In the financial sector for instance, the word is mainly used in terms of investment and credit risk, being regulated by law since 1998 in Germany [cf. KonTraG, 1998] and since 2006 in Europe [cf. Directive 2006/48/EC; Directive 2006/49/EC][1].

In the area of natural disasters, risk is often defined as being influenced by the probability or frequency of occurrence and the extent of loss (often the product of both) [cf. e.g. Helm, 1996; Smith, 1996]. While the probability or frequency of occurrence is often also described by or contained in the term *hazard*, the extent of loss is often expressed as a combination of the *elements at risk* and the *vulnerability* [cf. e.g. Granger et al., 1999] or the *exposure* and the *vulnerability* [cf. e.g. Crichton, 1999]. Consequently, the total risk can be said to depend on three elements: hazard (or probability), vulnerability and exposure (or elements at risk) [cf. e.g. Blong, 1996; Crichton, 1999; Granger et al., 1999].

In industry, the word risk is usually used in more technical terms in relation to technical failures in the operating procedure [cf. e.g. Hahn and Laßmann, 1999]. Failures in industrial operating procedures and the potentially arising emergency situations, however, can differ in many ways. Concerning their causes for instance, they may originate from the production process itself (or rather from losing control over the production process, i.e. the situation is *internally induced* or *man-made*) or may be induced externally, for

---

[1] The directives 2006/48/EC and 2006/49/EC can be regarded as the European implementation of the BASEL II accord.

instance by a natural disaster (i.e. the situation is *externally* or *naturally induced*). This is illustrated in Figure 1.1. The respective dimensions of the emergency situations' impact may differ considerably, too. Nevertheless, the dimensions are not immediately related to the causes, which means that the resulting consequences for the society and the environment can be very similar for internally and externally induced industrial emergencies. While emergency situations, in general, can differ substantially as regards their causes and the dimension of their respective impacts, as just mentioned, they share some common characteristics, such as the sudden onset or the necessity for a coherent and effective management of the crisis [Geldermann et al., 2007].

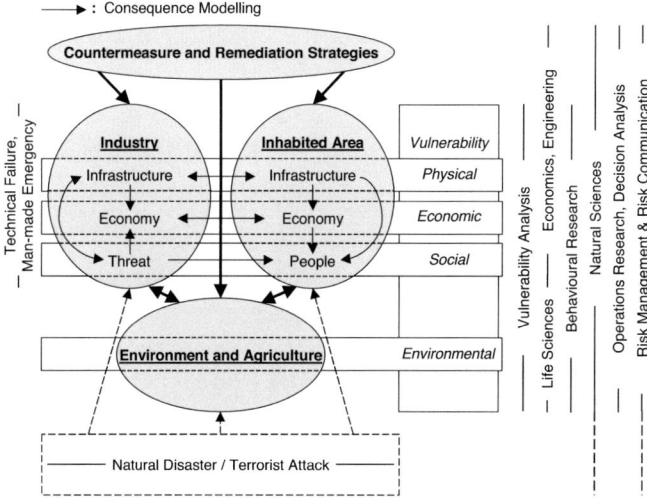

Figure 1.1: Framework of Industrial Risk Management

Furthermore, Figure 1.1 indicates that emergencies in industrial systems may be caused by a terrorist attack, a discussion which has recently gained much attention [cf. e.g. Esquivié and Wybo, 2003; Kincaid et al., 2003; Werner and Lechtenbörger, 2004; Richardson et al., 2006; Flaherty, 2007]. An emergency situation caused by an act of terrorism can of course not be called naturally induced but since it constitutes an external impact on an industrial system, it is shown in one "category" with natural disasters. However, the focus of this thesis shall not be on modelling the consequences of an external event on industrial systems, which is why the category of external influences on industrial systems is illustrated with dashed lines in Figure 1.1. Rather, emphasis is placed on providing support for the evaluation of countermeasure and remediation strategies in the aftermath of an industrial emergency. Thereby, special focus is put on analysing the consequences of industrial emergencies and alternative countermeasure and remediation strategies for the society and the environment (including agricultural land). In order to support a structured analysis, methods from the area of operations research will be applied. General links between the fields of operations research and environmental policy have for instance been discussed by Rentz [2004]. However, the knowledge acquired by such analyses can also be used for countermeasure planning purposes, for instance in emergency exercises, and can thus contribute to an improved emergency preparedness and risk awareness. The latter is also important with respect to spatial planning in the context of disaster risk reduction, a discussion that has recently gained increasing attention [cf. e.g. UNISDR, 2002; Kötter, 2003; Werner et al., 2004; Merz et al., 2007].

1.1.2 Multi-Criteria Aspects of Industrial Risk Management

Risks to people and the environment emerging from industrial production or the use and disposal of chemical substances are addressed in various initiatives. For instance, the "Toxic Substances Control Act" [cf. TSCA 15 U.S.C. S/S 2601 et seq. 1976] regulates production, import and use of chemicals potentially posing an environmental or human-health hazard in the United States. Accordingly, the new European chemicals regulation (REACH[2] [cf. Directive 2006/121/EC; Regulation (EC) No 1907/2006]) is aimed at improving the protection of human health and the environment in Europe. Besides the registration of chemical substances produced or imported into the EU and the identification of appropriate risk management measures, a basic principle of REACH is to put more responsibility for managing the risks from chemicals on the industry itself and to provide safety information which shall be passed through the supply chain. However, special attention must be paid when the individual production processes are coupled and when the time and length scales of the production processes within the supply chain are strongly disparate. The modelling of such processes necessitates integrated, multidisciplinary and multiscale approaches [cf. Charpentier, 2005]. The same holds for the management of the risks emerging from such processes at different time and length scales.

Besides acknowledging different time and length scales of industrial processes and risks, the handling of industrial risks, especially in the remediation or recovery phase of an emergency, involves the evaluation of various, at least partially conflicting objectives.

---

[2] REACH: "Registration, Evaluation and Authorisation of Chemicals", adopted in December 2006 and entering into force on 1 June 2007.

Perhaps most importantly, health and safety aspects, the environmental impact and the technical feasibility need to be considered besides the purely economic factors. An explicit examination of the trade-offs between these conflicting objectives plays an important role in providing a profound understanding of a decision situation.

Furthermore, as indicated in Figure 1.1, different levels of vulnerability need to be explored and knowledge from diverse scientific disciplines and methodologies must be brought together for an integrated evaluation of industrial risks.[3] Approaches from Multi-Criteria Decision Analysis (MCDA) can help to consider various incommensurable levels of information – quantitative as well as qualitative – and to take into account the (subjective) preferences of the responsible decision makers and thus contribute to transparency and traceability of decision making processes [Belton and Stewart, 2002; Geldermann et al., 2007].

Additionally, with the increasing demand from the media and the public for information and justification from authorities, methods are required to assess how decisions are taken [Wybo, 2006]. Providing a basis for participatory processes and group decisions, MCDA seeks to facilitate the communication with the public and the media and can be helpful in forming an audit trail and in enhancing public confidence and understanding in relation to complex group decisions [cf. Bose et al., 1997; Belton and Stewart, 2002; Bertsch et al., 2007b].

1.1.3   Uncertainties in Decision Processes

In practice, decision processes are usually affected by different sources of uncertainty. On the one hand, when evaluating alternative countermeasure and remediation strategies in the aftermath of an industrial emergency, the consequences of these alternative strategies with respect to the considered objectives/criteria can often not be determined deterministically. Such uncertainties, which eventually affect the input data of a decision model, may for instance be due to model approximations, measurements or inherent randomness. On the other hand, the subjective preferences of the responsible decision makers, which are explicitly taken into account in MCDA, constitute a major source of uncertainty – which is introduced during the decision process. Additionally, uncertainties may result from the fact that models are ultimately only simplifications of reality [cf. e.g. French

---

[3] The respective parts of the application ranges of the research disciplines covering the external influences on industrial systems are, again, illustrated by means of dashed lines in Figure 1.1 since these parts are not focussed on within this thesis.

and Niculae, 2005] but such uncertainties are usually difficult to quantify and can also be regarded as inherent to any model.

The presence of one or several types of uncertainty, however, influences the results of a decision model. Consequently, appropriate methods are required which allow to investigate the impact of the different sources of uncertainty on the results of the analysis. In particular, in order to be able to explore the robustness of decision processes, it is important to analyse which uncertainties are most relevant in terms of the results.

A demanding task in the context of complex production systems is the propagation of uncertainties through complex model chains. Especially, attention must be paid when encountered with nonlinear models within the model chain.

1.1.4   Risks in the Energy Sector

Energy supply is a very important part of critical infrastructure. An area-wide, secure electricity supply is essential for the functioning of a modern society [Ebeling and Böhmer, 2005]. However, critical infrastructure, such as energy transmission networks, can be severely damaged, destroyed or disrupted by technical failure (accidents), human failure (negligence), natural disasters, criminal activity or acts of terrorism [cf. e.g. Green Paper COM (2005) 576 final, of the European Commission] leading to supply interruptions which may have a severe impact on industry and economy as well as the society as a whole. Thus, crisis situations in the energy sector constitute a special challenge in comparison to emergency preparedness and management in many other areas which often involve contingency plans or checklists that have been prepared in advance and are more or less regularly utilised in emergency exercises.

Within the energy sector, risk management is especially relevant in nuclear power generation – inter alia because of the resulting severe and far-reaching consequences of a potential emergency. Furthermore, besides the fact that an increased awareness of the possibility of technical failure of industrial systems and an improved preparedness to deal with the risks and to cope with emergencies, are desirable in general, risk management and emergency planning are very important in nuclear power generation due to the fact that a large part of electricity is generated by nuclear energy – in Europe as well as world-wide.

World-wide, 437 nuclear power plant units with an installed electric net capacity of about 390 GW are in operation (status of December 2006) and 29 units with an approximate capacity of 25 GW are under construction [Nuclear Power World Report 2006]. The global net electricity generation from nuclear energy amounts to about 2 738 TWh in 2004, the total production since 1951 amounts to 51 375 TWh. The cumulative operating experience amounts to 11 500 years by the end of 2004.[4] Focussing on Europe, as of January 2006, there are a total of 204 nuclear power units with an installed net electric capacity of 171.99 GWe in operation and eight units with 7.93 GWe are under construction in four countries. In the countries of the European Union (EU-25), 32 % of electricity was generated by nuclear energy in 2006. Here, France holds the top position in electricity from nuclear energy with a share of 78 % followed by Lithuania (70 %), the Slovak Republic (57 %), Belgium (54 %) and Sweden (48 %). In Germany, where seven nuclear power plants of the top ten for world-wide electricity generation are located in 2006, electricity from nuclear energy has a share of 26 %. In addition, results of a model developed for France [cf. Fleury, 2005] show that the share of electricity from nuclear energy will remain similarly high at least until 2020 and that, under certain assumptions, the nuclear power plants decommissioned in the period 2020–2030 (assuming a life-time of 40 years for the existing nuclear power plants in France) will be replaced by new ones in order to satisfy the increasing energy demand.

Summarising, there are two major groups of reasons for which risk management, emergency preparedness and countermeasure planning are relevant topics in nuclear power generation. Firstly, although the frequency of occurrence of an emergency with a release of radioactive material is considered to be low, the consequences can be severe and far-reaching. Secondly, the security of electricity supply has recently attracted much attention [de Nooij et al., 2003]. Due to the substantial share of power generation from nuclear energy, these topics are not only relevant from the perspective of radiation protection. Concerning the first group of reasons, devising a contingency plan for nuclear emergencies that covers all imaginable eventualities is an impossible task. Hence, a flexible decision support system providing reliable information and guidance is needed in order to support those who are faced with the difficult job of managing such an emergency. In particular, the evaluation of long-term remediation strategies after a nuclear or radiological accident can benefit from operationally applicable multi-criteria methods and evaluation techniques to guide and support the responsible decision makers in the decision making process (see Figure 1.2).

In the immediate response phase, reliable information from powerful information systems is very important to enable decision makers to take fast decisions. In the remediation or recovery phase, the situation is more complex. Since the public acceptance of decisions in the late phase is essential for a successful implementation of the remediation strategies,

---

[4] See e.g. http://www.kernenergie.de as well as http://world-nuclear.org.

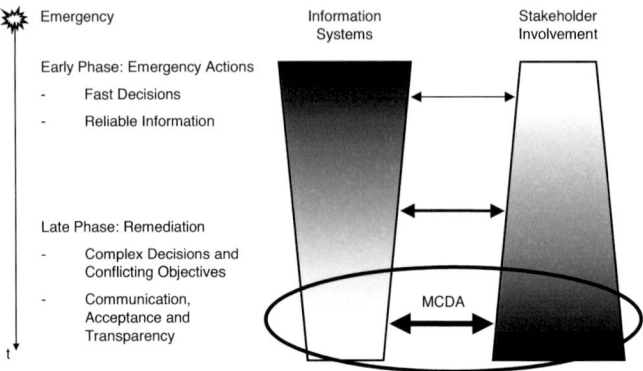

Figure 1.2: Decision Support in Different Phases of an Emergency

the affected stakeholders should not only be involved in the decision process but should also be considered as decision makers. It should be emphasised at this point that, in practice, decisions in the context of risk and emergency management are usually taken by groups of decision makers rather than by a single decision maker. Consequently, decision makers are referred to in plural throughout the whole thesis.

1.2   Objectives and Structure of the Thesis

Managing the risks emerging from today's complex and globally interlaced production networks has become increasingly important in the light of a rising number of emergencies and extreme events. The resolution of complex decision situations after a potential emergency involves the consideration of various criteria. A key challenge arises from the fact that, on the one hand, decision processes in practice are usually subject to different sources of uncertainty and that, on the other hand, especially on a political level, the way in which a decision is communicated is highly relevant, i.e. methods are needed to explain the rationale behind a decision.

Consequently, the main objective of this thesis is to develop an approach for an integrated uncertainty handling in decision support for industrial risk management. Rather than analysing the (economic) impact of industrial emergencies to the industry itself, i.e. assessing the occurring direct and indirect losses, the focus of this thesis is on analysing the impact on the society and the environment arising from such emergency situations and on providing support for the evaluation of alternative remediation strategies in the aftermath of an emergency using methods from the field of operations research. Thereby, special emphasis will be placed on appropriate graphical illustrations in order to support the tangibility of the results. In order to address these objectives, this thesis is structured as follows:

Providing the basis for the evaluation of various conflicting objectives and consequently for the resolution of complex decision situations, a general introduction into multi-criteria decision analysis is given in Chapter 2. After pointing out fundamental differences between MCDA and cost benefit analysis, an overview of multi-attribute value theory and multi-attribute utility theory is provided. The chapter is completed by a brief outline of Bayesian decision analysis and by a short summary of the relevance of the described methods.

The focus of Chapter 3 is the development of new approaches for uncertainty handling in MCDA. Firstly, an extensive classification of different types of uncertainty that may affect a decision is given. Secondly, simulation-based approaches to handle the different types of uncertainty are described with a special focus on visualising the impact of the occurring uncertainties on the results of the respective decision models. Chapter 3 is concluded by proposing approaches for a combined consideration of different types of uncertainty and by shortly summarising the added value of the described and developed methods.

Results of multi-criteria decision support for industrial risk management are presented for a case study in the area of emergency and remediation management in nuclear power generation in Chapter 4. The case study constitutes a major part of this research and demonstrates the features of the preceding chapters. After describing the general background of the case study, the different components of the real-time online decision support system for nuclear emergency management (RODOS) are introduced. Subsequently, the course of action as well as main results of a stakeholder workshop are described, in which the applicability of RODOS and MCDA to support a decision making process in the aftermath of a hypothetically assumed accident scenario at a nuclear power plant was demonstrated. Special emphasis within Chapter 4 is placed on the application of the developed and implemented approaches for uncertainty handling in MCDA in the context of the case study. Again, the value of visualisation techniques to support the communication of the effect of the different types of uncertainty on the achieved results is pointed out.

In Chapter 5, the main aspects of the methods developed within this thesis are discussed and the major contributions of this research are shown. This is pursued by a detailed discussion of the approaches, contrasting the advantages as well as the limitations. Additionally, potential areas of future research are highlighted.

The most important findings as well as possibilities for future research concerning the developed multi-criteria decision support approach for industrial risk management are summarised in Chapter 6.

These six chapters are complemented by two appendices. While Appendix A provides additional information on how the results of decision making processes can be explained by generating natural language reports, detailed information on the uncertainties in the underlying data set of the case study is compiled in Appendix B.

Chapter 2

Multi-Criteria Decision Analysis

Seeking to provide transparent and coherent support for the resolution of complex decision situations and aiming at facilitating the communication between all involved parties, much effort has been spent on the development of methods in the area of multi-criteria decision analysis (MCDA). As an alternative analytical approach, cost benefit analysis (CBA, cf. e.g. Brent [1996]; Pearce and Nash [1981]; Layard [1972] for a general introduction to CBA and its use) is frequently used in government and industry for a quantitative evaluation of risk related decisions [French et al., 2005]. The basic principle of CBA is the expression of all benefits and disadvantages of a decision in monetary terms, i.e. the value of a decision is determined by subtracting the net expected costs in monetary terms from the net expected benefits, again, in monetary terms. Proponents of CBA often claim that CBA is more objective than MCDA. However, this objectivity largely depends on the question whether or not all prices or, more generally, all consequences of a decision can be determined unambiguously. It should be noted that especially criteria such as the environmental impacts, safety, (ecological) risk and human values related to a decision cannot be easily condensed into a monetary value as required for CBA. For instance, environmental concerns often involve ethical and moral considerations which might not be related to any economic value [Linkov et al., 2004]. In addition, even if it were possible to transform all criteria into a monetary unit, this approach would not always be desirable since the stakeholders' preferences would presumably be lost in such a process [Kiker et al., 2005]. Hence, MCDA is strongly preferred for the context of this research since, by explicitly acknowledging the subjectivity in decision making processes, it provides a clear, transparent and traceable analysis as opposed to the illusory objectivity of CBA [French et al., 2005]. Additionally, by providing a sound framework for sensitivity analysis, MCDA offers valuable support for consensus finding within decision making groups.

2.1   Purpose and Scope of MCDA

Various MCDA methods, based on different theoretical foundations, have been developed. However, they all have in common that they evolved as a response to the inability of people to analyse multiple streams of unalike information in a structured way [cf. e.g. Linkov et al., 2004; Kiker et al., 2005] and that they are aimed at reducing incomparabilities between alternatives which would remain according to the "natural" dominance relation. According to this classical dominance definition, an alternative is said to dominate another if it is better on one criterion and at least as good as the other on all other criteria. If one alternative is better with respect to one criterion and another one is better with respect to another criterion, these two alternatives are incomparable [Brans and Mareschal, 2005]. Moreover, alternatives that are not dominated by any other alternative are called efficient [cf. also Koopmans, 1951]. The aim of MCDA methods is to reduce the incomparabilities by explicitly incorporating preferential information of the decision maker(s) [Brans and Mareschal, 2005; Treitz, 2006]. In general, two different types of preferential information can be distinguished:

1. Preferential information on the importance of differences of the performance scores of the different alternatives with respect to one criterion, i.e. comparisons within a criterion or *intra-criteria* preferential information.

2. Preferential information on the relative importance of the different criteria, i.e. comparisons between the criteria or *inter-criteria* preferential information.

In general, MCDA approaches can be subdivided into two classes: Multi-Objective Decision Making (MODM) approaches and Multi-Attribute Decision Making (MADM) approaches. While MODM methods are applied to continuous optimisation problems where several goals shall be optimised simultaneously, multi-attribute decision models have been successfully applied to support decision processes in many different contexts where the most preferable option was to be chosen from a (discrete) set of decision alternatives. The latter can be helpful for decision making in industrial risk management since the set of decision options is usually discrete in this context.

Within the field of MADM methods, the so-called "classical" approaches, such as multi-attribute value or multi-attribute utility theory (MAVT or MAUT) for instance, can be distinguished from outranking approaches such as e.g. PROMETHEE [Brans et al., 1984; Brans and Vincke, 1985] or ELECTRE [Roy and Bouyssou, 1993; Roy, 1996; Figueira et al., 2005]. In MAVT/MAUT as well as in outranking approaches, inter-criteria preferences are modelled by weighting factors. The main difference is in the modelling of the intra-criteria preferences. While the preference functions in outranking approaches are based on (relative) comparisons of the performances of the decision alternatives, the value functions in MAVT/MAUT are applied to the absolute performance scores of the alternatives.[5] The second basic difference is that MAVT/MAUT are fully compensatory approaches while outranking approaches also provide partial rankings, i.e. the incomparabilities are only partially resolved.

In practice, MADM problems can show various characteristics [cf. e.g. Belton and Stewart, 2002]. For instance, they can be classified according to the following properties:

- **Number of decision makers**: There may be a single person being responsible for a decision or there may be groups of different sizes where the different group members may have similar or very different goals, responsibilities and interests. While multi-attribute decision support can help a single decision maker to identify a decision directly in a transparent way, the main focus of using MADM methods in larger groups is the facilitation of consensus finding.

- **Presence of a moderator/facilitator**: This point is closely interconnected with the previous one. The individual steps within a MADM process are often carried out in a moderated/facilitated discussion, especially in larger groups of decision makers. However, single decision makers or smaller groups, who are experienced in applying MADM methods, may also want to carry out the decision making process by themselves. Nevertheless, since it is likely that decision making in industrial risk management involves rather large groups of decision makers, it is assumed in the following that there is a moderator/facilitator who guides the group through the MADM process.

- **Underlying data**: The input data of a decision model may be deterministic or may be subject to uncertainty. In practice, a decision making process is often affected by different types of uncertainty. The occurring uncertainties can be classified in several different ways [cf. for instance Gering, 2005; Bertsch et al., 2005; French, 1995; Morgan and Henrion, 1990]. According to their respective source, a distinction can be made between "data uncertainties" (uncertainties of the input data of a decision model), "parameter uncertainties" (uncertainties related to the subjective (preference) parameters of a MCDA model) and "model uncertainties" (uncertainties resulting from the fact that models are ultimately only simplifica-

---

[5] These different "schools of thought" are often discussed controversially in literature. However, they all have their (context-dependent) strengths and weaknesses [cf. Stewart and Losa, 2003] and such a discussion shall not be the focus of this research.

tions/approximations of reality [cf. French and Niculae, 2005]), where the latter are usually difficult to quantify and can also be regarded as inherent to the nature of any model. The presence of one or several types of uncertainty, however, should influence the choice of an appropriate MADM method. The topic of uncertainty handling in MADM will be dealt with in Section 2.3 as well as Chapter 3.

- **Time-frame of a decision**: Decisions may be operational, tactical or strategic, i.e. their time horizon may vary between hours or days and several years. Additionally, decisions may be taken at one single point or may be nested in a series of decisions which are related to each other. In the latter case, up-to-date data – if available – would be included for each new decision. The static or dynamic/sequential character of decision problems should be reflected by the decision support methods. However, in the following it is mostly assumed that the decisions can be taken at a single point.

In the following, the MAVT and MAUT approaches are described in more detail. Additionally, as one family of approaches within utility theory, the Bayesian decision paradigm is briefly outlined. MAVT and MAUT seem to be suitable to support decision making in industrial risk management because of their simple and transparent nature [cf. e.g. Papamichail, 2000]. Furthermore, they have already proved to suit for application in the context of emergency management [Geldermann et al., 2007; Hämäläinen et al., 2000; French, 1996]. Additionally, e.g. as far as radiation related risk management is concerned, the International Commission on Radiological Protection (ICRP) recommends MAVT in radiation protection [ICRP, 1989]. While in MAVT it is assumed that the underlying data of the decision analysis is deterministic, MAUT provides a formal framework for the modelling and handling of uncertainties. However, the algorithms associated with MAUT are much more complex which makes their applicability in practice problematic.

2.2 Multi-Attribute Value Theory

In the following it is assumed that the most preferable decision alternative is to be chosen from a (discrete) set of different alternatives. Thereby, the alternatives shall be evaluated with respect to different criteria. In order to support decision makers to find a solution to such a multi-criteria decision problem, multi-attribute value theory (MAVT) provides methods to structure and analyse such problems by means of an attribute tree (i.e. a hierarchy of criteria) and to elicit the relative importance of the criteria in such a tree

[Geldermann et al., 2007]. In an attribute tree the overall goal is divided hierarchically into lower level objectives (criteria) and – on the lowest level – measurable attributes.

The essential interactive steps in a MAVT analysis (see Figure 2.1) include firstly the structuring of the problem into an attribute tree and secondly the elicitation of the relative importance of the criteria. Subsequently, the elicited information is aggregated in order to obtain a ranking of the considered decision alternatives. An attribute tree allows to represent and evaluate the decision makers' priorities by an overall value score and break it down under different criteria as well as to study the sensitivity to changes in the weights.

Figure 2.1: Key Phases of MAVT [adapted from Belton and Stewart, 2002]

2.2.1   Steps in a MAVT Analysis

Within this thesis, the general notion for MAVT is as follows: m denotes the number of different alternatives which shall be evaluated with respect to a total of n attributes. Furthermore, a general decision alternative is denoted by a and $s_i(a)$ is the score of alternative a with respect to attribute i (where $1 \leq i \leq n$). Specific decision alternatives will be denoted by Alt_j (where $1 \leq j \leq m$). In order to describe the basic steps of MAVT, it is assumed that the task of a team of decision makers is to evaluate the four alternatives $Alt_1 - Alt_4$ with respect to the four attributes A_1, A_2, A_3, A_4 (i.e. $m = 4$ and $n = 4$). This example will be referred to throughout chapters 2 and 3.

For instance, assuming that a choice is to be made between different countermeasure or remediation alternatives $(Alt_1 - Alt_4)$ in the aftermath of an industrial emergency, various attributes $(A_1 - A_4)$ need to be taken into account. Besides the purely economic factors, it may be important to consider human health and safety aspects, the environmental impact and the technical feasibility related to a decision. However, the relevance of different attributes and criteria affecting a decision – quantitative as well as qualitative – and how they can be taken into account respectively will be dealt with in detail in the context of the case study in Chapter 4.

2.2.1.1   Problem Structuring

The process of problem structuring is concerned with appropriately formulating rather than solving a problem [Belton and Stewart, 2002]. It is a very important part of a MAVT analysis since it gives a better understanding of both, the problem and the values affecting a decision, and also serves as a basis for further analyses and as a common language for communication [Rosenhead and Mingers, 2001; Shaw et al., 2004]. In addition to identifying and specifying objectives (criteria) and attributes as well as decision alternatives, the aim of problem structuring is the hierarchical modelling of the criteria. Various techniques exist to stimulate the processes of identifying and selecting decision criteria and alternatives. However, the focus in this chapter is on the hierarchical modelling with the aim of constructing an attribute tree (see Figure 2.2) which can either be achieved by using a top-down or a bottom-up approach. The top-down approach can be referred to as strategic, starting with the determination of the most general objective (the overall objective or overall goal) which is subsequently successively divided into sub-objectives and – on the lowest level – measurable attributes. The bottom-up approach can be referred to as rather tactical, starting with listing all meaningful differences between the decision alternatives (identification of measurable attributes in which the performance of the alternatives differs) which are then combined and structured into higher level objectives.

If decision makers have a clear understanding of their objectives, a top-down approach is usually appropriate. Otherwise, a bottom-up approach might be more applicable. In practice, a combination of both approaches is often used. While structuring the objectives hierarchically, it should be checked that an objective is reasonably divided into lower-level objectives (i.e. the division clarifies the meaning of the upper-level objective and the relation between them is hierarchical) and that there are no unnecessary cross-links between a set of lower-level objectives and upper-level objectives (i.e. the set of lower-level objectives should be unique to the upper-level objective) [von Winterfeldt and Edwards, 1986; Keeney, 1992]. Furthermore, it should be checked that the set of objectives is exhaustive and non-redundant as well as essential (i.e. each of the alternatives included in the decision context can influence the degree to which the objectives are achieved) and controllable (i.e. all the decision alternatives that can influence the degree to which the objectives are achieved are included in the decision context, which may be difficult to achieve).

Finally, after an attribute tree has been constructed, it is worthwhile to check that it satisfies the following properties [Keeney and Raiffa, 1976]:

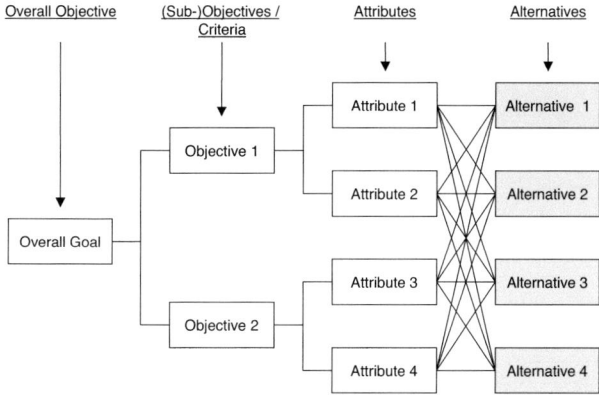

Figure 2.2: Example of an Attribute Tree (Hierarchy of Criteria)

- **Completeness**: All relevant objectives should be included in the hierarchy and the set of attributes completely defines the degree to which the overall objective is achieved.

- **Operationality**: Attributes should be meaningful and assessable.

- **Decomposability**: Attributes should be judgementally independent, that is, it should be possible to analyse one attribute at time.

- **Non-redundancy**: The set of attributes should be non-redundant to avoid double counting of the consequences.

- **Minimum size**: The set of attributes should be minimal.

As indicated before, besides structuring problems hierarchically, the aim of constructing an attribute tree is to break down the (strategic) objectives into measurable attributes. This means that for each attribute tree, a corresponding table can be compiled which contains the scores $s_i(a)$ of every single alternative a with respect to each attribute i ($1 \leq i \leq n$). This table is called decision table. Table 1 shows an exemplar decision table which corresponds to the attribute tree shown in Figure 2.2.

Table 2.1: Decision Table Corresponding to the Attribute Tree in Figure 2.2

Alternatives / Attributes [Units]	Alt_1	Alt_2	Alt_3	Alt_4
A_1 $[U_1]$	$s_1(Alt_1)$	$s_1(Alt_2)$	$s_1(Alt_3)$	$s_1(Alt_4)$
A_2 $[U_2]$	$s_2(Alt_1)$	$s_2(Alt_2)$	$s_2(Alt_3)$	$s_2(Alt_4)$
A_3 $[U_3]$	$s_3(Alt_1)$	$s_3(Alt_2)$	$s_3(Alt_3)$	$s_3(Alt_4)$
A_4 $[U_4]$	$s_4(Alt_1)$	$s_4(Alt_2)$	$s_4(Alt_3)$	$s_4(Alt_4)$

2.2.1.2   Preference Elicitation

After structuring an MADM problem into an attribute tree, it is necessary to construct a model that represents the preferences and value judgements of the decision makers. Such a preference model essentially consists of two components [Belton and Stewart, 2002; French, 2000]:

1. A model that scores each alternative against each individual attribute, enabling the comparison of different units (of the different attributes) on a common scale (i.e. a model for the *intra-criteria* preferences).

2. A model that allows comparisons amongst the different criteria which, in a subsequent step, enables to obtain an overall ranking of the alternatives (i.e. a model for the *inter-criteria* preferences).

The first component concerns the attributes. Let again a denote a decision alternative and $s_i(a)$ the score of alternative a with respect to attribute i ($1 \leq i \leq n$). As indicated in Table 2.1, the scores $s_i(a)$ of the alternatives may be measured in different units for the different attributes. Thus, before the alternatives can be compared to each other with respect to more than one attribute at the same time, all scores need to be mapped to a common (fictitious) scale ranging from 0 to 1 by a value function. For this, we first set $x_i = s_i(a)$. Then, a value function (an intra-criteria preference function) can be defined for each attribute i by

$$v_i : \begin{cases} \mathbb{R} & \to & [0,1] \\ x_i & \mapsto & v_i(x_i) \end{cases} \tag{2.1}$$

such that the "best" and "worst" possible outcomes correspond to 1 and 0 respectively. In general, many different value functions in the form of Equation 2.1 can be constructed. For instance, a linear value function for an attribute with increasing preferences can be defined by

$$v_i(x_i) = \frac{x_i - x_{min}^i}{x_{max}^i - x_{min}^i} , \tag{2.2}$$

where $x_{min}^i = \min_a\{s_i(a)\}$, $x_{max}^i = \max_a\{s_i(a)\}$ and "increasing preferences" means that a higher score x_i corresponds to a higher value $v_i(x_i)$. Similarly, a linear value function for an attribute with decreasing preferences (where a higher score corresponds to a lower value) can be defined by

$$v_i(x_i) = \frac{x_{max}^i - x_i}{x_{max}^i - x_{min}^i} . \tag{2.3}$$

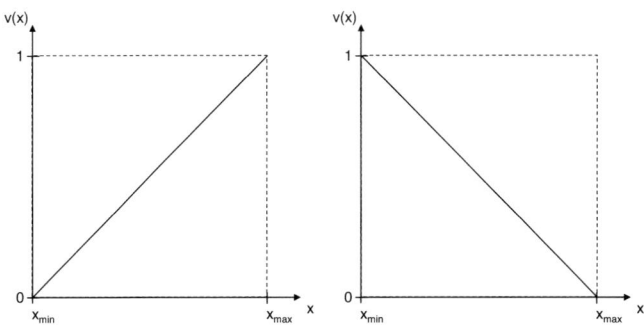

Figure 2.3: Linear Value Functions

Figure 2.3 shows linear value functions that correspond to the functions given in Equation 2.2 and 2.3 respectively. Of course, value functions do not necessarily need to be linear. In general, they can have any form that represents the preferences of the decision makers, as long as they are continuous. Often, exponential value functions may represent the preferences better than linear ones. For instance, for monotonically increasing or decreasing preferences, an exponential value function can be defined by the common one-parameter representation [cf. e.g. Kirkwood, 1997], where ρ_i defines the curvature of the value function of attribute i (see also Figure 2.4):

$$v_i(x_i) = \begin{cases} \dfrac{1-e^{-\frac{\Delta x_i}{\rho_i}}}{1-e^{-\frac{x_{max}^i-x_{min}^i}{\rho_i}}}, & \rho_i \neq \pm\infty \\[3ex] \dfrac{\Delta x_i}{x_{max}^i-x_{min}^i}, & otherwise \end{cases} \tag{2.4}$$

with

$$\Delta x_i = \begin{cases} x_i - x_{min}^i & \text{for increasing preferences}, \\ x_{max}^i - x_i & \text{for decreasing preferences}. \end{cases} \tag{2.5}$$

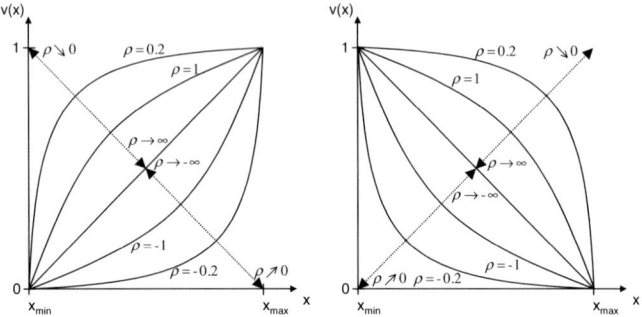

Figure 2.4: Exponential Value Functions

The determination of the form of the value functions is an important step within the preference elicitation. In many cases, if the differences between the outcomes of the alternatives are relatively small, the assumption of linear value functions can be justified. However, attention must be paid when outliers (of the performance scores of the alternatives with respect to the considered attribute) occur.

The second component of a preference model (cf. the beginning of this section) concerns the elicitation of the relative importance between the criteria and thus concerns all criteria (objectives) that are further subdivided into lower level criteria and attributes. These inter-criteria preferences are modelled by weights on each level in an attribute tree. The weight of each attribute can be obtained by multiplying the weights of the criteria on each level along the path in the attribute tree that corresponds to the attribute. The weighting vector $w = (w_1, ..., w_n)$ summarises the weights of all attributes. It is important to ensure that the w_i satisfy the constraint

$$\sum_{i=1}^{n} w_i \overset{!}{=} 1, \quad w_i \geq 0 \text{ for all } i\,, \tag{2.6}$$

i.e. they are normed. Weights can be elicited by different weighting procedures. The simplest way is to assign them directly by point allocation (DIRECT weighting). Alternatively, in the SWING procedure [cf. e.g. von Winterfeldt and Edwards, 1986], 100 points are first given to the most important attribute. Then, less points are given to the other attributes depending on the relative importance of their ranges. The SMART method is similar, but the procedure starts from the least important attribute keeping it as the reference [von Winterfeldt and Edwards, 1986; Edwards, 1977]. In SMARTER, the weights are elicited directly from the ranking of the alternatives [Edwards and Barron, 1994; Barron and Barret, 1996]. The Analytic Hierarchy Process (AHP) [cf. Saaty, 1980] has a fixed (pairwise) comparison procedure which includes redundancy and thus allows the estimation of the consistency of the statements, too. When the questions in the weight elicitation refer to value differences then the results from an AHP procedure can be shown to correspond with those of MAVT analysis [Salo and Hämäläinen, 1997]. A more detailed overview on the common weighting methods based on relative comparisons can be found in Belton and Stewart [2002]; Pöyhönen et al. [2001]; Weber and Borcherding [1993]. The different weighting methods can also be used in combination within one model.

2.2.1.3 Aggregation

The elicitation and modelling of preferential information is followed by aggregating the performance scores with respect to the individual criteria/attributes to an overall performance score taking into account the afore assigned weights w_i and value functions v_i. The most widely used approach for this is the additive aggregation rule which evaluates the overall value $v(a)$ of an alternative a as

$$v(a) = \sum_{i=1}^{n} w_i v_i(x_i), \qquad (2.7)$$

where, again, $x_i = s_i(a)$. The reason why this form is so commonly used is that it is comparatively easily explained to and understood by decision makers with various backgrounds and fields of expertise [Belton and Stewart, 2002].

However, certain properties of the preference structures are necessary for the use of the additive aggregation of the single-attribute value functions, namely the attributes need to be *mutually preferentially independent* [Keeney and Raiffa, 1976]. An attribute A_1 is called preferentially independent of an attribute A_2 if the preferences for certain outcomes (consequences) with respect to A_1 do not depend on the level of the outcomes with respect to attribute A_2 [cf. e.g. Keeney and Raiffa, 1976; French, 1986; Clemen and Reilly, 2001]. Mutual preferential independence additionally involves the independence of attribute A_2 of A_1. A set A of more than two attributes (e.g. $A = \{A_1, ..., A_4\}$ as in the example described at the beginning of Section 2.2.1) is said to be mutually preferentially independent if for all possible decompositions[6] (X, Y) of A, X is preferentially independent of Y [cf. e.g. French, 1986].

From a methodological point of view, the above described properties are necessary conditions for the use of additive aggregation. Thus, it is advisable to verify whether or not

---

[6] A decomposition (X, Y) of A satisfies: $X, Y \subseteq A$, $X \cap Y = \emptyset$ and $X \cup Y = A$.

the attributes in an attribute tree fulfill these properties before continuing the analysis. If
there is serious doubt about the assumptions, it is recommended to return to the problem
structuring phase [Belton and Stewart, 2002].

Besides the additive aggregation rule, other aggregation methods exist which necessitate
different properties of the preference structures. For instance, the use of a multiplicative
form is also common [Kirkwood, 1992]. However, this is not dealt with in detail here.
Because of the clearness of use and the consequential transparency, additive aggregation
is preferred for the context of this research.

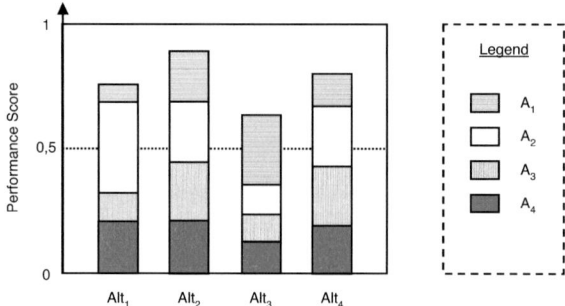

Figure 2.5: Performance Scores for the Example Illustrated as a Stacked-Bar Chart

After applying an aggregation rule, the performance scores can be visualised, for instance
as a stacked-bar chart as shown in Figure 2.5 for the example described at the beginning
of Section 2.2.1. Such a chart can not only illustrate the overall performance scores, but
also the contributions of the individual criteria/attributes.

2.2.1.4   Sensitivity Analysis

Since the determination of the preference parameters in a MAVT analysis is always subjective, sensitivity analyses play an important role in decision making [cf. e.g. Belton and
Vickers, 1990; Belton and Stewart, 2002]. By allowing the exploration of the robustness of
results to variations of the preferential parameters [cf. e.g. Saltelli et al., 2000], sensitivity
analyses can be especially valuable for groups of decision makers to investigate whether
or not differences in their value judgements do matter in terms of the results [Belton and
Vickers, 1990; French, 2003]. Inter alia, the motivations behind sensitivity analyses are
[French, 2003]:

- to support the elicitation of judgemental inputs to an analysis,

- to guide the making of decisions,

- to explore and build consensus,

- to build understanding about a given problem.

The most commonly used sensitivity analysis technique allows an examination of the effects (on the ranking) when the weight of a criterion is varied. Figure 2.6 for example, shows a sensitivity analysis graph for the example at the beginning of Section 2.2.1.

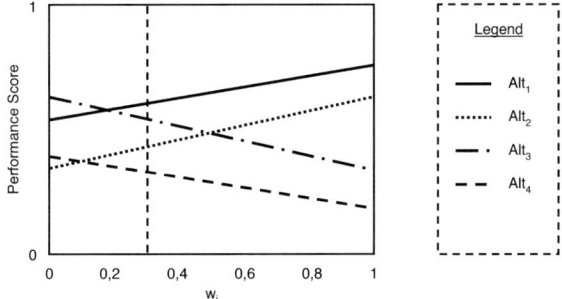

Figure 2.6: Sensitivity Analysis Graph for the Considered Example

The lines in the graph, each associated with one alternative, show the overall scores of the (associated) alternatives when the weight of a chosen criterion is varied from 0 % to 100 % and the black vertical line represents the status quo. The sensitivity analysis in Figure 2.6 shows that the decision is relatively robust against weight changes. However, if a sensitivity analysis shows that the ranking of alternatives is very sensitive to changes of a weight, the decision makers should carefully check if the weighting accurately reflects their preferences [cf. e.g. Belton and Vickers, 1990].

In addition to a sensitivity analysis as in Figure 2.6, spider diagrams can be used for the visual comparison of several alternatives with respect to the different criteria [Vetschera, 1994b]. Figure 2.7 shows a spider diagram for the considered example. The single-attribute performance scores (on a $[0, 1]$ scale) with respect to the individual attributes are shown on the axes where each axis is associated with one attribute and the outer boundary of each axis corresponds to the single-attribute performance score 1 while the origin corresponds to 0. Each alternative is represented by a line forming a polygonal traverse which connects the single-attribute values, i.e. the performance scores of an alternative relative to the individual attributes [cf. Treitz, 2006].

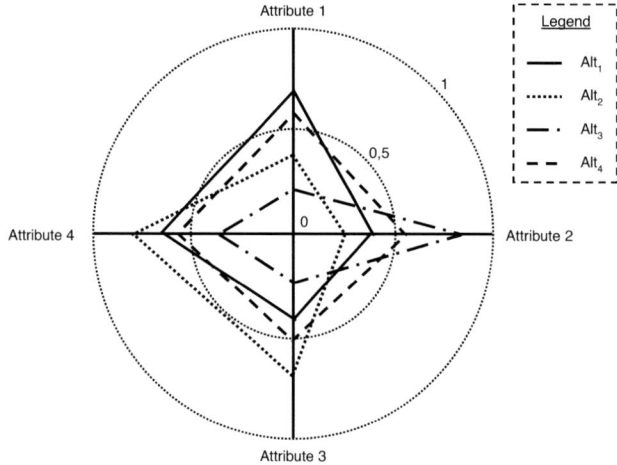

Figure 2.7: Spider Diagram for the Considered Example

A spider diagram such as in Figure 2.7 shows the performances of the different alternatives with respect to the different attributes but does not provide any information about the the weights of the attributes. In order to integrate information about the inter-criteria preference into a spider diagram, one possibility is to let the angles between the axes represent the attributes' weights (see Figure 2.8).

Rather than presenting precise values, the purpose of a spider diagram is to provide a holistic, overall impression of the decision problem [Vetschera, 1994b; Treitz, 2006]. However, the general overview becomes increasingly confusing with a growing number of criteria/attributes or alternatives. An aggregation of the attribute values is inevitable in such cases. Moreover, factor-analytic techniques can be helpful (cf. Section 3.3) [Timm, 2002; Hodgkin et al., 2005; Treitz, 2006].

2.2.2   Interpretation of MAVT as a Weighted Norm

It should be noted that in the aggregation step, all multi-criteria methods have in common that, in a way, they all make use of a (weighted) norm. Presuming that an MADM

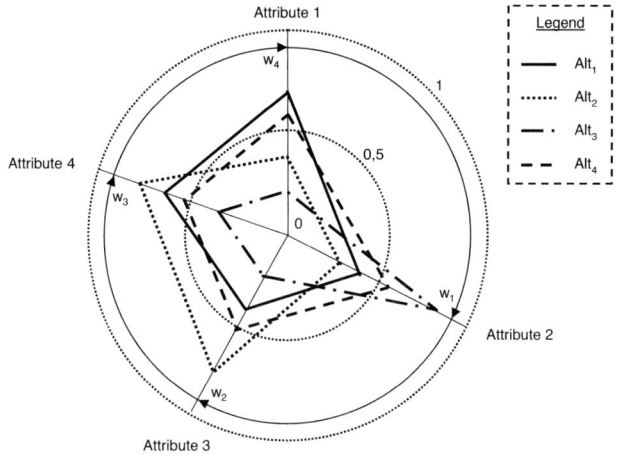

Figure 2.8: Illustration of a Spider Diagram Incorporating Weights

problem has been structured into an attribute tree and that the value functions have been determined for all attributes, an alternative Alt_k can be drawn in a coordinate system using the values $v_i(Alt_k)$ (where $v_i(Alt_k) := v_i(s_i(Alt_k))$). This is illustrated in Figure 2.9 for $n = 3$ attributes. Moreover, Figure 2.9 exemplarily shows two further fictitious alternatives which can be helpful to facilitate the interpretation:

- The *IDEAL* alternative, achieving theoretically "best" performance regarding all criteria (where $\forall i : v_i(IDEAL) = 1$).

- The *NADIR* alternative, showing theoretically "worst" performance with respect to all criteria (where $\forall i : v_i(NADIR) = 0$).

The concept of the IDEAL and NADIR alternatives is also well known for outranking approaches [cf. e.g. Munda, 1996]. The value of these two practically usually unattainable points particularly lies in the fact that decision makers can assess the quality of an alternative based on its relative position compared to the IDEAL or NADIR points [Treitz, 2006].

While Figure 2.9 already gives an impression of the performance of the different alternatives, the impact of the weighting factors is not yet visible. Moreover, it is not straightforward possible to read off the overall performance scores or relative performance differences

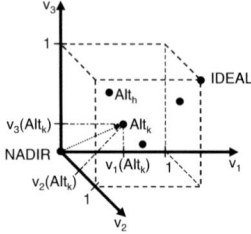

Figure 2.9: Exemplar Illustration of Different Alternatives in $\mathbb{R}^3$

between the alternatives (e.g. between Alt_k and Alt_h in Figure 2.9). For this, it is first necessary to carry out the aggregation step. Mathematically, the aggregation step can be compared to defining and using a general weighted p-norm:

$$\|\cdot\|_w^p : \begin{cases} \mathbb{R}^n & \to & [0,1] \\ x & \mapsto & \left(\sum_{i=1}^{n} w_i \cdot |x_i|^p\right)^{\frac{1}{p}}. \end{cases} \tag{2.8}$$

For instance, the additive aggregation (cf. Equation 2.7) corresponds to a weighted 1-norm (also known as "Manhattan norm"):

$$v(a) = \|a\|_w^1 = \sum_{i=1}^{n} w_i \cdot |v_i(s_i(a))| = \sum_{i=1}^{n} w_i \cdot v_i(s_i(a)). \tag{2.9}$$

The second equality in Equation 2.9 results from the definition of the value function (i.e. each v_i maps values from $\mathbb{R}$ to $[0,1]$, cf. Equation 2.1).

Figure 2.10 illustrates the so-called indifference surface for this norm allowing to assess trade-offs and compensation ratios. Mathematically, all points within an indifference surface (all points within the hatched area) are equally acceptable (show the same overall performance). In general, well balanced alternatives are preferred to "extreme" alternatives by using the 1-norm and the highest overall performance score can only be obtained by an alternative showing the best possible performance with respect to each individual criterion. Besides the 1-norm, other norms are also in use for aggregation purposes. For instance, the use of a 2-norm for performance evaluation has been proposed by Treitz et al. [2004] in the context of process design. Moreover, such a norm is often used in the outranking approach TOPSIS [Hwang and Yoon, 1981]. Finally, it should be emphasised that, while the $\mathbb{R}^n$ and the indifference surface corresponding to a norm are continuous,

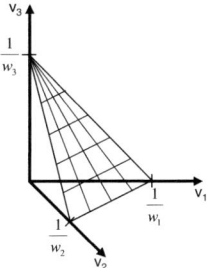

Figure 2.10: Exemplar Illustration of the 1-Norm in $\mathbb{R}^3$

only discrete decision alternatives within the continuous space are considered (as usual in multi-attribute decision making).

2.3   Multi-Attribute Utility Theory

The methods described in the last chapter, assume that the underlying data of the decision analysis is deterministic. Since a decision making process is often affected by different types of uncertainty in practice, the purpose of this chapter is to introduce multi-attribute utility theory (MAUT) [cf. Keeney and Raiffa, 1976] which provides a formal framework for the modelling and handling of uncertainties, particularly of the input data, by introducing utility functions which can be used to reflect the risk attitude of the decision makers.

Historically, Daniel Bernoulli was perhaps the first to introduce the concept of utility [cf. Bernoulli, 1738]. He pointed out that a rationally acting individual would use the expected utility rather than the expected value related to a game before deciding how much he or she was prepared to pay in order to participate in that game. Much later, von Neumann and Morgenstern [1947] developed their expected utility theory [cf. also Savage, 1954] to model the rational choices between alternatives under risk. Smidts [1997] emphasises that the utility models of Bernoulli and of von Neumann and Morgenstern are fundamentally different in that the value function in the former model is measured under riskless conditions and encodes the strength of preference for different outcomes while the utility function in the latter is determined by means of lotteries without explicitly referring to intensity of satisfaction [cf. e.g. Fishburn, 1989; Smidts, 1997; Papamichail, 2000]. Additionally, the curvature of the utility function represents the risk attitude in the latter model while to Bernoulli, the decreasing marginal value of outcomes is an explanation for the risk aversion of decision makers [Smidts, 1997]. In general, a utility function is used to measure the *utility* (to decision makers) related to an outcome rather than its *value*. An essential property of a utility function is that it preserves preferences for outcomes while its expectation preserves the preferences among gambles for such outcomes [Barron et al., 1984].

However, there are certain parallels between the concept of utility functions and that of value functions. Just as a value function, a utility function encodes the preferences of the decision makers, i.e. the value judgements about the relative worth of the consequences of the different alternatives [cf. French, 2000]. The difference is that these consequences are not assumed to be deterministic. In MAUT, the uncertain consequences, being influenced by unknown external "random" factors [cf. e.g. Belton and Stewart, 2002] are usually described by means of probability distributions instead of deterministic values. A problematic aspect in this context is that at least these probability distributions need to be known [cf. e.g. O'Hagan and Oakley, 2004].

2.3.1   Steps in a MAUT Analysis

In principle, a MAUT analysis follows the same key steps as a MAVT analysis (cf. Section 2.2.1). Nevertheless, differences occur in each of these steps. They are described in the following along with the main similarities.

2.3.1.1   Problem Structuring

The problem structuring process in MAUT is almost identical to that in MAVT. The main aim is the construction of an attribute tree for the decision problem. The difference, however, is in the decision table corresponding to the attribute tree. The data in this table is no longer deterministic but given by probability distributions. For discrete finite distributions, the deterministic decision table is simply replaced by a set of decision tables each of which can be related to a *scenario*, i.e. certain parameter settings/assumptions for the external environment.

2.3.1.2   Preference Elicitation

As regards the *inter-criteria* preferences, there are no differences which would be relevant for the purposes of this research. Concerning the *intra-criteria* preferences, the differences and parallels between value and utility functions have already shortly been addressed. The differences and similarities or, more generally, the relationships between value and utility functions have been discussed by many authors [cf. inter alia Belton and Stewart, 2002; French, 2000; Papamichail, 2000; Smidts, 1997; Kirkwood, 1992; French, 1986; Barron et al., 1984; Dyer and Sarin, 1982; Keeney and Raiffa, 1976]. However, the utility function u is often defined as a transformation of the value function v:

$$u = T(v) \, . \tag{2.10}$$

The form of the transformation function T reflects the risk attitude of the decision makers, i.e. whether they are risk averse, risk neutral or risk prone. In general, the published approaches differ in the following ways: They either define single-attribute utility functions $u_i(x_i)$ for all attributes i which are subsequently aggregated or they define the utility function as a transformation of the aggregated value function. Following the latter and letting $x = (x_1, ..., x_n)$ denote the consequence vector of an alternative a with respect to the n attributes, a utility function can for instance be defined by [cf. e.g. Papamichail, 2000]

$$u(x) = T(v(x)) = 1 - e^{-\frac{v(x)}{\kappa}} = 1 - e^{-\frac{\sum_{i=1}^{n} w_i v_i(x_i)}{\kappa}} \tag{2.11}$$

with $\kappa > 0$. Equation 2.11 indicates that the problem of assessing a multi-attribute utility function can be broken down into two stages (subproblems): defining a value function for each attribute and subsequently assessing a "composite" utility function (i.e. the risk attitude is expressed with respect to the overall goal or identically with respect to all attributes) [Papamichail, 2000]. The distinction between value and utility functions and the transformation of the former into the latter can help to simplify the process of assessing the functions [Barron et al., 1984]. For instance, value functions can be determined comparatively easily using common simple techniques as proposed by [Edwards, 1977]. The value functions can then be aggregated using the additive rule and transformed into a utility function. Additionally, a decomposition of the utility function assessment into two steps can help to separate the elicitation of trade-offs from that of risk attitude [French and Geldermann, 2005].

The parameter κ in Equation 2.11 determines the shape of a utility function and represents the risk attitude of the decision makers (see Figure 2.11). For $\kappa > 0$, Equation 2.11 represents a constantly risk averse utility function. The function is shaped concavely. Alternatively, a linear function can be used representing risk neutrality. Risk proneness can be represented by a convex utility function. For the purposes of industrial risk management it is often assumed that decision makers are rather risk averse [cf. e.g. Papamichail, 2000], even though Hämäläinen et al. [1998] have reported different results for Finland in the context of nuclear emergency management.

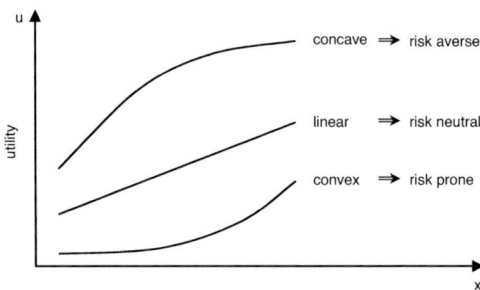

Figure 2.11: The Relation Between the Shape of a Utility Function and Attitude to Risk

There are well-documented approaches concerning the assessment of the parameter κ [cf. e.g. Keeney and Raiffa, 1976; Clemen and Reilly, 2001]. They are usually introduced in terms of gambles and preferences over lotteries. The most common way to elicit the risk attitude is based on determining the *certainty equivalent* of a lottery, i.e. an amount (of money) such that a decision maker is indifferent between taking this amount for certain and playing the lottery. A problematic aspect in this context is the dependency of the risk attitude on the framing of the decision context. For instance, it could be observed that decision makers are rather risk averse when an issue is framed in positive terms and, contrarily, that they tend to be risk prone when an issue is framed in negative terms [cf. for instance Tversky and Kahneman, 1981; Kahneman et al., 1982; Tversky and Kahneman, 1986].

Mathematically, the risk aversion in a point x (i.e. the *local risk aversion* in this point) corresponding to a utility function u can be "measured" by

$$r(x) = -\frac{u''(x)}{u'(x)}, \tag{2.12}$$

assuming that u is twice differentiable [cf. e.g. Pratt et al., 1964; French, 1986]. Furthermore, from Equation 2.12 and Figure 2.11 it can be derived that

$$\text{if } \forall x: \quad r(x) \begin{cases} > 0, & \Rightarrow \quad \text{risk averseness}, \\ = 0, & \Rightarrow \quad \text{risk neutrality}, \\ < 0, & \Rightarrow \quad \text{risk proneness}. \end{cases} \tag{2.13}$$

However, if a utility function such as in Equation 2.11 is to be scaled from zero to one, this can for instance be achieved by dividing u by $(1 - e^{-1/\kappa})$.

2.3.1.3 Aggregation

As indicated in Section 2.3.1.2, two basic principles of assessing and using utility functions can be distinguished within MAUT. Firstly, single-attribute utility functions can be defined for all attributes. Subsequently, these utility functions need to be aggregated. Secondly, the (additively) aggregated value of an alternative can be transformed using a composite utility function (as expressed, for instance, by Equation 2.11).

Concerning the first approach, a number of different methods can be used in the aggregation step assuming that a utility function has been assessed for each attribute. As in MAVT, the most commonly used approaches are the additive and the multiplicative aggregation rules. Again, an advantage of the additive rule is its transparency and comprehensibility. However, the required properties of the preference structure in order to be able to use the additive rule in MAUT are slightly different from those in MAVT. Mutual preferential independence is a necessary but not a sufficient condition [cf. e.g. Clemen and Reilly, 2001], i.e. stronger independence conditions are needed for preferences under uncertainty.

Utility independence is a stronger condition than *preferential independence*. An attribute A_1 is called utility independent of an attribute A_2 if the preferences for uncertain outcomes (consequences) with respect to A_1 are independent of the value of attribute A_2 [cf. e.g. Keeney and Raiffa, 1976; French, 1986; Clemen and Reilly, 2001]. If A_2 is also utility independent of A_1, then the two attributes are called mutually utility independent. A set A of more than two attributes (e.g. $A = \{A_1, ..., A_4\}$ as in the example described at the beginning of Section 2.2.1) is said to be mutually utility independent if for all possible decompositions (X, Y) of A (cf. Section 2.2.1.3 for the properties of a decomposition), X is utility independent of Y. Even though utility independence and preferential independence seem to be very similar, Keeney and Raiffa [1976] for instance, discuss an example where attributes are preferentially independent but not utility independent.

In order to be able to model preferences accurately using a purely additive aggregation method, *additive independence* is required – an even stronger condition than *utility independence*. According to Keeney and Raiffa [1976], two attributes A_1 and A_2 are *additively independent* if the pairwise preference comparison of any two lotteries defined by two joint probability distributions on $A_1 \times A_2$ depends only on their marginal probability distributions. Hence, the difference between additive independence and utility independence is that, for the former, changes in lotteries concerning one attribute do not affect the preferences for lotteries in the other attribute while, for the latter, changes in sure levels concerning one attribute do not affect the preferences for lotteries in the other attribute [cf. e.g. Clemen and Reilly, 2001]. Consequently, when assessing uncertain consequences for two attributes, it is sufficient to look at one attribute at a time (regardless of the uncertain consequences of the other attribute). It should be noted that in contrast to the other described independence conditions, additive independence is a reflexive property by definition. Analogously as for utility and preferential independence, a set A of more than two attributes (e.g. $A = \{A_1, ..., A_4\}$ in the considered example) is said to be additively independent if for all possible decompositions (X, Y) of A, X is additively independent of Y [cf. e.g. French, 1986].

Assuming that the preferences are additively independent and that a utility function has been determined for each of the n attributes, the total utility u of an alternative a can be evaluated as

$$u(x) = \sum_{i=1}^{n} w_i u_i(x_i), \tag{2.14}$$

with $x_i = s_i(a)$ (cf. Equation 2.7) and where, again, $x = (x_1, ..., x_n)$ is the consequence vector of the alternative a.

Additive independence is quite a strong condition for a preference structure whose fulfilment in practice is often questionable [von Winterfeldt and Edwards, 1986]. Nevertheless, the additive aggregation model may provide a good and useful approximation for many practical decision situations [Clemen and Reilly, 2001]. However, it is still important to bear the independence conditions in mind during the problem structuring process.

Concerning the second way of assessing and using utility functions (cf. the beginning of this section), a composite utility function can be used to transform the (additively) aggregated value of each alternative. Since the determination of utility functions involves many questions about lotteries [cf. e.g. Hämäläinen et al., 1998] in order to elicit the risk attitude of the decision makers, this second approach seems to be advantageous since the problem of utility function assessment is decomposed into the easier subproblems of assessing value functions and only one (composite) utility function (cf. Equation 2.11). Descriptions on how decision makers can derive utility functions from value functions taking their risk attitude into account can for instance be found in Keeney and Raiffa [1976]; Krzysztofowicz [1983]. However, being equivalent to the multiplicative aggregation of utility functions (since the sum is in the exponent in Equation 2.11) as studied, for instance, by Keeney and Raiffa [1976], the exponential utility transform 2.11 requires mutual utility independence [cf. Papamichail, 2000].

Generalising Equation 2.11, [Keeney and Raiffa, 1976] have proved that u must have one of the following forms, given that mutual preferential independence holds and that at least one attribute is utility independent of the others:

$$u(x) \sim \begin{cases} -e^{-cv(x)}, & c > 0, \\ v(x), & \\ e^{cv(x)}, & c < 0. \end{cases} \qquad (2.15)$$

If the utility is to be scaled from zero to one, this can, again, be achieved by dividing the utility u in Equation 2.15 by $(1 - e^{-c})$.

An aggregated utility function, such as in Equation 2.11, measures the utilities of the uncertain consequences x_i. Thus, the ranking of the alternatives is based on calculating their *expected utilities* $E[u(x)]$, i.e. the most preferred alternative is the one with the highest expected utility. Assuming that the probability distribution of the real-valued consequence vector $x = (x_1, ..., x_n)$ is known and that its density is f, then the expected utility of an alternative can be calculated by

$$E[u(x)] = \int_{\mathbb{R}^n} u(x) \cdot f(x) \, dx. \qquad (2.16)$$

When calculating the expectation of the exponential utility function u, it should be noticed that this expectation has the same functional form as the so called moment generating function. In general, the moment generating function of a random variable X is defined as

$$g(t) = E[e^{tX}], \tag{2.17}$$

introducing the new parameter t [cf. e.g. Grinstead and Snell, 1997]. The kth moment of X can be calculated as the kth derivative of g for $t = 0$ (where e.g. the first moment is the expectation and the second moment is the variance of X). However, for a number of well-known probability distributions, the respective moment generating functions are very helpful to calculate the expected utilities.

For instance, if X is normally distributed with mean μ and standard deviation σ, it can be shown [cf. e.g. Grinstead and Snell, 1997] that

$$E[e^{tX}] = e^{t\mu + \frac{\sigma^2}{2}t^2}. \tag{2.18}$$

For a negative exponent as in Equation 2.11 it can be derived [cf. e.g. Keeney and Raiffa, 1976] that

$$E[e^{-tX}] = e^{-(t\mu - \frac{\sigma^2}{2}t^2)}. \tag{2.19}$$

Setting $X = \sum_{i=1}^{n} w_i v_i(x_i)$, it follows that

$$\mu = \sum_{i=1}^{n} w_i \mu_i, \tag{2.20}$$

where μ_i denotes the mean of $v_i(x_i)$ and

$$\sigma^2 = w^T C w, \tag{2.21}$$

where w denotes the weighting vector and C the covariance matrix (of the $v_i(x_i)$). Hence, setting $t = \frac{1}{\kappa}$, it can be followed for a utility function u as in Equation 2.11 that [cf. Papamichail, 2000; Papamichail and French, 2000]

$$E[u(x)] = 1 - e^{-(\frac{\sum_{i=1}^{n} w_i \mu_i}{\kappa} - \frac{w^T C w}{2\kappa^2})}. \tag{2.22}$$

After calculating the expected utilities, they can be visualised. The total expected utilities can, for instance, be displayed in a bar chart (see Figure 2.12). Illustrating the results in the form of a stacked-bar chart, similar as in MAVT, is not straightforwardly possible since the information about the contributions of the individual criteria is only available in the exponent.

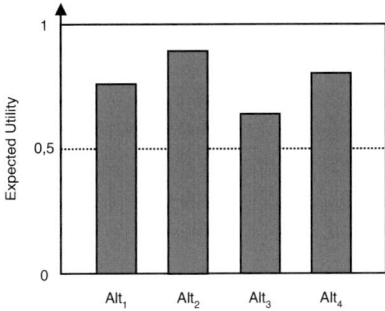

Figure 2.12: Expected Utilities for the Considered Example Illustrated as a Bar Chart

However, since exponentiation is a monotonic operation, it is suggested by Papamichail and French [2000] that it is sufficient to evaluate the alternatives according to

$$\sum_{i=1}^{n} w_i \mu_i - \frac{w^T C w}{2\kappa} \tag{2.23}$$

instead of Equation 2.22. This means that an alternative can be evaluated by subtracting the term depending on the associated covariance matrix from a linear function. It is discussed by Papamichail [2000] that Equation 2.23 simplifies the assessment process since it does not explicitly require to deal with probability distributions. Additionally, it should be emphasised that, in the event that all alternatives are subject to the same uncertainty, they can simply be ranked according to the first term since the second term would be identical for all alternatives.

Examining the second term in Equation 2.23 which is quadratic in w in more detail, it can be expected that it takes high values if the weights on the attributes with a high covariance are high. Thus, alternatives showing a high covariance on the attributes with high weights will be ranked comparatively lower since a larger number is subtracted from the first term.

However, in the above equations 2.17–2.23 it is assumed that the underlying data is normally distributed. In practical applications such an assumption cannot always be justified. Especially, when uncertainties are observed empirically, discrete probability distributions may provide much better approximations than continuous ones [cf. e.g. Collender and Chalfant, 1986]. In this case, the integral in Equation 2.16 is replaced by a sum. If all empirically determined realisations of a random variable X are equally probable (or if no other information is available), a discrete uniform distribution can provide an adequate approximation. In general, the discrete uniform distribution is a discrete probability distribution that can be characterised by the property that all realisations of a finite set of possible realisations are equally probable. Thus, if the discrete random variable X is uniformly distributed and the set of possible outcomes is $\{x^1, ..., x^\nu\}$, i.e. its cardinality is ν, the probability of each outcome (realisation) for X is $\frac{1}{\nu}$. The moment generating function for X is then given by [cf. e.g. Grinstead and Snell, 1997]

$$g(t) = E\left[e^{tX}\right] = \frac{1}{\nu}\sum_{h=1}^{\nu} e^{tx^h} \,. \tag{2.24}$$

Again, X is not a common univariate random variable but is to be replaced by $X = \sum_{i=1}^{n} w_i v_i(x_i)$. Each realisation x^h of X $(1 \leq h \leq \nu)$ can be obtained by $\sum_{i=1}^{n} w_i v_i(x_i^h)$, where for each alternative a, x_i^h is the hth realisation of the consequence with respect to the ith attribute. Setting $t = \frac{1}{\kappa}$, again, it follows for the utility function u of 2.11 together with Equation 2.7 that

$$E\left[u(x)\right] = 1 - \frac{1}{\nu}\left(\sum_{j=1}^{\nu} e^{-\frac{1}{\kappa}\sum_{i=1}^{n} w_i v_i(x_i^h)}\right) = 1 - \frac{1}{\nu}\left(\sum_{j=1}^{\nu} e^{-\frac{1}{\kappa}v^h(a)}\right) \,. \tag{2.25}$$

A similar function has been proposed by Collender and Chalfant [1986] where it is called "empirical moment generating function". One of the main differences between this function and that of Equation 2.22 is that Equation 2.25 cannot explicitly be decomposed into a linear function and a quadratic term. Consequently, no covariance matrix needs to be calculated explicitly.

2.3.1.4 Sensitivity Analysis

As in MAVT, the determination of preference parameters is always subjective in MAUT and thus, the motivations to perform sensitivity analyses are generally the same (cf. Section 2.2.1.4). In fact, when introducing utility functions, there is an additional subjective parameter to be analysed by sensitivity analyses: the risk attitude parameter κ. However, the focus of this section is first on differences or similarities between weight sensitivity analyses in MAVT and MAUT and, subsequently, a sensitivity analysis approach for κ is discussed.

In principle, the ways in which a sensitivity analysis can be visualised are the same as in MAVT. A major difference is that the lines in the graph, which are associated with the different alternatives, do not necessarily need to be linear. Especially, concerning the quadratic term in equations 2.23 and 2.22, if a normal distribution can be assumed, the lines can take parabolic shapes. This means that it is possible that the lines associated with two alternatives intersect twice in the diagram (such as the lines corresponding to Alt_1 and Alt_2 in Figure 2.13) which constitutes a new challenge for sensitivity analysis in multi-attribute decision making. However, the main question is the same as in MAVT: if a sensitivity analysis shows that the ranking of alternatives is very sensitive to changes of a weight, the decision makers should carefully check if the weighting accurately reflects their preferences.

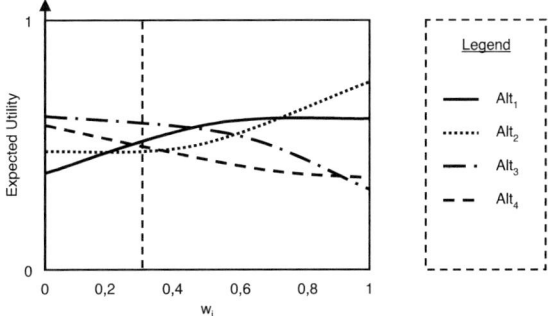

Figure 2.13: Weight Sensitivity Analysis in MAUT for the Considered Example

As mentioned above, the determination of the parameter κ, representing the risk attitude of the decision makers, is subjective, too. Hence, it is also important to carry out a sensitivity analysis with respect to κ [cf. e.g. Keeney and Raiffa, 1976]. One possibility is to examine the expected utility of the different alternatives when varying the parameter κ within a certain interval. For instance, Figure 2.14 illustrates such a sensitivity analysis for κ in the interval $[0, 1]$.

If the ranking of the alternatives remains the same for all examined values of κ, the results can be regarded as robust. However, the vertical dashed line at $\kappa = 0,55$ in Figure 2.14 indicates that, for values of κ above this point, Alt_1 has the highest expected utility, while for values below, Alt_3 has the highest expected utility. Thus, if the decision makers determined a value for κ close to this line, it is advisable to check if the determined value really accurately represents their risk attitude. Figure 2.14 also indicates that Alt_1 and Alt_3 dominate the two other alternatives which means that the decision problem is reduced to the choice between Alt_1 and Alt_3.

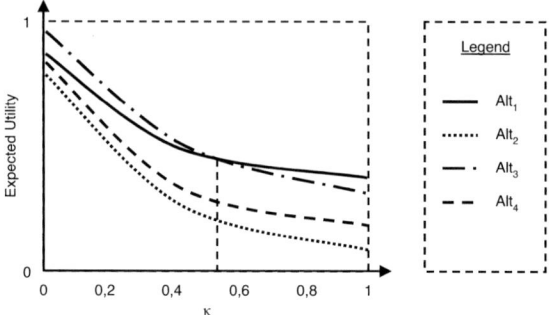

Figure 2.14: Risk Attitude Sensitivity Analysis in MAUT for the Considered Example

2.3.2 Bayesian Decision Analysis

As a formal framework to probabilistically deal with uncertainty in decision making, utility theory has been introduced above. Within this framework, the uncertain consequences
are described by means of probabilities. However, a problematic aspect in this context,
as mentioned above, is that at least the probability distributions need to be known or
assessable in an adequate way [cf. O'Hagan and Oakley, 2004]. While, for the classical approaches within utility theory, it is assumed that these probability distributions
can be assessed objectively, the Bayesian paradigm is based upon the view that decision
makers should be able to incorporate their subjective beliefs and experiences when assessing probability distributions, i.e. they should be allowed to define and use subjective
probabilities.

The conceptual framework of Bayesian decision analysis was laid down by Savage [1954].
Since then, it has developed into a sophisticated methodology aimed at providing support
for decision making under uncertainty. The uncertain consequences of different alternatives are determined as interactions of the alternatives with an unknown "state of the
world" [cf. e.g. French, 2000]:

$$alternative \oplus state \longrightarrow consequence\,, \tag{2.26}$$

where the $\oplus$ in Equation 2.26 is meant to indicate the interaction which is usually non-
additive.

In principle, the steps within Bayesian decision analysis are the same as those described
in sections 2.2 and 2.3, i.e. problem structuring, preference elicitation, aggregation and

sensitivity analysis.[7] As indicated above, however, the main methodological difference is the following: While the "usual" utility theory, as described in Section 2.3.1, provides methods to cope with uncertain consequences by calculating expected utilities based on known, *objective* probability distributions, Bayesian decision analysis is based on obtaining the uncertain consequences on the foundation of the *subjective* beliefs of the decision makers about the unknown state of the world and it provides support for decision making under uncertainty by calculating subjective expected utilities. This difference particularly concerns the elicitation phase in which, besides determining the usual preference parameters, subjective probability distributions representing the decision makers' beliefs and knowledge need to be assessed. Thus, according to the Bayesian paradigm, decisions are taken on grounds of knowledge and beliefs about data and facts rather than on grounds of the data and facts themselves. Therefore, knowledge can be regarded as context-dependent and having knowledge means having understanding, experience and expertise [French et al., 2007].

In statistics, the above two different approaches are also known as the frequentist and the Bayesian approach. In the frequentist sense, probability is objective and defined as the long-term relative frequency of occurrence of an ideally infinitely repeatable experiment. From the Bayesian point of view, probability is subjective. Detailed discussions on the distinction between both can for instance be found in French [1986]; Fienberg [2006].

In general, for two events B and D, Bayes' theorem says

$$P(D|B) = \frac{P(B|D) \cdot P(D)}{P(B)}$$
$$\propto P(B|D) \cdot P(D), \qquad (2.27)$$

where $P(B|D)$ is the conditional probability of event B under the assumption that event D has happened and $\propto$ stands for "is proportional to". In other words, the *a posteriori* probability of D, knowing that B has happened, is the *a priori* probability of D multiplied by the conditional probability of B assuming that D has happened, also known as the *likelihood*. The proportionality in Equation 2.27 is generally obtained in such a way that $P(\cdot|B)$ sums (or integrates) to 1.

The following nomenclature will help to link Equation 2.27 to utility theory [cf. e.g. French and Smith, 1997; French and Ríos-Insua, 2000]: Let Θ denote the set of all possible states of the world and let $\theta \in \Theta$ denote an unknown state. Furthermore, let a denote a single decision alternative (action) and $x(a, \theta)$ the uncertain consequence of applying a when

---

[7] Even though some authors [such as Savage, 1954] do not see any value in sensitivity analysis within the Bayesian framework, the role of analysing the sensitivity of probabilities and utilities in Bayesian decision analysis has for instance been clearly pointed out by French [2003].

the state of the world is θ (where x is usually multi-attributed). Then, according to the Bayesian paradigm, the decision makers encode their beliefs and preferences through two functions:

- a *subjective (prior) probability distribution* $P_\Theta(\cdot)$ representing the beliefs about the unknown state of the world;

- a *utility function* $u(x)$, for instance in the form of Equation 2.11, representing the preferences.

Assuming that a decision is to be taken after having made an observation $Y = y$ (in general, an outcome of some experiment that depends on θ), Bayes' theorem is used to update the prior knowledge or belief $P_\Theta(\cdot)$ in the light of this observation to obtain the posterior probability distribution [cf. e.g. French and Smith, 1997]:

$$P_\Theta(\theta|y) \propto P_Y(y|\theta)P_\Theta(\theta). \tag{2.28}$$

This means that the knowledge of the world can be continuously updated by observations. Subsequently, it is possible to aggregate the preferences (utilities) and probabilities (beliefs) by determining the subjective expected utility of an alternative a as [cf. e.g. French, 2003]

$$E_\theta\left[u(x)|\,y\right] = E_\theta\left[u\left(x(a,\theta)\right)|\,y\right] = \int_\Theta u\left(x(a,\theta)\right)f_\theta(\theta|y)d\theta, \tag{2.29}$$

where f_θ is the density function, $E[\cdot|y]$ is the conditional expectation having observed $Y = y$ and, again, the integral is replaced by a sum for discrete distributions. Then, following the Bayesian paradigm, the alternative with the maximal subjective expected utility is the one to be chosen.

Figure 2.15 summarises the main elements of a Bayesian decision process as described above, combining elements from the fields of decision analysis, consequence modelling as well as statistical inference and forecasting. More detailed descriptions and discussions of Bayesian decision analysis can for instance be found in Berger [1985]; French [1986]; Dorfman [1997]; French and Smith [1997]; French and Ríos-Insua [2000]; Fienberg [2006].

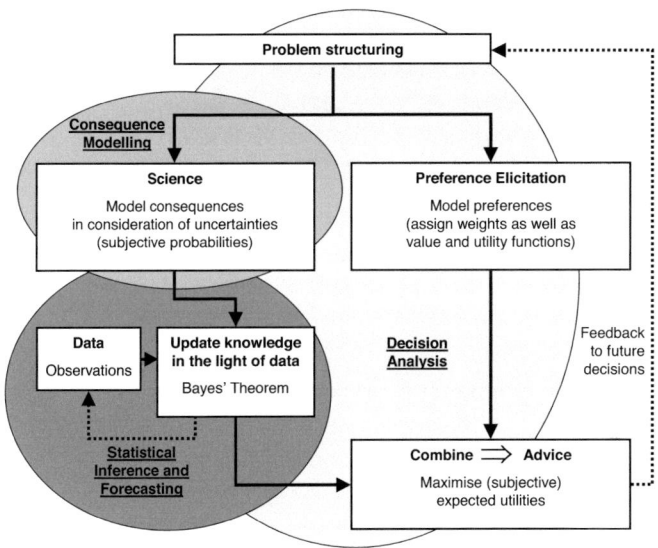

Figure 2.15: Process of Bayesian Decision Making [adapted from French, 2003]

2.4   Summary

Complex decision situations in industrial risk management require the consideration of different, usually conflicting criteria. Providing the basis for the evaluation of such conflicting criteria, a general introduction into MCDA has been given. It has been argued that MCDA is strongly preferred to cost benefit analysis because of its transparent nature which, inter alia, results from the explicit recognition of subjectivity in decision making processes.

Within the field of MCDA, the MAVT and MAUT approaches have been described in detail since they have already proved to be suitable to support decision making in industrial risk management in consequence of their operational applicability. Furthermore, the ICRP recommends MAVT in the context of nuclear emergency management. While MAVT provides a transparent framework for deterministic decision analyses, MAUT offers a formal possibility for the modelling and handling of uncertainties arising in a decision process. In addition to the classical MAVT and MAUT approaches, the Bayesian decision paradigm has been outlined, as one family of approaches within utility theory. In contrast to the classical approaches within utility theory, Bayesian decision analysis is based upon the view that probabilities are subjective, seeking to facilitate the process of assessing probability distributions. Fundamental approaches for sensitivity analysis, allowing to analyse the robustness of the results with respect to variations of the subjective parameters, have been described for the MAVT as well as for the MAUT methods.

The application of the described methods is demonstrated in the context of the case study in Chapter 4. Furthermore, the described approaches can be applied in other contexts to support decision makers in resolving complex decision situations. For instance, MCDA can be used to criteria such as risk exposure into account in site selection decisions of expanding companies as shortly sketched at the beginning of Section 2.2.1. However, while MAUT offers a way to formally treat the uncertainty arising in a decision making process, it should be noted that the uncertainty is contained implicitly in the results and usually cannot be visualised explicitly in order to support the communication of the impact of the uncertainties on the results. The simulation based approaches for uncertainty analysis introduced in Chapter 3 are aimed at overcoming this drawback.

Chapter 3

Simulation-Based Uncertainty Analysis

The focus of this chapter is on approaches for uncertainty handling in multi-attribute decision analysis, particularly on new simulation-based approaches which will be motivated below. While the prime purpose of Chapter 2 was a general introduction into MCDA, it also became apparent that a decision analysis process, in practice as well as in theory, may be subject to various types of uncertainty. A formal framework to deal with uncertainty in MCDA probabilistically has been introduced in Section 2.3 and it was mentioned that, within this framework, two schools of thought can be distinguished [cf. e.g. French, 1986; Morgan and Henrion, 1990; Basson, 2004]:

- The *frequentist* school, according to which probability is *objective*, i.e. it is understood as the long-run frequency of occurrence and its estimation requires the gathering of empirical data.

- The *Bayesian* school, according to which probability is *subjective*, i.e. persons may be able to assess a probability based on their knowledge, experience and beliefs, even when there is insufficient empirical data. Or, contrariwise, even in the presence of empirical data it might not be possible to assess a probability distribution objectively.

While the advantages and drawbacks of the frequentist as opposed to the Bayesian approaches are discussed controversially in literature [cf. e.g. Savage, 1954; Edwards, 1972; Kahneman et al., 1982; French, 1986; Paté-Cornell, 1996; Gilboa et al., 2007], the approaches have in common that the uncertainty is treated in terms of probability. However, even though the probabilistic treatment of uncertainty is the most widely used formalism for the quantification of uncertainty [cf. e.g. Morgan and Henrion, 1990; Bedford and Cooke, 2001], a large problem is that there are types of uncertainty for which it is difficult or impossible to assess a probability – even a subjective one [cf. e.g. O'Hagan and Oakley, 2004; Basson, 2004]. This means that it is likely that, by attempting to describe uncertainty by means of a probability distribution, new uncertainty is introduced which would make the value of modelling uncertainty at all questionable.

Different types of uncertainty need to be treated in different ways [cf. e.g. Morgan and Henrion, 1990; Helton, 1993, 1996; Bedford and Cooke, 2001]. Thus, a classification of uncertainties that may arise in a decision making process and corresponding ways of treatment is very important [cf. e.g. Basson, 2004]. However, there are many different ways to classify the occurring uncertainties. But, even though the classification itself is subject to uncertainty, it provides several advantages including [cf. e.g. Bonano, 1995]

- Consistent propagation of uncertainties into the results of an analysis resulting in more transparent decision making;

- Simpler identification of the most significant uncertainties;

- Easier possibility to include new developments in treating specific uncertainties into the decision making approach.

This is especially important in the context of industrial risk management since the arising uncertainties can have a substantial impact on the outcome of a decision making process. An adequate categorisation of the uncertainties and the assignment of appropriate ways of treating the uncertainties within the different categories respectively is needed to support decision makers in coping with the uncertainties. In order to increase the robustness and reliability of decision making in risk management, it is important to support the communication of the impact of the uncertainties on the results of the analysis.

3.1   Classification and Treatment of Uncertainties

In the field of risk analysis, uncertainties are often divided into two categories [cf. e.g. Helton, 1993; Paté-Cornell, 1996; Helton, 1996; Bedford and Cooke, 2001; Basson, 2004]:

- *Aleatory* uncertainties, arising because the system under study can behave in many different (most likely unpredictable) ways

- *Epistemic* uncertainties, arising from a lack of knowledge about the system under study

While aleatory uncertainty is a property of the observed system, epistemic uncertainty "belongs" to its observer (and his or her knowledge). Thus, epistemic uncertainty can be seen as theoretically reducible in contrast to the irreducible aleatory uncertainty.

Another categorisation has for instance been proposed by Morgan and Henrion [1990] for the area of policy analysis. They distinguish, inter alia, the following sources of uncertainty:

- Empirical quantities

- Decision variables

- Value parameters

- Model domain parameters

- Defined constants and index variables (which are said to be certain by definition)

Within the group of empirical quantities, they further investigate the potential sources from which these uncertainties may arise, including:

- Statistical variation

- Subjective judgement and systematic errors

- Linguistic imprecision

- Variability (over time and/or space)

- Inherent randomness and unpredictability

- Approximation

In the above list of the sources of empirical uncertainties, Morgan and Henrion [1990] do not explicitly differentiate between aleatory and epistemic uncertainties but it is argued that uncertainties originating from inherent randomness and unpredictability are unlikely to be reducible whereas the uncertainties arising from the other sources may, at least in theory, be reducible. In this way, the two attempts to categorise uncertainties are linked with each other. Though, by explicitly considering model and value parameters, the categorisation of Morgan and Henrion [1990] can be said to go beyond the distinction between aleatory and epistemic uncertainties. Additionally, they consider uncertainty about the form or structure of a model which, according to them, can have a substantial impact on the results on the one hand but, on the other, is difficult to quantify and analyse. However, an exact distinction between their categories "uncertainties about model domain parameters", "uncertainties about model structure" and "uncertainties arising from approximation" does not seem to be straightforward. Rather, the uncertainties occurring as a result of approximation can be regarded as being directly linked to the model structure since a model can always only be an approximate version of the real-world system under consideration [French and Niculae, 2005]. Even though models are often iteratively refined until they describe a certain part of the real world sufficiently well[8], the refinement cannot be an infinite process in practice [French, 1995]. Thus, these uncertainties can be seen as inherent to all models.

There are many other approaches to classify uncertainties. For instance, French [1995] and later also Mustajoki et al. [2006] proposed to group the uncertainties according to the different steps of the modelling process in which they can occur:

- Constructing the model
  - Uncertainty about what can happen and what can be done
  - Uncertainty in consequence of ambiguity in terminology
  - Uncertainty about related decisions
- Exploring the model
  - Physical randomness and lack of knowledge
  - Uncertainty about current beliefs and preferences as well as their future evolution
  - Accuracy of calculations
- Interpreting the model results
  - Uncertainty about the choice of a model
  - Uncertainty about the depth to which the analysis should be conducted

Based on the classification suggested by Bonano [1995], a differentiation between *technical* and *valuation* uncertainties is described in Basson [2004]. There are obviously many relations and overlappings between the above described classification approaches and they

---

[8] Such models are also called *requisite* decision models [e.g. in Phillips, 1984].

all have their context-dependent strengths and weaknesses. However, from the point of view of MADM, a distinction can be made between uncertainties

- in the alternatives' values with respect to the different attributes, i.e. uncertainties in the input data of an MADM model;

- of the subjective parameters of a decision model, i.e. the uncertainties introduced during the multi-attribute evaluation of a set of alternatives [cf. also Basson, 2004];

- related to the structure of the MADM model.

The first group will be reflected in uncertainties in the data of the decision table which is why they will be referred to as *data uncertainties* in this thesis [cf. also Gering, 2005; Bertsch et al., 2005]. The second group concerns the (subjective) preference parameters of an MADM model. They are denoted *parameter uncertainties* or *preferential uncertainties* within this thesis [cf. also Bertsch et al., 2006a, 2007a]. Uncertainties of this second group can be further subdivided into uncertainties associated with the *intra-criteria* and *inter-criteria* preference parameters (cf. Section 2.2.1.2). Uncertainties of the third group are referred to as *model uncertainties* in this thesis. It has already been mentioned that the uncertainties of the third group are difficult to quantify and can be regarded as inherent to any model [French and Niculae, 2005]. They are thus not quantitatively analysed within this thesis. However, the impact of model uncertainties on decision making in industrial risk management could be explored by using different attribute trees (i.e. choosing different sets of decision criteria) or, more generally, different MADM models in a series of stakeholder workshops and by subsequently comparing the respective results. Figure 3.1 shows one potential overall classification scheme for uncertainties arising in an MADM process which summarises the most relevant aspects for the purposes of this thesis.

The classification into data, parameter and model uncertainties does not take account of the respective origins of the uncertainties, especially within the group of data uncertainties. This is because the focus of this Chapter is on describing methods that allow to investigate what the occurring uncertainties mean for the decision and which uncertainties are most relevant. Aspects of information quality and individual sources of uncertainty will be considered in conjunction with the case study in Chapter 4. For the case study in the context of emergency management in the nuclear power generation sector, the modelling of empirical uncertainties and their propagation through a chain of models is described in detail in sections 4.2.2 and 4.5. The effect they can finally have on the results of a decision making process is shown in Section 4.6.

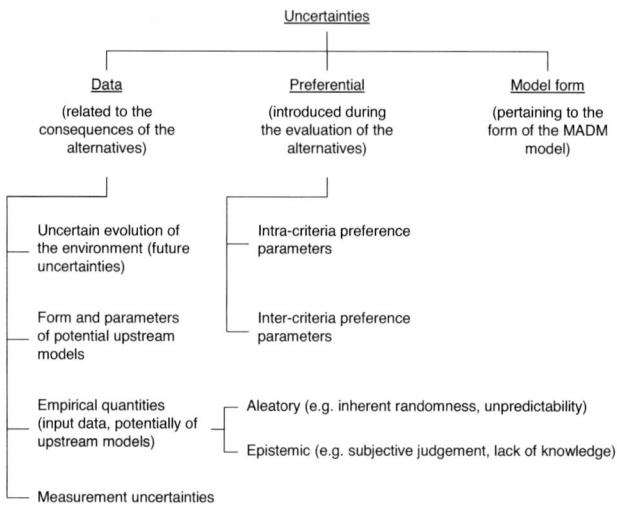

Figure 3.1: Classification of Uncertainties [adapted from Basson, 2004]

Concerning appropriate approaches of treatment corresponding to the different classes of uncertainty, Morgan and Henrion [1990] emphasise that, within their categorisation, uncertainty of empirical quantities is the only type of uncertainty which may be appropriately modelled by probability distributions on the grounds that empirical quantities are the only quantities which can have a true in contrast to a good or appropriate value. For preferential uncertainties, a probabilistic treatment is strongly disadvised since this may hide the impact of the uncertainties on the results. Instead, it is proposed to treat them parametrically (i.e. repeating the analysis for a range of possible values of the preference parameters) providing more insight into the situation.

The choice of an approach for uncertainty handling in multi-attribute decision making should depend on the particular decision context [Basson, 2004]. Besides the model nature (e.g. linear / non-linear) and the type(s) of uncertainty, relevant factors include the time needed to acquire profound knowledge about the approach or the easiness in explaining the approach to other parties (e.g. stakeholder groups).

In Monte Carlo simulation [cf. e.g. Fishman, 1996; Frey and Nießen, 2001, for a rigorous introduction], a random value is drawn for each input variable or parameter according to some distribution. It should be noted that, in this context, distribution does not necessarily mean a continuous well-explored probability distribution. If no exact information about the distribution type of some model input is available, the use of empirical distributions or, if information about a range of values is available, the use of uniform distributions is often more advisable. The set of randomly sampled values, one for each input, then defines a *scenario*. However, random sampling is not the only way to define scenarios. It is also common to incorporate expert knowledge or subjective beliefs into the process of creating plausible scenarios (plausible futures). The latter approach (the "manual Monte Carlo method") is called scenario analysis rather than Monte Carlo analysis but the distinction between the two is not always clear-cut. In both cases, the scenarios are subsequently used as parallel model input, i.e. the process is repeated (or carried out in parallel) for each scenario. Monte Carlo Simulation provides a number of desirable properties concerning the handling of uncertainties in decision making [Morgan and Henrion, 1990; Helton, 1993]. These include inter alia:

- Possibility to sample the full range of all input data and parameters and to subsequently use all points as model input

- Capability of propagating uncertainties through a sequence (or chain) of models (including non-linear ones)

- Conceptually simple, often used, easy to understand/explain, operationally applicable and straightforwardly implementable

Perhaps not the only, but the major disadvantage of Monte Carlo Simulation is the large number of required model evaluations. This fact can constitute a computational limitation (or simply a time constraint) but within the scope of the application to the case study (cf. Chapter 4), such limitations did not occur. According to Basson [2004], when using Monte Carlo methods in practice, factors to be considered are for instance the choice of a sampling technique, the sample size and possible correlations between the model input. All these factors are strongly context-dependent. Concerning the choice of a sampling method, an increasingly widely used and recommended approach is "Latin Hypercube sampling"[9] [Iman et al., 1980; Morgan and Henrion, 1990; Helton and Davis, 2002]. However, it should be emphasised that the focus in this chapter is on describing methods that allow to investigate the ranges in which the results can vary in consequence

---

[9] To generate samples with this technique, each distribution is divided up into equiprobable intervals. Subsequently the sampling itself is carried out within these intervals according to the probability distribution, resulting in more uniformly spread values than strict random sampling.

of the variations of input data and parameters rather than comparing the use of different sampling techniques.

Yet another approach to address uncertainty in multi-criteria methods is carried out by fuzzy approaches [cf. e.g. Zadeh, 1965; Bellman and Zadeh, 1970; van Laarhoven and Pedrycz, 1983; Buckley, 1985; Boender et al., 1989; van de Walle and de Baets, 1995; de Baets et al., 1995; Carlsson and Fullér, 1996; Ribeiro, 1996; Geldermann, 1999; Geldermann et al., 2000]. Instead of describing the uncertainty probabilistically, a *possibility theory* [cf. Zadeh, 1978] has been developed within the fuzzy framework and for the uncertainty itself, terms such as *fuzziness* or *imprecision* are often used. In fuzzy set theory, imprecisions arising in a decision process can for instance be grouped into the classes "intrinsic imprecision", "relational imprecision" and "informational imprecision" [cf. e.g. Rommelfanger, 1994; Oder, 1994]. In the context of emission reduction strategies for energy systems, Oder [1994] further distinguishes different sources, besides linguistic ambiguity, from which the informational imprecisions may arise. These include *measurement*, *time*, *place* (or *location*) as well as the *environment* [cf. also Geyer-Schulz, 1986].

The use of fuzzy approaches as opposed to, for instance, probabilistic approaches is discussed controversially in literature. But such a discussion shall not be the focus of this thesis. However, the ranking of the alternatives using fuzzy approaches is usually based on defuzzfied values. It should be emphasised that the methods proposed in this thesis are aimed at communicating and visualising the ranges in which the results can vary due to the uncertainties in contrast to the results that would remain after a procedure such as the defuzzification (or after calculating expectation values in the case of probabilistic approaches).

Thus, Monte Carlo analysis is used for uncertainty handling within this thesis, providing an appropriate framework to address the different types of uncertainty in MADM (e.g. data and preferential uncertainties) in an understandable and transparent way. Moreover, Monte Carlo simulation has shown to be operationally applicable in the context of the case study and a combined consideration of the different types of uncertainty is easily possible. Further fields, in which Monte Carlo simulation has already been successfully applied include, for instance, uncertainty handling in time and motion studies in the sector of vehicle refinishing [cf. Schollenberger, 2006] or treatment of data as well as preferential uncertainties in multi-criteria decision support for production process design [cf. Treitz, 2006]. It should be noted that the use of Monte Carlo simulation for uncertainty handling does not contradict the opinion of Morgan and Henrion [1990] that, besides empirical uncertainties, it is advisable to treat the occurring uncertainties parametrically rather than probabilistically. But since it would be very time-consuming to investigate all reasonable parameter combinations one at a time [cf. e.g. Butler et al., 1997], Monte Carlo simulation is applied to speed up the process. Thus, the approaches elaborated within this chapter, especially those in Section 3.3, can be described as "Parametric Monte Carlo Techniques".

Having motivated the use of Monte Carlo techniques above, a Monte Carlo based approach to handle data uncertainties is introduced in Section 3.2. Subsequently, Section 3.3 deals with new Monte Carlo methods to cope with preferential uncertainties. Two ways allowing a simultaneous consideration of the effects of data and preferential uncertainties are described in Section 3.4. Equivalent approaches for a combined analysis of these two types of uncertainty and their respective impacts on the MADM results have not been mentioned in literature so far. A short methodic summary is given in Section 3.5.

3.2   Data Uncertainty

Data uncertainties, as described above, may arise in consequence of the uncertain evolution of the environment, form or parameters of potential upstream models, empirical uncertainties (aleatory as well as epistemic) or measurement uncertainties. The uncertainties of the data in a decision table can thus have many different reasons/sources. Consequently, a merely probabilistic treatment, as it could be done for empirical, especially aleatory, uncertainties is problematic as discussed before.

3.2.1   Modelling and Propagation of Data Uncertainties

When handling the data uncertainties by means of Monte Carlo simulation, as proposed in this thesis, several scenarios are treated in parallel. The scenarios are either obtained by randomly sampling values for each input according to some distribution or they may be available ready for use in the event that the sampling step had already been carried out before running a potential upstream model. In both cases, an adequate and reliable uncertainty assessment is required before the actual sampling. In the event that information is only available on the range of an input value but not on the specific distribution within the range, a uniform distribution can provide an appropriate approximation. If different (discrete) observations (or measurements) of one input value exist, they may also be represented in terms of a discrete probability distribution. Alternatively, the different scenarios can be defined as plausible futures using expert knowledge and experience.

In any case, the scenarios are used as parallel model inputs. If the sampling is carried out before an upstream model, the samples are used as input data for multiple parallel runs of this model, leading to multiple results for the consequences of the different decision alternatives. Hence, by using Monte Carlo simulation, uncertainties can be easily propagated through large model chains, including complex upstream or downstream models. The importance of this property of Monte Carlo simulation for decision support in risk management is described in detail in the context of the case study in Chapter 4. The subsequent multi-attribute decision analysis is not based on one (deterministic) decision table but on a set of decision tables where each table corresponds to one sample (realisation/scenario). The different decision tables are simultaneously evaluated, i.e. the MADM process is carried out in parallel for each scenario.

3.2.2   Visualisation of Data Uncertainties

In general, there are many different ways to visualise the results of a multi-attribute decision analysis [cf. e.g. Vetschera, 1994b,a; Hodgkin et al., 2005]. The focus in this section, however, is on visualising results under data uncertainty. In contrast to the approaches, which are based on calculating expected utilities (cf. Section 2.3), the main intention within this section is aimed at explicitly illustrating the spread of the results, i.e. the ranges in which the results can vary in consequence of the uncertain data in the decision table. A challenge in this context is that providing too much information about the uncertainties may easily cause an information overload which needs to be avoided.

An easy and understandable way to represent the uncertainty in decision analysis results is to simply illustrate the overall performance score for each alternative in each scenario. Assuming that there are ten possible scenarios (decision tables) or that ten possible realisations could be observed for the example described at the beginning of Section 2.2.1, such a visualisation of uncertainties is shown in Figure 3.2.

The advantage of such an illustration is that it is immediately possible to read off the percentage (of scenarios) at which an alternative receives the highest overall performance score. While in the left diagram of Figure 3.2, the results are simply sorted by the scenarios, they are sorted by alternative Alt_4 in the right diagram. With the latter illustration it is often easier to acquire a rapid overview. Furthermore, information about the exact percentage at which an alternative is ranked first can more clearly be read off from the right diagram. For instance, Alt_4 comes off best in 80 % of the scenarios for the considered example. Alternatively, the ranking of the alternatives could be visualised separately for each scenario by means of a stacked-bar chart as in Figure 2.5 (page 22).

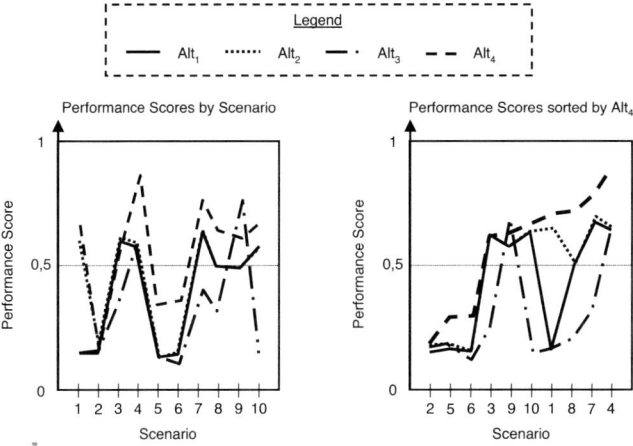

Figure 3.2: Representation of Uncertainties in Results by Showing Results for all Scenarios (Left); Same Results Sorted by Alt$_4$ (Right)

A drawback of both procedures, however, is that they quickly result in an information overload when the number of scenarios increases.

In order to avoid such an overload, it is advisable not to visualise all simultaneously calculated results. Here, the notion of *quantiles*[10] is helpful. The α-quantile of a distribution of a random variable X is for instance defined as the value x such that

$$P(X \leq x) \geq \alpha,\qquad(3.1)$$

where P denotes the probability [cf. e.g. Henze, 2006].

Transferring the concept of quantiles to the problem of illustrating the uncertainty ranges, the results of the scenarios corresponding to the 5 %- and 95 %-quantiles (of the overall performance score) can be shown alongside the results of the most probable scenario (cf. Figure 3.3) [Bertsch et al., 2005; Geldermann et al., 2006]. For a given alternative this means, for instance, that the probability that the overall performance score of this alternative in a (randomly picked) scenario is smaller than the score in the scenario corresponding to the 95 %-quantile is at least 95 %. The 5 %- and 95 %-quantile scenarios can also be referred to as *worst case* and *best case* scenarios respectively.

---

[10] Alternatively, the notions *percentile* or *fractile* are used in literature.

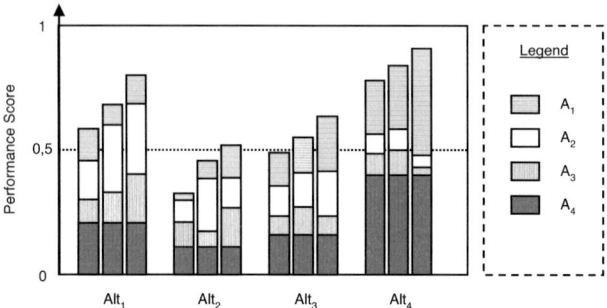

Figure 3.3: Representation of Uncertainties in Results by Means of a Stacked-Bar Chart

An illustration as in Figure 3.3 can provide important information for the decision makers. Similar to the results under certainty, a stacked-bar chart not only illustrates the uncertainty ranges of the overall goal but also indicates which of the considered attributes are subject to uncertainties and shows the uncertainty ranges of the individual attributes as well as their contribution to the uncertainties in the overall ranking. Furthermore, taking uncertainties into account in the decision making process allows to graphically analyse whether or not the considered alternatives are distinguishable from each other [cf. Basson, 2004].

An exact percentage at which an alternative receives the highest overall performance score cannot be read off from an illustration as in Figure 3.3 but the representation still sheds light on whether or not there are alternatives which are dominated by others. Another advantage of using the 5 %- and 95 %-quantiles instead of showing the results of all scenarios including the absolute minimum and maximum scores respectively is that potential outliers are usually eliminated. Not treating the outliers adequately may result in "squeezing" the rest of the data (when being mapped to a [0, 1] scale by a value function) and consequently in reducing the discriminating power of the attribute [Mavrotas and Trifillis, 2006].

In both representations (Figure 3.2 and Figure 3.3), the most important question is if the ranking (or at least the alternative with the highest performance score) remains the same for the different scenarios [Bertsch et al., 2005]. If it does, the results can be regarded as robust. Otherwise, it is important to investigate the reasons for the changes in the ranking, i.e. to relate the uncertainty in the results to the uncertainty in the input data.

3.2.3   Principal Component Analysis (PCA)

An additional way of visualising uncertainties in the results of MADM problems is provided by *Principal Component Analysis (PCA)* [cf. e.g. Timm, 2002; Härdle and Simar,
2003]. Since decision problems are usually characterised by a multiplicity of variables resulting in high-dimensional (often strongly correlated) data sets, appropriate multivariate
statistical techniques, such as PCA, are needed for a graphical illustration of such data
sets.

In general, principal component analysis is aimed at projecting high dimensional data
onto a lower dimensional space, most commonly a two-dimensional plane, with minimal
loss of information.[11] The axes of the target space of the transformation, the *principal
components*, are linear combinations of the axes of the original data space which are
composed in such a way that the principal components are uncorrelated (i.e. they are
orthogonal to each other). Thus, by applying PCA, the number of correlated variables is
reduced and, since the minimal loss of information corresponds to a maximum preservation
of variance, the (uncorrelated) principal components successively describe a maximum of
variance (information) [Timm, 2002; Härdle and Simar, 2003].

It should be noted that, in a first step, PCA is simply a rotation of the coordinate system
and that both, the original data space as well as the target space are n-dimensional. In a
second step, the desired reduction of dimension is attained by only using a subset of the
target coordinate system, often by only using the first two principal components.

3.2.3.1   Basics of Principal Component Analysis in MADM

The application of multivariate statistical techniques to support the visualisation of
MADM problems and results has been proposed by Stewart [1981]. In view of the reduction in dimension and, at the same time, the preservation of as much information as
possible, PCA is powerful in providing a rapid overview of the results of multi-attribute
decision analyses [cf. e.g. Hodgkin et al., 2005; Basson and Petrie, 2007]. Additionally,
similarities and dissimilarities of the different decision alternatives can be easily identified.

In order to apply PCA in MAVT, let V denote the matrix of the single-attribute performance scores of the different alternatives, i.e. each row of V corresponds to an alternative
and contains values out of $[0, 1]$ representing the performance scores with respect to the
individual attributes. Then, let $\mu(V)$ denote a matrix whose rows are all identical and
where the kth element within each row is the mean of the kth column of V. $\mu(V)$ is

---

[11] In linear algebra, the procedure is also known as *Principal Axis Transformation*.

needed for centring purposes, i.e. $\mu(V)$ is subtracted from V which does not affect the variance but the values of $V - \mu(V)$ are centred around zero and consequently the values in the PCA plane will later be centred around the origin. In order to perform a PCA, the eigenvalues and eigenvectors of the covariance matrix $\Sigma = cov(V - \mu(V))$ need to be calculated.[12] Since the covariance matrix Σ is symmetric, a "spectral decomposition"

$$\Sigma = \Gamma \Lambda \Gamma^T \tag{3.2}$$

exists according to the spectral theorem [cf. e.g. Beutelspacher, 1995], where the matrix Γ contains the eigenvectors $\gamma_1, ..., \gamma_n$ of Σ as columns and Λ is a diagonal matrix consisting of the eigenvalues $\lambda_1, ..., \lambda_n$ of Σ. Starting from Equation 3.2, it can furthermore be shown that the eigenvalue λ_i equals the variance of the jth *principal component* y_j for the transformation

$$Y = (V - \mu(V))\Gamma, \tag{3.3}$$

where the vector y_j is the jth column of the matrix Y [cf. e.g. Härdle and Simar, 2003]. Hence, for a maximum preservation of variance, the eigenvectors are sorted according to the magnitude of the corresponding eigenvalues (starting with the highest). Letting $\hat{\Gamma}$ denote the matrix of the sorted eigenvectors, the principal component transformation is given by

$$Y = (V - \mu(V))\hat{\Gamma}. \tag{3.4}$$

The y_j resulting from the transformation in Equation 3.4 are linear combinations of the axes of the original data space. The 1st principal component y_j is the linear combination with the largest variance and the 2nd principal component, which is orthogonal to the 1st, represents the largest part of the remaining total variance. By projecting the alternatives from the $\mathbb{R}^n$ onto the plane of the 1st and 2nd principal component, the dimension is reduced while preserving the maximum information in the $\mathbb{R}^2$.

Hence, the sorted eigenvalues are a measure for the ratio of the total variance, represented by the principal components. It can thus be calculated how much variance (information) is represented by the 1st and 2nd principal component. In general, the relative proportion

---

[12] For the outranking method PROMETHEE, for instance, this is much easier: Here, the matrix M of the *single criterion net flows* is "automatically" centred and in consequence of the inherent structure of M, its covariance matrix can be obtained as $M'M$. The PCA plane has a special name in PROMETHEE, it is called the *GAIA plane* (**G**eometric **A**nalysis for **I**nteractive **A**id) [cf. e.g. Brans and Mareschal, 2005].

of the variance represented by the first q principal components in comparison to the total variance can be measured as [cf. e.g. Härdle and Simar, 2003]

$$\delta_q = \frac{\sum\limits_{i=1}^{q} \lambda_i}{\sum\limits_{i=1}^{n} \lambda_i} \; ; \quad q \leq n \, . \tag{3.5}$$

In practice, more than 60 % or even 80 % of the total variance is often represented by the first two principal components [cf. e.g. Brans and Mareschal, 2005]. However, the ratio yet depends on the number of alternatives and attributes under consideration and it should be noted that there are many cases where less information is represented by the first two components. In such cases it is questionable whether or not the visual representation in the PCA plane is meaningful for the decision problem [cf. e.g. Basson, 2004].

In addition to the total variance ratio, the correlation of the new principal axes and the axes of the original data space may be of interest. In general, the correlation between two variables X and Y is defined as

$$\chi_{XY} = \frac{cov(X,Y)}{\sqrt{Var(X)Var(Y)}} \, . \tag{3.6}$$

Consequently, letting x_i denote the variable corresponding to the ith attribute, the correlation between the jth principal component y_j and the ith attribute can be measured as

$$\chi_{x_i y_j} = \frac{\gamma_{ij} \lambda_j}{(\sigma_{ii} \lambda_j)^{1/2}} = \gamma_{ij} \left(\frac{\lambda_j}{\sigma_{ii}} \right)^{1/2} , \tag{3.7}$$

where σ_{ii} is the ith diagonal element of the covariance matrix Σ (i.e. the variance of x_i) and γ_{ij} is the ith component of the jth eigenvector [cf. e.g. Härdle and Simar, 2003]. Equation 3.7 can be used to investigate how well the axis corresponding to the ith attribute is represented by the PCA. The decision makers can use this information to explore the representativeness of the 1st and 2nd principal component with respect to the ith attribute.[13]

3.2.3.2 Interpretation of the PCA Plane

The alternatives are plotted as triangles in the PCA plane and the unit vectors of the axes of the original data space (the attributes) are displayed as straight lines emanating from the origin (cf. Figure 3.4). The alternative vectors are usually longer than one. Thus, the

---

[13]Note that $\sum_{j=1}^{n} \chi_{x_i y_j} = 1$.

triangles corresponding to the alternatives are projected relatively far away from the origin for a growing number of attributes and, consequently, the attributes appear comparatively small which makes the interpretation more difficult. Therefore, the alternative vectors can optionally be normalised. In this case, the end points of the unit vectors of the alternatives are projected onto the plane and the projections of the alternatives thus move towards the origin. Thereby, the relative positions amongst the projections remain unchanged and the meaning is thus not affected. Since the performance scores are centred before PCA is applied, as explained in Section 3.2.3.1, the centre of the alternatives is located in the origin of the projection plane, i.e. an imaginary alternative with exactly average performance with respect to all attributes would be projected onto the new origin [Belton and Stewart, 2002].

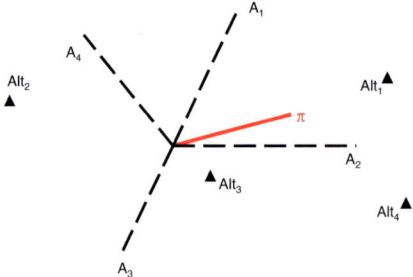

Figure 3.4: Alternatives and Attributes Evenly Spread in the PCA Plane

Alternatives projected close together in the PCA plane show similar characteristics and, correspondingly, strongly differing alternatives are usually projected distant from each other [Treitz, 2006]. Alternatives plotted in the direction of an attribute show good performance with respect to the attribute. Concerning the projections of the attributes, their length is a measure of the influence of the respective attribute on the decision problem, i.e. a long projection of the unit vector of an attribute on the plane corresponds to an attribute which is important in differentiating between the different alternatives and vice versa. Additionally, attributes whose projections approximately point in the same direction are positively correlated, while negatively correlated attributes have rather opposite orientations in the plane. Orthogonal attributes, however, imply independence of the attributes as regards their impact [cf. e.g. Brans and Mareschal, 1994].

Moreover, the PCA plane can lay open the representativeness of the selected attributes and the independence of the attributes concerning the considered alternatives can be investigated. In Figure 3.4 for instance, the attributes' projections point in all directions while in Figure 3.5 there are no attributes pointing in the direction of alternative Alt_2 indicating that the solution space is not adequately represented by the considered attributes.

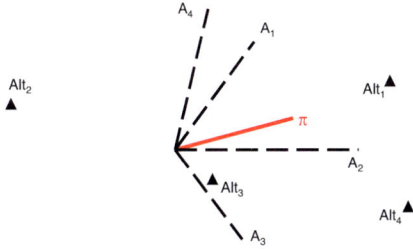

Figure 3.5: Alternatives and Attributes Unevenly Spread in the PCA Plane

However, it should be emphasised that the PCA plane provides an unweighted representation of the decision problem under consideration. Thus, while it provides a valuable overview of the performance of the alternatives relative to the different attributes and shows similarities or dissimilarities between alternatives, an aggregated ranking of the alternatives cannot be read off immediately from this illustration. For the latter, the so-called *decision axis* π, i.e. the projection of the normed weighting vector w, is usually displayed in the PCA plane in addition to the alternatives and attributes (see Figures 3.4 and 3.5). π points in the direction of the preferred alternatives according to the preferences of the decision makers, i.e. for different weights, π points in different directions and possibly different alternatives are preferred. While the normed weighting vector w always has the same length by definition, the length of its projection may of course change.[14]

An aggregated ranking can be obtained by projecting the alternatives orthogonally on the weighting vector (in the n-dimensional original data space) and by subsequently de-

---

[14]In studies in which PROMETHEE is used for instance, it is stated that the position of π determines the *decision power* [cf. e.g. Brans and Mareschal, 2005; Treitz, 2006]: In cases where w is comparatively flat in relation to the plane and therefore π is relatively long, alternatives projected far from the origin in the direction of π can usually be considered as well performing. If w is almost orthogonal to the plane, however, π is rather short. This can imply strongly conflicting objectives potentially resulting in difficulties in the determination of a preferred alternative.

termining the order of the respective perpendiculars on w. This is exemplarily shown in Figure 3.6, where the alternatives in the original data space, illustrated as small points, and the corresponding projections of the alternatives in the PCA plane, illustrated as slightly larger triangles, are labeled identically for reasons of clarity.

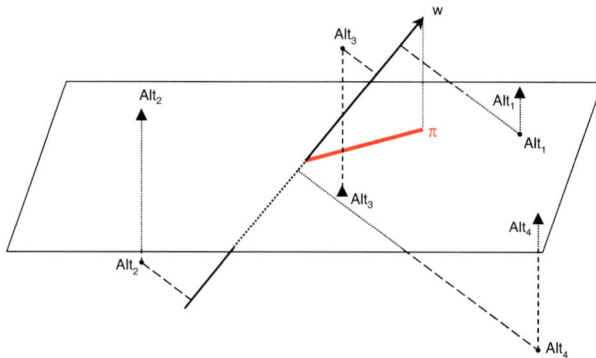

Figure 3.6: Projections of the Alternatives on the PCA Plane and on the Weighting Vector

Then, by "projecting these projections" onto the PCA plane, the aggregated ranking can also be visualised in the $\mathbb{R}^2$. It is obtained by determining the order of the intersections of the projected projections with the decision axis $[-\pi, +\pi]$ (see Figure 3.7). The performance score of an alternative equals the distance between the respective intersection and the origin on π.

In addition to the alternatives under consideration, it can be helpful to further consider the two fictitious alternatives *IDEAL* and *NADIR* in the PCA plane, which have already been introduced in Section 2.2.2. As pointed out in Section 2.2.2, these two practically unattainable points can provide valuable support in assessing the quality of the alternatives based on their relative positions in comparison to these points, i.e. alternatives projected close to the *IDEAL*, have high performance scores, while alternatives projected near the *NADIR* do not correspond to the preferences of the decision makers. The projections of the *IDEAL* and *NADIR* alternatives intersect the decision axis in π and $-\pi$ respectively (in the axis' ends, see Figure 3.7).

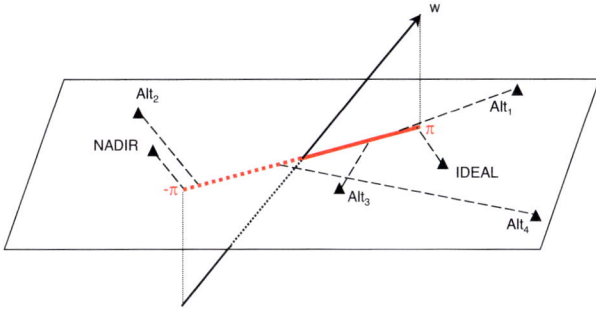

Figure 3.7: Visualisation of an Aggregated Ranking in the PCA Plane

3.2.3.3   PCA for the visualisation of data uncertainties

The value of PCA for the visualisation of data uncertainties is rooted in the possibility of its straightforward combination with Monte Carlo simulation. Assuming that the uncertainties of the data in the decision table have been modelled and propagated by means of Monte Carlo analysis, several points in the original data space, instead of only one, correspond to each alternative. More precisely, if ν denotes the number of (observed or sampled) scenarios, each alternative is represented by a cloud of ν points each of which is projected onto the PCA plane resulting in a scatter plot of triangles (cf. Figure 3.8).

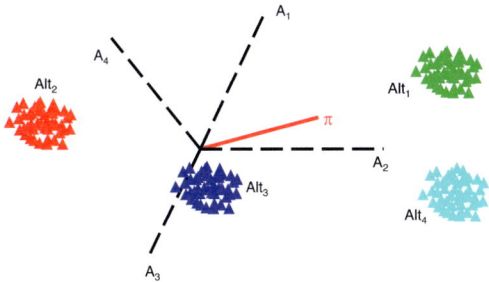

Figure 3.8: Representation of Data Uncertainty in the PCA Plane: Clearly Distinguishable Scatter Plots

This combination of PCA and Monte Carlo analysis provides a good graphic overview on the effect of the data uncertainties and allows to carry out a *distinguishability analysis* [cf. Basson, 2004; Basson and Petrie, 2007]. The *distinguishability* of alternatives can be explored graphically in the PCA plane, i.e. it is possible to explore whether or not the different alternatives can be evaluated meaningfully based on the considered attributes and the uncertainties afflicted with the data in the decision table. The complete set of points in the plane corresponding to one alternative represents the range of variation due to the underlying data uncertainty. For instance, in Figure 3.9, the alternatives Alt_1 and Alt_4 are not clearly distinguishable as a result of the uncertainties.

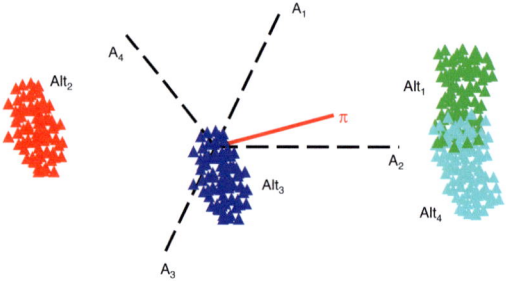

Figure 3.9: Representation of Data Uncertainty in the PCA Plane: Scatter Plots are not Clearly Distinguishable

In addition, an analytical evaluation of the distinguishability of the alternatives based on the calculation of a so-called *distinguishability index (DI)* has been suggested by Basson [2004]; Basson and Petrie [2007]. However, it should be noted that, while distinguishability of alternatives in the PCA plane implicates distinguishability of alternatives in the original data space, the situation is different for indistinguishability. Alternatives being indistinguishable in the plane do not necessarily imply that they are indistinguishable in the original data space. Before such conclusions can be drawn, additional analyses in the high-dimensional data set are necessary.

3.3 Parameter Uncertainty

In Section 3.2, Monte Carlo based methods have been introduced that allow to explore the effect of data uncertainties on the results of an MADM process. Some authors, however, argue that in practice it can often be observed that the impact of the data uncertainties is negligible, i.e. a common deterministic decision analysis will often lead to the same results as the more complex methods which are capable to cope with uncertainties [cf. e.g. von Winterfeldt and Edwards, 1986; Kirkwood, 1992; Papamichail, 2000; Papamichail and French, 2000]. Nevertheless, data uncertainties may of course cause changes in the ranking of the alternatives and the question whether or not they do, certainly depends on the individual context and the magnitude of the uncertainties. While the impact of data uncertainties in the context of a concrete case study will be investigated in Chapter 4, the particular focus of this section is the introduction of operationally applicable approaches for examining the effect of the preferential uncertainties (within certain boundaries), i.e. the uncertainties of the parameters introduced during the evaluation process.

While methods such as SWING and SMART [cf. Edwards, 1977; von Winterfeldt and Edwards, 1986] seek to support decision makers (or their advisers) in eliciting appropriate weights for the different criteria by allowing the assignment of weight ratios instead of direct weights, the most difficult problem is often the determination of precise weights or precise weight ratios. Experiences gained from conducting scenario-focused decision making workshops[15] and also training courses on the use of decision analysis, have shown that decision makers (or their advisers) do in general appreciate the benefits from applying MCDA but that they need more guidance. They were often unsure about an exact quantification of the modelled preferences due to the inherent degree of subjectivity contained within the preferential parameters [cf. e.g. Geldermann et al., 1999; Belton and Stewart, 1999; Bertsch et al., 2006a]. Hence, an appropriate handling of the preferential uncertainties is of particular importance.

The problem of preferential uncertainties is closely interconnected with the field of group decision processes [cf. e.g. Salo, 1995; Zhang, 2004]. It is suggested to allow the assignment of ranges (intervals) for the preference parameters instead of precise values since this could facilitate the preference elicitation process (for single decision makers but, in particular, also for groups). Furthermore, it should be noted that preferences may certainly vary according to value systems that are influenced by culture which, in particular, has to be accounted for when decision groups involve persons with different cultural backgrounds. Using approaches for sensitivity analysis that allow to find out whether or not the variation of certain weights has an impact on the ranking of the alternatives, disagreements which do not affect the results can be eliminated from debate and the group can focus on discussing the differences that do matter in terms of the results [French, 2003; Bertsch et al., 2006a].

---

[15] For instance, a series of such workshops has been organised across Europe within the European research project EVATECH ("Information Requirements and Countermeasure Evaluation Techniques in Nuclear Emergency Management", see: http://cordis.europa.eu/fp5-euratom/src/index.htm)

Sensitivity analyses, in general, are very helpful to examine the impact of variations of the preference parameters. The most frequently applied sensitivity analysis technique for multi-criteria problems, which simply allows an examination of the robustness of the choice of an alternative with respect to changes of the weight of a criterion, has been described as the fourth elementary step in a MAVT analysis in Section 2.2.1.4. Such one-dimensional sensitivity analyses are very helpful since they allow an assessment of the robustness of a decision and thus provide a deeper insight into the decision situation. However, a major drawback is that the procedure is limited to varying the weight of one criterion at a time. Consequently, the aim is the elaboration of an approach that allows to analyse the variation of several parameters at a time. While in Section 3.3.1 and Section 3.3.2, approaches to treat uncertainties in the inter-criteria and intra-criteria preference parameters will be described respectively, the main emphasis of this section is aimed at introducing an approach for investigating simultaneous variations of all parameters. For both, the inter-criteria as well as the intra-criteria preferences, intervals can be used to replace the precise parameters. Subsequently, since it would be very time-consuming to investigate all reasonable parameter combinations one at a time [cf. e.g. Butler et al., 1997], Monte Carlo simulation can be applied to draw samples within the intervals and to perform a multi-dimensional sensitivity analysis in order to explore the effect of the "preferential uncertainties" within the afore assigned intervals.

The problem of preferential uncertainties, however, is not new. It has been addressed by many researchers and practitioners in the field of decision analysis. For instance, the use of mathematical programming techniques to explore the sensitivity of multi-criteria decisions when simultaneously varying different decision parameters is proposed by Ríos-Insua and French [1991]; Proll et al. [1993]. Saaty and Vargas [1987] propose the use of interval judgments in the comparison matrix of the analytic hierarchy process (AHP [cf. Saaty, 1980]). In "Preference Programming", the interval judgments within AHP are interpreted as linear constraints and a series of linear programming problems is solved [Arbel, 1989; Salo and Hämäläinen, 1995]. Mustajoki et al. [2005] discuss "interval SMART/SWING", an approach that generalises the SMART and SWING methods by allowing the choice of an arbitrary attribute as reference attribute and by allowing interval judgments for the weight ratios. Chevalier and Téno [1996] use interval calculation techniques to model inaccurate data in the context of life cycle assessment (LCA). Lahdelma and Salminen [2001] and also Mavrotas and Trifillis [2006] propose to explore the weight space (i.e. describing the valuations which would make each alternative the most preferred one) when preference information is afflicted with uncertainties, missing or only partially available. Morgan and Henrion [1990] distinguish between probabilistic and parametric treatment of uncertainty. For preferential uncertainties, parametric sensitivity analyses [cf. also

Dinkelbach, 1969] are strongly preferred on the grounds that treating the uncertainties probabilistically may hide the impact of the uncertainties on the results while treating them parametrically potentially provides more insight into the situation. The use of simulation techniques for sensitivity analyses has for instance been proposed by Butler et al. [1997]; Mateos et al. [2006]. For outranking approaches, such as PROMETHEE for instance, the problem of preferential uncertainties is e.g. dealt with in Mareschal [1998]; Hyde et al. [2003]; Zhang [2004]; Treitz [2006].

As indicated above, many different methods to handle preferential uncertainties have previously been proposed in literature. However, an equivalent sensitivity analysis approach for the value functions including an investigation of their domains' boundaries and the simultaneous consideration of varying the different preferential parameters, as described later in this section, has not been mentioned in the existing literature so far. While a framework for multi-dimensional sensitivity analysis based on mathematical programming has already been proposed by Ríos-Insua and French [1991], an operationally applicable implementation has not been presented at that time. The rapid technological development in the area of information systems since the early 1990's now allows to close this gap. Thus, one aim within this thesis is the implementation of the proposed Monte Carlo approach in a usable tool. Furthermore, a large part of the existing literature is focussed on the theoretical foundations of the approaches and the presented examples are often of artificial nature. As it will be demonstrated in Chapter 4, large emphasis is placed on applying the presented approach to a case study in the context of industrial risk management and on supporting the communication of results by providing comprehensible visualisations throughout the decision making process.

3.3.1   Multi-Dimensional Inter-Criteria Sensitivity Analysis

A multi-dimensional approach is introduced to allow the consideration of simultaneous variations of the weights within a decision model and to facilitate the weight elicitation process by allowing the assignment of intervals instead of discrete weights. It should be emphasised that this approach is not aimed at substituting but at complementing the one-dimensional sensitivity analysis. Assuming, again, that n attributes are considered ($n \in \mathbb{N}$), this means that instead of assigning one exact weight w_i to each attribute i ($i \in \{1, ..., n\}$), it is sufficient to assign an interval $I(w_i)$ by determining a lower (w_i^l) and an upper (w_i^u) bound:

$$I(w_i) = \left[w_i^l, w_i^u\right] . \tag{3.8}$$

In groups, the intervals could for instance be obtained by permitting each group member
to define his or her weights individually and then defining the intervals as the superset
of the individual weights. Alternatively, the group members could be permitted to use
intervals, too, and the group interval could be obtained by using the superset of the
individual intervals. However, the uncertainties of the inter-criteria preferences for all n
attributes can then be described by the n-dimensional interval

$$C_w = \prod_{i=1}^{n} I(w_i) = \left[w_1^l, w_1^u \right] \times ... \times \left[w_n^l, w_n^u \right] , \qquad (3.9)$$

which can also be regarded as a generalised cuboid. However, not all points within C_w
represent valid weight combinations since they do not necessarily fulfill the constraint that
the sum of the weights of all attributes is equal to one. This constraint is represented by
the hypersurface

$$H = \left\{ w \in \mathbb{R}^n : w_i \geq 0, \sum_{i=1}^{n} w_i = 1 \right\} . \qquad (3.10)$$

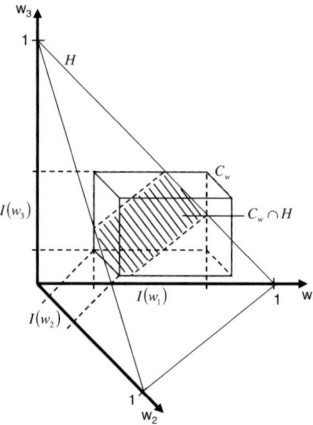

Figure 3.10: Intersection of the Weight Intervals and the (Hyper-)Surface Representing the Valid
    Weights in 3D

Hence, the intersection $C_w \cap H$ is the set of valid weight combinations within the n-
dimensional weighting interval. Thus, this is the basic set for the Monte Carlo Simulation
(see below). For $n = 3$ the set $C_w \cap H$ can be illustrated as the hatched area in Figure 3.10.
For higher dimensions, such a graphic illustration is not directly possible. However, the
method can nevertheless be applied for any dimension. The set $C_w \cap H$ of valid weight

combinations is also called *weight space* in literature [cf. e.g. Lahdelma and Salminen, 2001; Hodgkin et al., 2005; Mavrotas and Trifillis, 2006].

It is important to choose the weight intervals and thus C_w in such a way that $C_w \cap H \neq \emptyset$. It is of course possible to construct intervals that result in $C_w \cap H = \emptyset$. A procedure providing usable results for such parameter input would necessitate scaling up or down the input and would thus result in weights lying outside the afore assigned intervals (at least for some weights). Rather than considering such procedures, it is argued that, in practice, there should always be a facilitator who guides the decision making group in order to avoid the occurrence of such problems, to ensure that $C_w \cap H \neq \emptyset$ and to explain the difficulty to the members of the group of decision makers if necessary. For instance, a comparison of the ranges of the assigned weight intervals and the ranges of the actually drawn weights can provide the basis for a consistency check. The latter will be picked up again in more detail in Chapter 4.

Monte Carlo simulation can then be used to draw multiple samples of valid weight combinations, where "valid" means that the samples are drawn under the constraint that the sum of the weights of all attributes must be equal to 1. Uniform distributions of the weights within the assigned intervals are presumed for the analyses carried out, if no other information is available. On the one hand, this assumption was made for reasons of simplicity. But on the other hand, the most important (and most understandable) part in a practical application, is to illustrate the spread of the results (the ranges in which the results can vary) and not the probabilistic structure inside the spread [Bertsch et al., 2007c]. Thus, when drawing the samples, all elements of the set $C_w \cap H$ are considered to be equiprobable.

While the restriction of the simulation space to the set $C_w \cap H$, as illustrated in Figure 3.10, is conceptually simple, the question arises how this problem can be tackled computationally. Because of its straightforward implementability and its computation rate in practical applications, an approximate procedure as illustrated in Figure 3.11 is proposed. This procedure allows the sum of the attributes' weights to vary within the interval $[1 - \epsilon, 1 + \epsilon]$ whose size is determined by the *accuracy factor* ϵ ($\epsilon > 0$).

The accuracy factor ϵ certainly influences the computation rate. However, it could be observed in practical case studies that setting $\epsilon = 10^{-3}$ or $\epsilon = 10^{-4}$, for instance, gives good results in combination with an acceptable computation rate. Concerning the influence on the calculation speed, the same holds for the desired sample size τ. Here, practical experiences have shown that setting $\tau = 1000$ or $\tau = 10000$ usually leads to sufficiently good results, i.e. a graphical comparison has shown that the drawn samples provide a

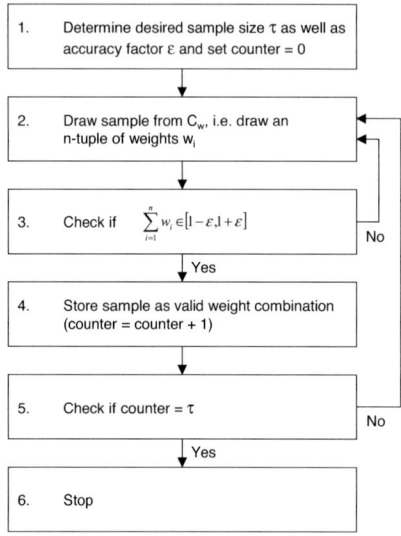

Figure 3.11: Proposed Procedure to Ensure that the Sum of the Weights is Equal to 1

good representation of the full range of the theoretical distribution. Once the samples are drawn, the approach is in principal straightforward and furthermore computationally easily feasible, i.e. the analysis is carried out in parallel for all samples.

As mentioned above, uniform distributions are used for the sampling of the weights w_i within the respective intervals $I(w_i)$. It should be noted that it can thus be concluded that the resulting weight combinations, sampled according to the proposed procedure, are also uniformly distributed (in $C_w \cap H$). However, such a conclusion cannot be drawn for arbitrary distributions.

3.3.2   Multi-Dimensional Intra-Criteria Sensitivity Analysis

Besides the elicitation of the inter-criteria preferences, i.e. the weights, the determination of the intra-criteria preferences, i.e. value functions' shapes, is a difficult task in practice. Thus, it is important to provide methods that allow to investigate the impact of varying the shape(s) of the value function(s) within certain intervals [cf. also Bertsch et al., 2007a]. In comparison to exploring the impact of simultaneously varying the weights, the procedure is much simpler for value functions since there is no constraint such as that their sum needs to be equal to 1 as for the weights.

In addition to varying the value functions' shapes it is also interesting to investigate the effect of varying their domains' boundaries. In practice, the boundaries are often defined by the minimum and maximum scores actually achieved by the different alternatives (with respect to the considered attributes). By following this approach, theoretically possible better or worse outcomes are neglected. However, the estimation of reasonable values for these theoretically possible boundaries is a difficult task. Thus, in order to support a decision making team in coping with this task, it is suggested to analyse whether or not the variation of the boundaries has an impact on the results.

Bearing the definition of an exponential value function (cf. Equation 2.4 on page 19) in mind, this means that the modelling of the uncertainties of the intra-criteria preferences concerns the parameters ρ_i (see Section 3.3.2.1) as well as x^i_{min} and x^i_{max} (see Section 3.3.2.2). Both procedures are very similar. In both cases, Monte Carlo simulation can be used to draw the samples.

3.3.2.1 Varying the Value Functions' Shapes

In the following, the impact of varying the parameters ρ_i (i.e. varying the shape(s) of the value function(s)) shall be analysed. For high positive and high negative values of a ρ_i, the exponential expression in Equation 2.4 almost equals a linear value function. For small positive values of ρ_i, the value function becomes concave (which means that differences between the scores are perceived to be more important in the lower half of the scale) and for small negative ρ_i, the function becomes convex (implying that differences between the scores are perceived to be more important in the upper half of the scale respectively) However, let now $\rho = (\rho_1, ..., \rho_n)$ denote the vector of the value functions' shape parameters. In order to explore the effect of simultaneously varying the value functions' shapes, it is proposed to assign an interval $I(\rho_i)$ to each attribute i by determining a lower (ρ^l_i) and an upper (ρ^u_i) bound instead of assigning a discrete value ρ_i:

$$I(\rho_i) = \left[\rho^l_i, \rho^u_i\right] . \tag{3.11}$$

The uncertainties with respect to the value functions' shapes can then be described by the n-dimensional interval

$$C_\rho = \prod_{i=1}^{n} I(\rho_i) = \left[\rho^l_1, \rho^u_1\right] \times ... \times \left[\rho^l_n, \rho^u_n\right] . \tag{3.12}$$

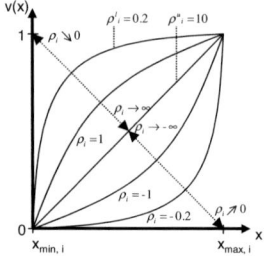

Figure 3.12: Value Function Shapes for Different Values of the Parameter ρ_i and Illustrative Visualisation of an Interval $I(\rho_i)$

For an increasing value function, the exemplar interval $I(\rho_i) = [0.2, 10]$ is illustrated as the grey area in Figure 3.12. Monte Carlo simulation can be used to draw samples of the vector ρ. Because of the exponential function in the definition of the value function (cf. Equation (2.4) on page 19), it is not advisable to simply presume a uniform distribution of the elements of the set C_ρ. For instance, there is not much difference in the curvature of the value functions corresponding to the parameters $\rho_i = 5$ and $\rho_i = 10$, whereas the difference is much larger for the functions corresponding to $\rho_i = 0.2$ and $\rho_i = 0.3$. Thus, a logarithmic transformation is performed at first and then, it is assumed that the elements of the transformed set can be considered to be equiprobable.

3.3.2.2   Varying the Value Functions' Domains

Besides varying the value functions' shapes, the effect of varying their domains' boundaries shall also be investigated [cf. also Bertsch et al., 2007a]. The procedure is very similar to the one described in the last section. Instead of varying the parameters ρ_i, the boundaries x^i_{min} and/or x^i_{max} are varied within their lower (e.g. $x^{i,l}_{max}$) and upper (e.g. $x^{i,u}_{max}$) bounds (see Figure 3.13):

$$I(x^i_{max}) = \left[x^{i,l}_{max}, x^{i,u}_{max}\right] . \tag{3.13}$$

These uncertainties can thus be described by the n-dimensional interval

$$C_{x_{max}} = \prod_{i=1}^{n} I(x^i_{max}) = \left[x^{1,l}_{max}, x^{1,u}_{max}\right] \times ... \times \left[x^{n,l}_{max}, x^{n,u}_{max}\right] . \tag{3.14}$$

The intervals $I(x^i_{min})$ and $C_{x_{min}}$ can be defined analogously. However, the upper bounds $x^{i,u}_{min}$ of the intervals of the lower boundaries and the lower bounds $x^{i,l}_{max}$ of the intervals of

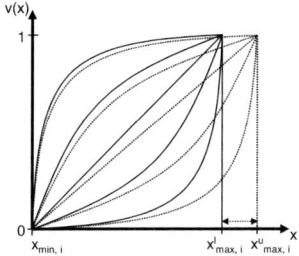

Figure 3.13: Value Function Shapes for Different Values of the Parameter x^i_{max}

the upper boundaries of the value functions' domains should be chosen in such a way that they correspond to the minimum and the maximum of the occurring scores respectively. This is important to ensure that the actually occurring scores cannot exceed the domains' boundaries.

3.3.3   Visualisation of Parameter Uncertainties

After presenting new methods for the modelling of preferential uncertainties in Sections 3.3.1 and 3.3.2, multi-dimensional sensitivity analyses can be performed for one or several preference parameter(s) from the set $\{w, \rho, x_{min}, x_{max}\}$, where each of the parameters is n-dimensional (and n is still the number of considered attributes). In practice, the parameter x_{min} is often equal to zero for at least some of the considered attributes in which case it is not varied since negative values would not make sense [Bertsch et al., 2007c]. However, comprehensible illustrations are very important to support the communication of the results of the multi-dimensional sensitivity analyses. Thus, the aim within this section is to propose understandable visualisations whose explanatory power goes beyond the often used box plots which are for instance used in the decision support tool GMAA.[16] Figure 3.14 shows possible results for the example described at the beginning of Section 2.2.1 for $\tau = 1000$ samples of the (n-dimensional) random quadruple $(w, \rho, x_{min}, x_{max})$.

As for the data uncertainties, taking preferential uncertainties into account allows to examine whether or not the considered alternatives are distinguishable from each other (from a preferential perspective). The left diagram shows the spread (the minimum, the maximum and the mean) of the overall performance scores as a result of the preferential

---

[16] GMAA: "Generic Multi-Attribute Analysis", see http://www.dia.fi.upm.es/~ajimenez/GMAA as well as Ríos-Insua et al. [2003]; Jiménez et al. [2005]; Mateos et al. [2006].

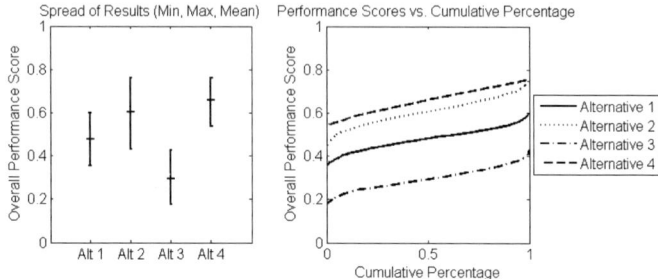

Figure 3.14: Possible Results for the Considered Example when Varying the Quadruple $(w, \rho, x_{min}, x_{max})$

uncertainties. Figure 3.14 shows that Alternative 1, Alternative 2 and Alternative 4 are not clearly distinguishable from each other in this example. But the results in the left diagram do show that, even in the "worst cases", Alternative 2 and Alternative 4 have a higher performance score than the Alternative 3 in the "best case" which means that the latter is dominated by Alternative 2 and Alternative 4.

While the left diagram provides a good overview on the impact of the uncertainties of the preferential information, it is not possible to read off information about the relative frequency of the performance scores of the different alternatives (i.e. performance scores at the lower and upper bound of the shown ranges will usually occur less frequently than those in the middle of the ranges). However, such information is provided in the right diagram. The illustration by means of plotting the performance scores versus the cumulative percentage has also been proposed by Butler et al. [1997]. This visualisation is favoured over a box plot since more proper information of the complete distribution of the results is provided.

It is important to note that the performance scores of the different alternatives at an imaginary "perpendicular cut" through the diagram of the cumulative percentage do not necessarily belong to only one parameter combination. Thus, information about the exact percentage at which a certain alternative is ranked first cannot be read off from this diagram immediately. This means, for instance, that it cannot be concluded from the right diagram of Figure 3.14 that Alternative 4 receives the highest overall performance score for all drawn parameter combinations. However, an illustration as in Figure 3.15 (where Alternative 4 is visualised as in Figure 3.14 but the other alternatives are sorted in such a way that their scores at an imaginary "perpendicular cut" do belong to the same parameter combination) or an analytical evaluation can be helpful to provide such accurate information. For the considered example, Alternative 4 is ranked first for 86.5 %, Alternative 2 for 13 % and Alternative 1 for 0.5 % of the drawn weight combinations. Additionally, a visualisation as in Figure 3.15 can provide insight into potential correlations between the different alternatives. For example, Figure 3.15 indicates a correlation between Alternative 4 and Alternative 2.

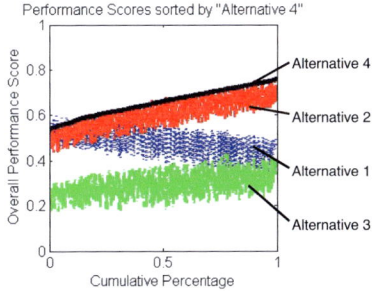

Figure 3.15: Possible Results Sorted by Alternative 4

In addition, a *backwards calculation* can help to investigate the origin of potential differences in the results (see Figure 3.16). Beyond the information provided in Figure 3.14 and Figure 3.15 it would for instance be very helpful for a decision making team to explore which preference parameter combinations result in Alternative 2 and which combinations result in Alternative 4 as the alternative with the highest performance score. For the weights, Figure 3.16 provides such information in an easily understandable way. The upper diagram shows all drawn weight combinations (i.e. the complete weight space). The lower diagram only shows those weight combinations for which Alternative 2 has the highest overall performance score. While the intervals in both diagrams seem to be more or less the same for almost all attributes, differences can be seen for Attribute 2. While the interval assigned to Attribute 2 allows the weight to vary between 0.05 and 0.2, the weights of Attribute 2 for which Alternative 2 turns out to be the most preferred alternative are not higher than 0.08. Such information can be very valuable for groups so that their discussion can focus on the most important preference parameters in terms of their respective impact on the results.

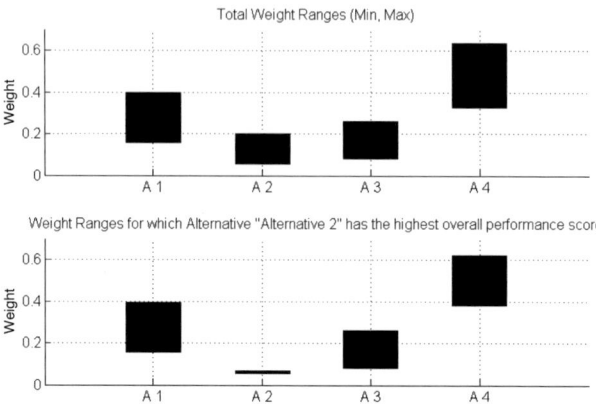

Figure 3.16: Backwards Calculation

3.3.4   Principal Component Analysis (PCA) for Parameter Uncertainties

For the visualisation of MADM results under data uncertainty, PCA has been described as a powerful method to provide a fast overview of the impact of the underlying uncertainties (cf. Section 3.2.3). Thus, beyond the visualisation techniques for preferential uncertainties introduced in Section 3.3.3, the use of PCA for visualising the impact of the uncertainties of the preference parameters is described in this section, eventually also providing the basis for a combined consideration of data and parameter uncertainties in the PCA plane (cf. Section 3.4.2). While Section 3.3.4.1 deals with the projection of the uncertainties with respect to the inter-criteria preferences onto the PCA plane, the projection of the intra-criteria preferential uncertainties is described in Section 3.3.4.2.

3.3.4.1   Projecting the Weight Space onto the PCA Plane

It should be noted that the basic principle of projecting alternatives and attributes from an n-dimensional space onto a plane by PCA, as described in Section 3.2.3.1, remains unchanged. In Section 3.2.3.2, however, the decision axis π, i.e. the projection of the normed weighting vector onto the PCA plane, has been introduced. The aim of this section is to link the concept of π to the procedure allowing to simultaneously vary the weights (cf. Section 3.3.1). Each (sampled) valid weight combination of the set $C_w \cap H$ represents a different (normed) weighting vector w. Projecting each of the τ weighting vectors onto the plane would result in τ different decision axes π which cannot be simultaneously visualised without causing confusion. But the endpoints of the weighting vectors, representing the set $C_w \cap H$ (i.e. the weight space), can be projected onto the plane and the convex hull of the projections can be illustrated. The projection of the weight space or, more precisely, its convex hull will be denoted by Ω in the following. Ω surrounds the endpoint of π and marks the range in which π can move when varying the weights within the defined interval limits (see Figure 3.17).[17]

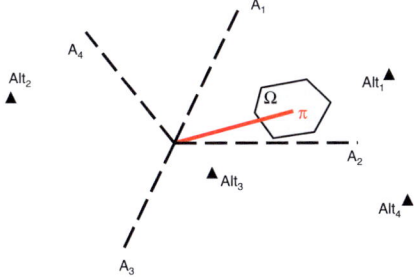

Figure 3.17: Projected Weight Space Ω in the PCA Plane

It should be noted that the position of Ω relative to the origin in the plane gives a general impression of the magnitude of the impact of the inter-criteria preferential uncertainties. In the event that Ω is situated in the plane as in Figure 3.17, not including the origin, it can be argued that all valid weight combinations point at least in a similar direction. Consequently, the alternatives lying in this direction will in general be preferred. In the event that Ω is located centrally in the plane, including the origin, π – representing the valid weight combinations – can point in any direction. Thus, for each direction of π, different alternatives will be preferred resulting in a more difficult decision problem. More detailed discussions on so-called "hard" and "soft" problems can for instance be found in Brans and Mareschal [1995]; Treitz [2006].

---

[17]Projecting the convex hull of all valid weighting vectors on the PCA plane is well known for the outranking method PROMETHEE, too. There, the generated convex polygon on the plane is called the *PROMETHEE VI Area* or sometimes also the *Human Brain (HB)*, as it visualises the preference perceptions of the decision makers [Brans and Mareschal, 1995]. However, problems concerning the calculation speed for the determination of this convex hull, as reported by Treitz [2006] for instance, could not be observed using the procedure of Figure 3.11 since the drawn samples representing the weight space only need to be projected onto the plane.

However, an exact determination of the effects of simultaneously varying the weights within their intervals based on the projected weight space Ω and the decision axis π is problematic. For this, insights as offered by the backwards calculation (see Figure 3.16) need to be made available in the PCA plane. This means that a possibility should be provided to partly project the weight space, i.e. to only project those weight combinations onto the plane for which a certain alternative is the most preferred. Such a so-called *preference region*[18] [cf. e.g. Hodgkin et al., 2005] can be denoted by Ω_j in the plane, where $j \in \{1, ..., m\}$ denotes the index of the most preferred alternative (as Ω_4 in Figure 3.18 denotes the projection of the weights for which Alternative 4 is most preferred). Hodgkin et al. [2005] describe a way to show a preference region in a triangular plot. In the context of this thesis, the projection of such a preference region is displayed in the PCA plane together with the complete projected weight space in order to provide an overall overview (see Figure 3.18).

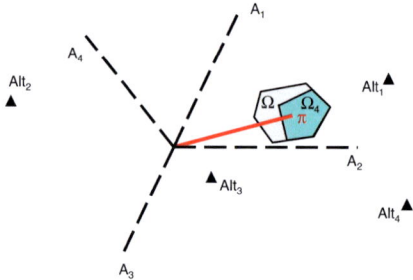

Figure 3.18: A Preference Region within Ω in the PCA Plane

3.3.4.2   Intra-Criteria Preferential Uncertainties in the PCA Plane

As described in Section 3.2.3.1, the projection by PCA is based on the matrix V of the single-attribute performance scores of the different alternatives, i.e. the original values of the decision table have already been transformed, each on a $[0, 1]$ scale, by the corresponding value functions. Thus, a variation of the intra-criteria preference parameters affects the matrix V and consequently also the position of the alternatives' projections in the plane. This effect of the intra-criteria preferential uncertainties shall also be visualised in the PCA plane. In principle, the procedure is similar to that described for the data uncertainties in Section 3.2.3.3. While in Section 3.2.3.3, the performance scores of the

---

[18] The notion *stability interval* is also used in literature [cf. e.g. Zhang, 2004; Treitz, 2006].

alternatives for each of the ν scenarios were projected onto the plane, the alternatives' scores for each of the τ samples are now projected and illustrated. In order to distinguish between data and parameter uncertainties in the PCA plane, the alternatives are now plotted as points instead of triangles in the plane or, more precisely, each alternative is now represented by a cloud of points in the plane (see Figure 3.19). The spread of points in the plane corresponding to one alternative represents the range of variation in consequence of the underlying intra-criteria uncertainty.

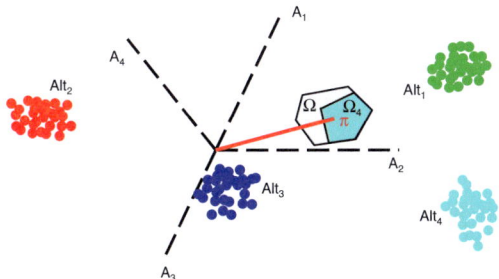

Figure 3.19: Combined Illustration of all Preferential Uncertainties in the PCA Plane

Similar to the scatter plots for the data uncertainties (see Figures 3.8 and 3.9), Figure 3.19 provides a graphical facility to explore whether or not the alternatives are distinguishable from each other in the light of the underlying parameter uncertainties. As for the methods introduced in Section 3.3.2, a separate investigation of the impact of varying the value functions' shapes and that of varying their domains' boundaries can provide further insight into the relevance of each of the parameters concerning the corresponding effect on the results. Altogether, showing the projected weight space Ω in addition to the intra-criteria scatter plots, Figure 3.19 provides a holistic impression of the impact of the complete preferential uncertainty on the MADM results.

3.4 Combined Consideration of Data and Parameter Uncertainties

When motivating the use of Monte Carlo analysis for uncertainty handling in MADM in Section 3.1, one point that has been stressed was the straightforward possibility to simultaneously consider the different types of uncertainty in an understandable and transparent

way. Section 3.4.1 deals with the incorporation of the simulation based approaches for
preferential uncertainty handling, described in Section 3.3, into the framework of MAUT
(cf. Section 2.3). In Section 3.4.2, an illustration for the simultaneous consideration of
data and parameter uncertainties in the PCA plane is introduced.

3.4.1   Integration of the Simulation Based Approaches for Parameter Uncertainties into MAUT

In Section 2.3, approaches for data uncertainty handling have been introduced which
are based on calculating expected utilities – in the Bayesian case subjective expected
utilities. In contrast to the methods described in Section 3.2, these methods are not
aimed at explicitly illustrating the range in which the results can vary in consequence of
the data uncertainties since, after the aggregation into an expected utility, all information
about the uncertainties is (implicitly) included in this utility.

However, this section is aimed at introducing a sensitivity analysis concept for the methods
presented in Section 2.3 allowing to investigate the robustness of MAUT results with
respect to parameter variations [cf. e.g. Ríos-Insua and Ruggeri, 2000]. Thus, the multi-
dimensional sensitivity analyses introduced in Section 3.3 shall now be integrated into
MAUT, i.e. the preference parameters – especially the weights – in equations 2.22 and
2.25 will be simultaneously varied allowing to investigate the corresponding impact on
the expected utilities and thus allowing to consider data and parameter uncertainties
at the same time. In addition, the impact of the risk attitude, encoded in κ, will be
explored. In particular, it seems to be important to analyse the impact of the weights
on the expected utility calculated according to Equation 2.22 which includes a quadratic
term of the weighting vector w.

The procedure is very similar to the one described in Section 3.3. The samples of the
preference parameters are generated exactly as proposed in Sections 3.3.1 and 3.3.2. Each
of the τ samples is then processed in parallel and the expected utilities are calculated
according to either Equation 2.22 or 2.25. Since an illustration of the results as in Figure
3.15 seems to be very powerful concerning the insight that it provides, such a visualisation
is also suggested for the combined consideration of data and parameter uncertainties. The
analysis can then be repeated for different values of κ in order to analyse the sensitivity
with respect to the risk attitude. Figure 3.20 shows the results of such an analysis when
the weights are varied. However, varying the value function parameters in addition (or
instead) is straightforwardly possible, too. In general, the expected utilities in the right
diagram are much smaller than those in the left which is understandable, bearing Equation

2.25 in mind according to which the utilities have been obtained. However, besides the general altitude of the utilities, there are no differences between the left and the right diagram, i.e. there are no changes in the ranking in consequence of varying κ. In both cases, the exemplar results show Alternative 4 to be the most preferred alternative for 100 % of the drawn weight combinations.

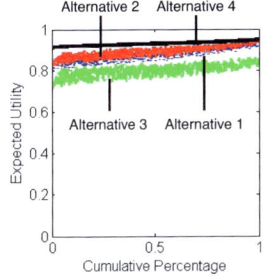 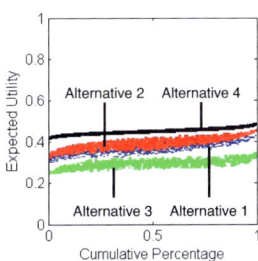

Figure 3.20: Expected Utilities Sorted by Alternative 4 for $\kappa = 0.25$ (left) and $\kappa = 1$ (right)

As mentioned above, it is especially important to analyse the impact of varying the weights when an expected utility of the form of Equation 2.22 is used, i.e. when the data is normally distributed. It has been described in Section 2.3.1.3 that, in consequence of the monotonicity of exponentiation, Equation 2.22 can be reduced to the simplified evaluation rule in Equation 2.23. The second term of Equation 2.23 $\left(\frac{w^T C w}{2\kappa}\right)$ is particularly interesting since it is quadratic in w. Additionally containing the covariance matrix C and the risk attitude κ, this term basically includes all information about the uncertainties and will thus be called *uncertainty factor* henceforth. Figure 3.21 shows exemplar results of the uncertainty factor for two different values of κ presuming that the data in the example described at the beginning of Section 2.2.1 is normally distributed.

However, as already indicated in Section 2.3.1.3 it becomes apparent from Equation 2.23 that, besides the value of κ, the interaction of the weighting vector w and the covariance matrix C plays an important role in determining the magnitude of the uncertainty factor. It can be expected that the uncertainty factor is large if the weights on the attributes with a high covariance are high. In order to gain further insight into this interaction of w and C, it is proposed to compute the covariance matrix on the one hand and, on the other hand, to perform a slightly modified backwards calculation in comparison to the one described in Section 3.3.3. Instead of examining which parameter combinations lead to which preferred alternative, it is now suggested to analyse which weight combinations

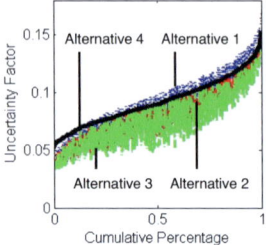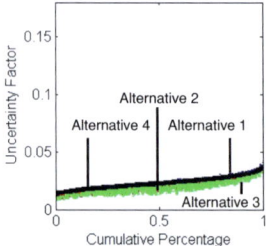

Figure 3.21: Uncertainty Factor for Different Values of κ (Left: $\kappa = 0.25$, Right: $\kappa = 1$)

result in a high uncertainty factor. For instance, Figure 3.22 shows the weights related to the highest 5 % of the uncertainty factor of Alternative 4 of the example in comparison to the total weight ranges.

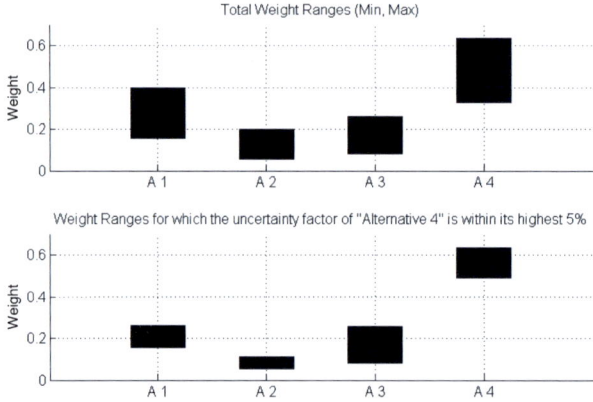

Figure 3.22: Weight Space Exploration for Uncertainty Factor

A comparison of the covariance matrix C and the results from a visualisation as in Figure 3.22 can give valuable insights into the robustness of the expected utility calculations. For instance, Figure 3.22 shows for Alternative 4 in the example that the weights drawn for attribute A_4, which can be associated with the highest 5 % of the uncertainty factor, are all in the upper third of the complete weight range assigned to A_4. Accordingly, the highest value of the covariance matrix corresponding to Alternative 4 is the variance of attribute A_4. Hence, for normally distributed data, a procedure has been elaborated in order to determine whether or not the underlying uncertainty can significantly affect the expected utilities. Since several alternatives are compared by this procedure, the alternative index j ($j \in \{1, ..., m\}$) is included into Equation 2.23:

$$\sum_{i=1}^{n} w_i \mu_{i,j} - \frac{w^T C_j w}{2\kappa} . \tag{3.15}$$

Then, the procedure can be summarised by the following six steps:

1. Determine, for each alternative j, the covariance matrix C_j, the mean performance score $M_j = \sum_{i=1}^{n} w_i \mu_{i,j}$ and the uncertainty factor $U_j = \frac{w^T C_j w}{2\kappa}$.

2. Determine $M_{j_{max}} = \max_{j=1}^{m} \{M_j\}$ and $M_{j_{second}} = \max_{\substack{j=1 \\ j \neq j_{max}}}^{m} \{M_j\}$.

3. Select the covariance matrices $C_{j_{max}}$ and $C_{j_{second}}$ for the two alternatives j_{max} and j_{second}, i.e. the alternatives with the highest and second highest mean performance score.

4. Determine $\Delta M = M_{j_{max}} - M_{j_{second}}$ and $\Delta U = U_{j_{max}} - U_{j_{second}}$.

5. Check if a sample $k \in \{1, ..., \tau\}$ exists with

$$\frac{(w^k)^T C_{j_{max}} w^k}{2\kappa} - \frac{(w^k)^T C_{j_{second}} w^k}{2\kappa} > \Delta M , \tag{3.16}$$

$$\Longleftrightarrow \quad \Delta U > \Delta M , \tag{3.17}$$

   where w^k denotes the kth sampled weighting vector.

6. Store and visualise (for example as in Figure 3.22) all samples k for which equations 3.16 and 3.17 become true. If such samples exist, the weight intervals and the assessed risk attitude κ should be re-examined. If such samples do not exist, the underlying uncertainties will not affect the results for the determined risk attitude and preference parameter intervals. This means, that in such cases, it is sufficient to calculate the mean performance scores.

The above procedure has been described to analyse if changes in the ranking of the alternatives with the highest and second highest performance score can occur. However, if the decision makers are interested in rank reversals of other alternatives besides those with the two highest scores, the procedure can be applied analogously. It should be stressed, however, that the fact that no preference parameter samples exist which fulfil Equation 3.16 or Equation 3.17 does not automatically imply that evaluating each of the ν scenarios deterministically, gives the same results.

3.4.2   Combined Consideration of Data and Parameter Uncertainties in the PCA Plane

The combined exploration of the impact of data and parameter uncertainties in the PCA plane is very similar to the simultaneous consideration of intra-criteria and inter-criteria preferential uncertainties in the PCA plane as described in Section 3.3.4.2. While Section 3.4.1 dealt with the incorporation of the Monte Carlo based approaches to handle preference parameter uncertainties (cf. Section 3.3) into the concept of utility theory (cf. Section 2.3), where the ranges in which the results can vary due to the uncertainties are usually not explicitly illustrated, this section is aimed at combining the methods described in Sections 3.2 and 3.3, in particular those of the Sections 3.2.3 and 3.3.4. This means that, in contrast to the previous section, the approach described in this section seeks to explicitly visualise the spread of the results due to the different types of uncertainty.

While the uncertainties of the inter-criteria preference parameters can be visualised in the PCA plane in the form of the projected weight space Ω, the uncertainties of the intra-criteria preference parameters and the data uncertainties both affect the values in the matrix V of the alternatives' single-attribute performance scores upon which the PCA projections are based. Influencing the position of the alternatives' projections in the plane, the latter two types of uncertainty are visualised as scatter plots. Simultaneously considering data and parameter uncertainties instead of considering each type individually means that each of the τ drawn parameter combinations is associated with each of the ν scenarios resulting in $\nu \cdot \tau$ projections per alternative. As for the data uncertainties (cf. Section 3.2.3.3), they are shown in the form of triangles in the plane (see Figure 3.23).

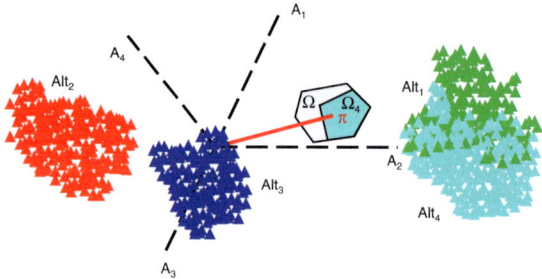

Figure 3.23: Combined Consideration of Data and Parameter Uncertainties in the PCA Plane

Again, the spread of the projections corresponding to an alternative represents the range of variation and it is possible to graphically explore whether or not the alternatives are distinguishable from each other in the light of the underlying uncertainty. As a result of the higher number of projections per alternative when simultaneously considering data and parameter uncertainties, it is likely that the spread of each alternative increases and thus, that the distinguishability decreases accordingly. Showing the projected weight space Ω as well as the scatter plots, representing the data and the intra-criteria preferential uncertainties, Figure 3.23 provides an overall overview of the impact of the different types of uncertainty on the MADM results.

3.5 Summary

Decision making processes in the context of industrial risk management are subject to various sources of uncertainty. Starting from a structured uncertainty classification, new simulation based methods have been elaborated and introduced seeking to provide operationally applicable decision support in the light of different types of uncertainty. The approaches for uncertainty handling have been presented with a special focus on visualisation techniques and are aimed at explicitly illustrating the spread, i.e. the ranges in which the MADM results can vary in consequence of the uncertainties.

Since, as described in Section 2.1, one of the basic principles of MCDA is the explicit recognition of subjectivity in decision making processes, sophisticated sensitivity analysis approaches are important to investigate the impact of variations of the many subjective preference parameters. In particular, the approaches for multi-dimensional sensitivity analysis (cf. Section 3.3) can contribute to facilitate the preference elicitation and consensus building in decision making groups. It is likely that different members of a group argue for different preference parameters. The proposed methods can provide valuable insights into the robustness of a decision which is especially important for industrial risk management. Furthermore, they allow to explore trade-offs between conflicting objectives. The results of the different analyses lead to a deeper understanding of decision problems.

The added value of the described methods is particularly to be seen in the framework for value function sensitivity analysis, i.e. the analysis of the intra-criteria preferential uncertainties – including an investigation of the impact of varying the boundaries of the value functions' domains and furthermore in the approaches for simultaneously considering different types of uncertainty. The introduced approaches to perform backwards calculations are especially valuable in order to link the uncertainties in the MADM results to the uncertainties in the MADM input data and parameters. Consequently, the decision makers are able to evaluate the influence of the chosen preference parameters and to investigate the sensitivity in the light of uncertainty. Allowing the assignment of intervals for the preference parameters seems to provide a more adequate model of human preferences than sharply defined values.

The case study in the next chapter (Chapter 4) shows the application of MCDA and the various simulation based approaches for uncertainty handling and visualisation. The methods described above have been implemented in a software prototype in MATLAB[19] within this thesis in order to demonstrate their respective functionalities in the context of the case study. It should be noted, however, that the described approaches are universally applicable and can be applied in a straightforward way in any context where multi-criteria decision analysis is used to support decision makers or their advisers in resolving complex decisions.

---

[19] For further information see: http://www.mathworks.com

Chapter 4

Decision Support for Nuclear Emergency and Remediation Management

An important and challenging area within the field of industrial risk management is nuclear emergency and remediation management involving various stakeholder and expert groups with diverse background knowledge in the decision making process. Know-how from economic, ecological, engineering and natural sciences must be brought together, taking into account political and socio-psychological factors resulting in a typical MCDA problem. Thus, the focus of this chapter is the application of the newly developed methods described in Chapter 2 and Chapter 3 to a hypothetical case study from nuclear emergency and remediation management.

Before the actual application, the general background of the case study is described in Section 4.1 and the different components of the decision support system RODOS are introduced in Section 4.2. Subsequently, the hypothetical case study, which was used within a moderated decision making workshop in Germany in order to discuss agricultural countermeasure and remediation alternatives, is presented in Section 4.3. The course of action as well as the main results of the corresponding workshop are illustrated in Section 4.4. After describing how the uncertainties of the input data and the preference parameters can be modelled for the case study (Section 4.5), special focus within Section 4.6 is put on the application of the new approaches for uncertainty handling to the case study. The main results of the case study are discussed and summarised in Section 4.7.

4.1 Background and General Setting

One of the major observations following the nuclear accident from Chernobyl in 1986 was that decision making needs to be harmonised between and in individual countries [Ehrhardt et al., 1993; Ehrhardt and Weiss, 2000; French, 2000; Raskob et al., 2005a]. Initiatives emerged to overcome this problem and the development of a common Decision Support System (DSS), suitable to be applied in the whole of Europe, became one of the major tasks in the area of radiation protection of the European Commission's Framework Programmes. The development, starting in 1989 and involving more than 40 research institutions and national emergency management organisations in over 20 European countries, resulted in the RODOS[20] system which provides consistent and comprehensive decision support at different levels in the event of a nuclear or radiological emergency in Europe.

In order to test the applicability of RODOS, a series of moderated stakeholder workshops was organised across Europe.[21] These workshops were inter alia aimed at familiarising the responsible persons with the capabilities of the system and at gathering feedback in order to ensure that the developments meet the requirements of the potential users [cf. e.g. Geldermann et al., 2005; Sinkko et al., 2005]. In these workshops, moderation techniques [cf. e.g. Seifert, 2002] were applied in combination with MCDA.

In the following, fundamentals about events at nuclear installations are introduced, providing the basis for classifying such events according to their severity. Subsequently, similarities between moderation methods and MCDA are pointed out followed by describing their application within the workshops.

4.1.1 Events at Nuclear Installations

Nuclear power plants have multi-level safety devices and, in addition, there are pre-planned safety procedures in order to prevent the occurrence of a nuclear accident with large-scale radiological consequences. Nevertheless, incidents and accidents did occur in the past. So far, the accident in Chernobyl in 1986 had the most serious consequences,

---

[20] RODOS: Real-time Online Decision Support System for Nuclear Emergency Management (see: http://www.rodos.fzk.de)

[21] Within the EVATECH project ("Information Requirements and Countermeasure Evaluation Techniques in Nuclear Emergency Management"), a total of nine workshops were organised in Belgium, Denmark, Finland, Germany, Poland, the Slovak Republic and the UK.

116 000 people were evacuated and additional 220 000 people were relocated in the following years [UNSCEAR, 2000].

For the characterisation and classification of events at nuclear power plants, an "International Nuclear Event Scale (INES)" (cf. Table 4.1) was designed by an international group
of experts convened jointly in 1989 by the International Atomic Energy Agency (IAEA)
and the Nuclear Energy Agency (NEA) of the Organisation for Economic Co-operation
and Development (OECD). By using consistent terms to communicate the safety significance of events, the scale can facilitate a common understanding amongst the nuclear
community, the media and the public and can thus also contribute to safety improvements.
It is successfully being used in over 60 countries [IAEA, 1999].

Table 4.1: The International Nuclear Event Scale (INES) [cf. IAEA, 1999]

	Level – Descriptor	Examples
	7 – Major accident	Chernobyl, Soviet Union (now Ukraine), 1986
	6 – Serious accident	Kyshtym reprocessing plant, Soviet Union (now Russia), 1957
Accident	5 – Accident with off-site risk	Windscale (now Sellafield), UK, 1957
		Three mile island (Harrisburg), USA, 1979
	4 – Accident without significant off-site risk	Windscale reprocessing plant (now Sellafield), UK, 1973
		Saint-Laurent, France, 1980
		Buenos Aires, Argentina, 1983
Incident	3 – Serious incident	Vandellos, Spain, 1989
	2 – Incident	
	1 – Anomaly	(*)
Deviation	0 – No safety significance	

(*): The majority of reported events are found to be below Level 3. No specific examples of
these events are given here. Countries in which the scale is used usually provide information
on events at the lower levels individually [For Germany for instance, cf. e.g. Lindauer, 2005;
Borst et al., 2006, as well as http://www.bfs.de/kerntechnik/ereignisse/berichte].

4.1.2 Moderated Workshops

Decisions in the context of emergency and remediation management involve many parties
who usually have different views, responsibilities and interests [Hämäläinen et al., 2000;
Sinkko, 2004; Carter, 2005; French and Geldermann, 2005; Geldermann et al., 2005, 2007].

Priorities must be set and a consensus must be found for the different parties involved in the decision making process. Decision makers (DMs) are those responsible for the decision. Stakeholders share, or perceive that they share, the impacts arising from a decision and therefore they claim that their perceptions should be taken into account. Experts provide economic, engineering, scientific, environmental and other professional advice. Analysts are concerned with the synthesis of the DMs' and stakeholders' value judgments and the experts' advice [Belton and Stewart, 2002]. In addition, they guide and assist the DMs and are experienced in applying MCDA.

The stakeholder workshops, organised across Europe, can also be seen as emergency exercises, which are important since the identification of responsibilities and authorities is vital to implementing a rapid response in emergency and remediation management [Geldermann et al., 2007]. In these workshops, moderation techniques [cf. e.g. Seifert, 2002] have been applied in combination with MCDA, i.e. the decision making process and, in particular, the processes of problem structuring and preference elicitation were guided by a moderator/facilitator whose responsibility is to lead the discussion and to introduce the individual work steps. This aspect is very important in multi-stakeholder settings in order to reduce potentially arising tensions. Furthermore, moderators steer the group with questions as the work continues and manage the interactions with and between participants. Without actively interfering into the discussion, their task is to resolve disagreements and to foster consensus building [cf. e.g. Geldermann and Rentz, 2004].

MCDA, as a tool, can be very helpful in structuring such moderated discussions. Additionally, the comprehensive possibilities of visualising results as well as sensitivity analyses constitute a valuable benefit for a moderator and eventually also for the group responsible for the decision. The close relation between the phases of moderation and those of multi-criteria decision analysis is visualised in Figure 4.1.

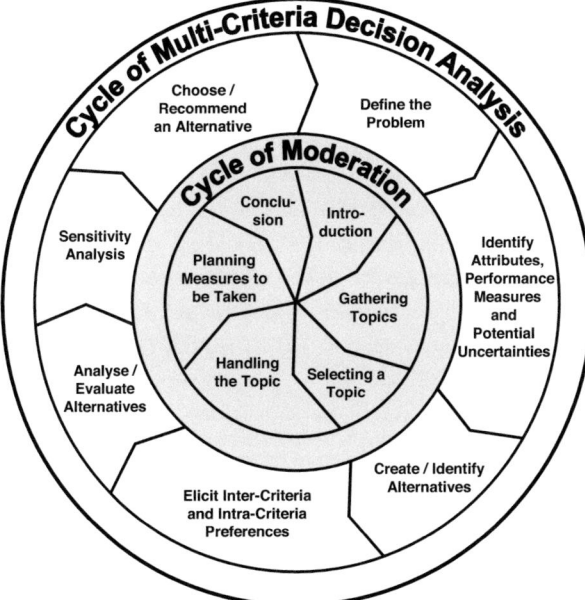

Figure 4.1: Steps of a Moderation Cycle and of Multi-Criteria Decision Analysis [adapted from Geldermann and Rentz, 2004]

4.2 RODOS

The real-time online decision support system RODOS is designed to provide consistent and comprehensive decision support at different levels in the event of a nuclear or radiological emergency in Europe. The support offered by RODOS ranges from largely descriptive reports, such as maps of the predicted, possible and, later, actual contamination patterns and dose distributions, to a detailed evaluation of the benefits and drawbacks of various countermeasure or remediation strategies and their ranking according to the societal preferences as perceived by the decision makers [Ehrhardt et al., 1993; Ehrhardt and Weiss, 2000; French et al., 2000; Raskob et al., 2005a]. Models and databases within RODOS contain extensive information about site and plant characteristics of the different nuclear power stations in Europe and the geographical, climatic and environmental variations. Its operational application requires online coupling to radiological and meteorological real-time measurements and meteorological forecasts from national weather services. The main users of the system are those responsible for emergency management at the local, regional, national and supra-national levels.

4.2.1   The Conceptual Structure

RODOS is intended to support decision making throughout all phases of emergency management – from the early phase through to medium-term and long-term countermeasure or remediation strategies implemented weeks, months or years after an accident. Figure 4.2 shows its conceptual structure which comprises three subsystems: The "Analysing Subsystem (ASY)", the "Countermeasure Subsystem (CSY)" and the "Evaluation Subsystem (ESY)".

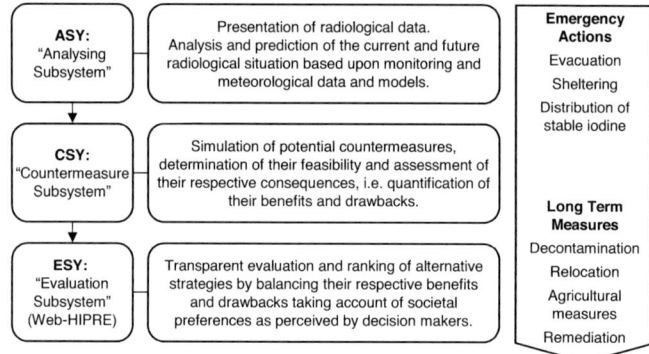

Figure 4.2: The Conceptual Structure of RODOS [cf. e.g. Ehrhardt and Weiss, 2000; French et al., 2000]

Basis of any decision is the analysis of the radiological situation which comprises the estimation of contamination levels in the environment. This can be either based on simulation models for the dispersion of radionuclides in the atmosphere, hydrosphere and the food chain or rely on monitoring results from fixed stations or mobile teams [cf. e.g. Bertsch et al., 2006b]. Thus, the ASY consists of a model chain starting with models for calculating the atmospheric dispersion in the near and far range, followed by a model for calculating the deposition to soil and plants, and finally food chain and dose models for simulating the transfer of radionuclides from the deposition into foods, as well as resulting radiation exposure. If needed a hydrological model chain (considering run-off of radionuclides from watersheds, transport in river systems, behaviour in lakes and reservoirs) can be inserted in between the deposition model and the food chain and dose models [Bertsch et al., 2005; Gering, 2005]. The prediction of the radioactive dispersion through the various pathways and thus the prediction of the radiation exposure of the population during and after a nuclear event is an important part within nuclear emergency management.

In the early phase, emergency management involves decisions on measures of disaster response, such as evacuation, sheltering or distribution of stable iodine tablets. Such measures are usually limited to areas within a few tens of kilometers of the nuclear accident. Since decisions on whether or not to implement such measures depend to a great extent on the spread of the radioactive plume and the estimated contamination levels, emergency management in the early phase is closely related to the predictions of the ASY (see Figure 4.2). In the longer term, more complex decisions on decontamination and remediation strategies, restricted access measures (e.g. relocation) and agricultural countermeasures are required [cf. e.g. Bertsch et al., 2006b; Geldermann et al., 2007]. Many parties with different viewpoints are involved and many conflicting objectives must be resolved. Priorities must be set, and perhaps most importantly, a consensus must be found for the various perspectives of the many stakeholder groups. Both, the early and later phase emergency management are part of the calculations of the CSY (Countermeasure Subsystem). However, due to the higher complexity in the later phase, the ESY (Evaluation Subsystem) was developed to support the evaluation of the alternative countermeasure and remediation strategies, whose potential benefits and drawbacks are quantified by the CSY (see Figure 4.2).

4.2.2   Data Assimilation and Uncertainties in RODOS

The model predictions of RODOS play an important role for the rapid assessment and prognosis of the possible (radiological) consequences in nuclear emergency management [Rojas-Palma et al., 2003; Raskob et al., 2005b]. The predictions concerning the atmospheric dispersion are based on a Gaussian model in RODOS [cf. e.g. S. Thykier-Nielsen and S. Deme and E. Láng, 1995; T. Mikkelsen and S. Thykier-Nielsen and P. Astrup and J. M. Santabárbara and J. H. Sørensen and A. Rasmussen and L. Robertson and A. Ullerstig and S. Deme and R. Martens and J. G. Bartzis and J. Päsler-Sauer, 1997; Mikkelsen et al., 1998]. Besides the Gaussian approach, several other models for meteorological dispersion calculations are discussed in literature [cf. e.g. Sennewald, 1996]. However, all model predictions are inherently afflicted with uncertainties. Radiological observations, such as dose rate measurements, can be used to improve the model predictions. The process of combining model predictions and measurements is usually referred to as *data assimilation* [cf. e.g. Ghil and Malanotte-Rizzoli, 1991; Tilmes, 1999; Wergen, 2002; Rojas-Palma et al., 2003; Gering, 2005]. In this way, data assimilation techniques can contribute to a smooth transition from pure model predictions (in the pre-release phase) to a real situation (in the post-release phases) [cf. e.g. Rojas-Palma et al., 2003; Raskob et al., 2005b].

Especially, at the beginning of the post-release phase, when more and more measurements are available but "gaps" still need to be filled with results from models, data assimilation is a very important tool to provide a consistent analysis of the radiological situation [Raskob et al., 2005a]. In this period, analysing the radiological situation purely relying on atmospheric dispersion calculations is no longer sufficient as a basis for decision making. Decisions will be mainly based on measurements in this phase but simulation models are nevertheless required to estimate the evolution of the contamination in future (i.e. for an "extrapolation into the future"). This is particularly important for inhabited areas, in which safe living conditions must be established and thus decontamination might be necessary, and in agricultural areas where production of clean food needs to be assured [Raskob et al., 2005a].

In RODOS, data assimilation is based on *Kalman filtering*. The Kalman filter is a recursive, linear, minimum mean-squared error estimator which was introduced in the 1960's by Kalman [1960] for application in linear systems. For nonlinear systems, extensions such as the *extended Kalman filter* have for instance been proposed [cf. Gelb, 1974]. The data assimilation based on the recursive algorithm of the Kalman filter consists of two steps, a prediction step and a correction step, where in the correction step, the predictions are linearly combined with measurements [cf. e.g. Rojas-Palma et al., 2003; Gering, 2005]. Kalman filters have been extensively applied in fields such as the navigation of aeroplanes and spacecrafts as well as in meteorology.

One of the main challenges for an operational application of the Kalman filter is the topic of uncertainty modelling and propagation [cf. Rojas-Palma et al., 2003]. The *ensemble Kalman filter*, a Monte Carlo version of the Kalman filter originally introduced for assimilation purposes in oceanography by [Evensen, 1994], provides a framework for representing uncertainties by ensembles of possible sets of input data as well as model parameters according to their respective probability distributions [cf. Gering, 2005]. Consequently, the data assimilation modules within the RODOS model chain are based on the ensemble Kalman filter [cf. Rojas-Palma et al., 2003]

Beyond the general conceptual structure of RODOS (Figure 4.2), Figure 4.3 shows the model chain within RODOS, especially within the ASY, in more detail including three data assimilation modules. In addition, it is indicated that input data of RODOS is subject to uncertainties and that uncertainties due to model imperfectness and parameter uncertainties are introduced in each of the three subsystems. The uncertainty propagation is based on Monte Carlo analysis, i.e. the uncertainties are propagated from upstream to downstream models by ensembles.

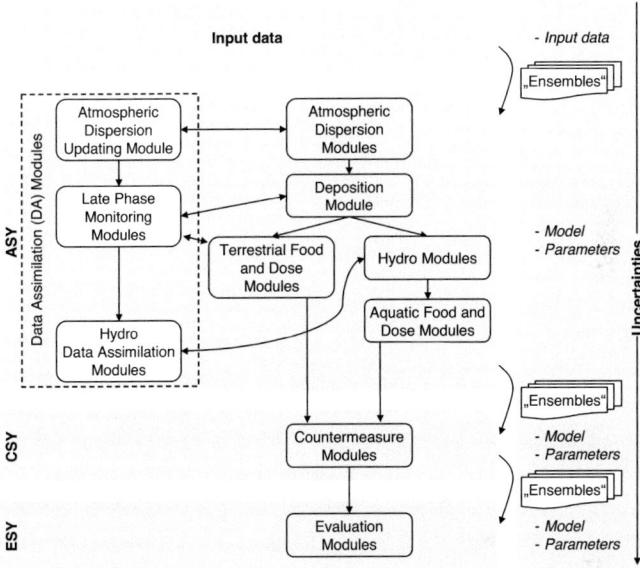

Figure 4.3: Data Assimilation and Uncertainties in the RODOS Model Chain [adapted from Rojas-Palma et al., 2003]

It should be noted that, from a theoretical point of view, the conceptual framework of Bayesian decision analysis (cf. Section 2.3.2) provides a sound basis capable to address all requirements with respect to uncertainty handling and data assimilation in a coherent manner [cf. e.g. Caminada et al., 2000; French, 2003]. Combining, inter alia, elements from the fields of consequence modelling and statistical inference and forecasting (see Figure 2.15 on page 41), Bayesian decision analysis is inherently in accordance with the principles of data assimilation. A problematic aspect of Bayesian decision analysis, however, is that the uncertainty is treated probabilistically and that, as mentioned already, the assessment of probabilities (including subjective ones) can be difficult or impossible in practice [cf. e.g. O'Hagan and Oakley, 2004; Basson, 2004].

4.2.3   Economic Consequence Modelling in RODOS

The model for economic consequence assessment in RODOS is very elementary. It gives a rough overview of the incurring direct costs by calculating unit costs of decontamination techniques in inhabited areas [cf. Schieber and Benhamou, 1999a] as well as agricultural countermeasures [cf. Schieber and Benhamou, 1999b]. Concerning the decontamination techniques, the total cost of each technique is evaluated on the basis of the following parameters which are stored separately in a data base, in order to facilitate their update [cf. Schieber and Benhamou, 1999a]:

- Unit cost of manpower (€/man-hour)

- Unit cost of consumable (€/km^2)

- Unit cost of equipment (or investment) (€/km^2)

For the determination of the costs of the consumables, purchase prices need to be estimated and regularly updated, for instance for diesel, water, sand or electricity. The consumable needs (e.g. kg, litres or kWh needed for decontaminating a contaminated surface of 1 km^2) as well as the manpower needs (necessary man hours for decontaminating a contaminated surface of 1 km^2) have been elicited in various expert interviews. The costs of equipment include – inter alia – hiring fees for plants or lorries. The costs of waste disposal, including the transport of waste, are not included in the current model for decontamination techniques in inhabited areas.

Data concerning the costs of the agricultural countermeasures considered in RODOS have mostly been collected via European statistic data bases published by EUROSTAT[22]. In cases, in which the relevant data were not officially available on a European level, private firms and experts, who accepted to communicate their own data and knowledge, have been interviewed directly [cf. Schieber and Benhamou, 1999b].

In general, food production losses need to be evaluated for all the agricultural countermeasures considered in RODOS, since the loss of production applies to all of them when a banning of food is necessary. Schieber and Benhamou [1999b] assume that the loss due to not selling the products is an appropriate indicator for the production losses. Consequently, they evaluate the unit cost of the food production losses (in €/kg) through the average selling price of the food under concern.

Another cost element that applies to all countermeasures is the cost of food disposal since it is necessary to dispose the amount of food exceeding the intervention levels [cf.

---

[22] cf. e.g. Eurostat [2002] and the references therein and see: http://ec.europa.eu/eurostat

Schieber and Benhamou, 1999b]. However, it is difficult to suggest a general procedure to determine the cost of disposal of contaminated food since such costs depend, to a large extent, on the available technical facilities. For instance, there is a notable difference between burning and putrefying radiologically contaminated agricultural waste.

Other countermeasures, for which the unit costs are modelled in RODOS, include the processing of food aiming at a decrease of the concentration of radioactivity, the storage of food, removal of animals from contaminated pasture and substitution of contaminated with clean feed, adding of sorbents to the feed and the treatment of soils with ameliorants to improve their quality and reduce the uptake of radionuclides by plants. Concerning the storage of food, a difference is made between loose and pallet storage (both at ambient temperature), refrigerated storage and freezing storage. However, all of the above unit costs are calculated in €/kg. In addition, the costs for the decontamination of pasture and farmland can be calculated by RODOS (in €/km^2). As the costs of decontamination techniques in inhabited areas, the latter are calculated on the basis of unit costs of manpower, consumables and equipment.

It should be noted, however, that the calculation of costs, as described above, requires regular updating since salaries as well as selling and purchasing prices are highly time-variant. In addition, they are country specific and thus need to be customised for each individual country.

Moreover, it should be stressed that the above method can only provide a very course estimation of the costs for conducting countermeasures as well as costs related to food production losses. Costs associated with the damage to human health and the environment induced by a nuclear emergency cannot be assessed using this approach. Furthermore, the method does not reflect costs in relation to the damage caused within industrial production networks (i.e. indirect costs). Moreover, economies of scale are not considered at all. The suitability of the cost model within RODOS for a profound economic impact assessment of a nuclear emergency is thus very limited.

In order to improve the assessment of economic consequences within RODOS, a quantitative approach for the modelling of the direct as well as the indirect losses is needed.[23] van der Veen and Logtmeijer [2005] for instance, discuss the application of approaches such as input-output analysis, being standard in economics, to compute the effects of an emergency for the economy as a whole. Furthermore, recent overviews of methods for

---

[23] The Institute for Industrial Production (IIP) is involved in the "Asset Estimation Group" of the Center for Disaster Management and Risk Reduction Technology (CEDIM), whose current work is focussed on the estimation of direct losses, while future work will concentrate on the development of approaches for the assessment of indirect losses in industry.

both types of losses can e.g. be found in Cochrane [2004]; van der Veen [2004]; Merz et al. [2007].

4.2.4   Web-HIPRE

The multi-criteria decision support tool Web-HIPRE[24] has recently been integrated into RODOS as the evaluation subsystem. As a web-based Java applet, Web-HIPRE is simultaneously accessible from different places and is thus suitable to allow geographically dispersed groups of decision makers to share their knowledge (for instance, in the form of a decision model). Furthermore, it can be used on any computer with a Java enabled web browser without the need of being installed beforehand. The underlying theory is multi-attribute value theory (MAVT). In principle, Web-HIPRE provides user-friendly support for all key steps of a MAVT analysis as described Section 2.2.1.

Besides the basic steps of MAVT, the new evaluation subsystem within RODOS provides "background information" for the alternative countermeasure and remediation strategies (see Figure 4.4). Data sheets are linked to the different strategies and can be accessed directly in Web-HIPRE. These data sheets have been developed as a part of the handbooks, which were developed for decision support within the STRATEGY[25] and FARMING[26] projects (FP 5) and further refined in the EURANOS[27] project (FP 6) [cf. e.g. Nisbet et al., 2006; Brown et al., 2007].

In this context, "background information" does not only denote a detailed description of the general objective(s), benefit(s) and target group(s) or area(s) of a measure but also information on (legal) constraints, feasibility aspects, cost estimations and other effects such as the social impact related to a measure. For instance, Figure 4.4 shows an extract of the data sheet with background information on the alternative "Proc" standing for "processing of milk" (after an accidental release of radionuclides). Such information on preconditions and implications as well as side effects of performing a measure enhances the understanding of what exactly is meant by the decision alternatives. Moreover, the availability of detailed information for the various countermeasure and

---

[24] Web-HIPRE: "HIerarchical PREference analysis on the World Wide Web" [cf. Hämäläinen and Mustajoki, 1998; Mustajoki and Hämäläinen, 2000], see: http://www.hipre.hut.fi

[25] STRATEGY: "Sustainable restoration and long-term management of contaminated rural, urban, and industrial ecosystems", see: http://cordis.europa.eu/fp5-euratom/src/index.htm

[26] FARMING: "Food and agriculture restoration management involving networked groups", see: http://cordis.europa.eu/fp5-euratom/src/index.htm

[27] EURANOS: "European approach to nuclear and radiological emergency management and rehabilitation strategies", see: http://www.euranos.fzk.de

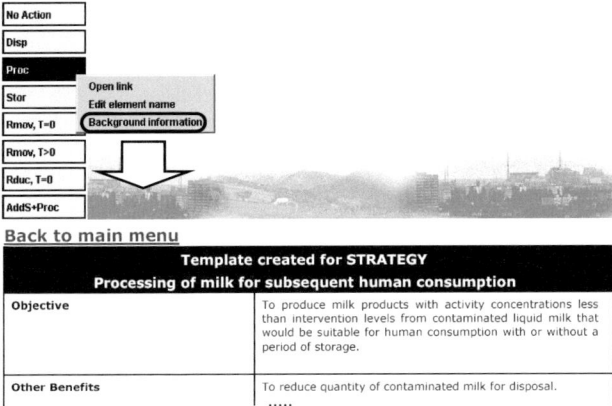

Figure 4.4: Access to Background Information in Web-HIPRE [cf. Bertsch et al., 2006b]

remediation strategies facilitates the communication with different stakeholder groups, the mass media and the public [cf. e.g. Renn, 2001].

4.2.5   The Explanation Module

After ranking the alternative countermeasure or remediation strategies, it is possible to generate explanation reports that justify this ranking. Explanation facilities contribute to positive user attitudes and improve user performance [Gregor and Benbasat, 1999] They have proved to be useful to users, experienced professionals as well as novices [Mao and Benbasat, 2000; Arnold et al., 2006]. They influence user perceptions such as trust, confidence and satisfaction and increase levels of acceptance and learning [Dhaliwal and Benbasat, 1996].

An Explanation Module has thus been developed to justify the advice of the evaluation subsystem of RODOS and to increase the trust and confidence of the DMs in the results of the system [Papamichail, 2000; Papamichail and French, 2003]. In practice, the executive DMs do usually not operate the system themselves, but by generating an audit trail the Explanation Module seeks to help the emergency management team, advising the DMs, in communicating the results in an understandable way. The Explanation Module adds transparency to the ranking process, by generating two reports:

- A "Comparative Report" that interprets the evaluation results and compares two strategies by discussing how well a strategy rates with respect to the evaluation criteria, outlines arguments for and against each strategy, examines how much better a strategy is over another and highlights factors that differentiate between two strategies.

- A "Sensitivity Analysis Report" that interprets sensitivity analysis graphs, illustrates the effect of changing the weight of an attribute in the ranking of alternative strategies and discusses the robustness of the results.

The input of the Explanation Module comprises qualitative data in the form of an attribute tree as well as quantitative data in the form of a decision table (containing the scores of the alternative strategies) or in the form of values of decision parameters (such as the weights). The Explanation Module then applies natural language techniques [cf. Reiter and Dale, 2000] and statistical methods [cf. Klein, 1994] to generate understandable reports in English. The natural language generation process involves three stages:

1. *Content determination* which involves what type of report to generate (i.e. comparative report or sensitivity analysis report) and what type of explanations to convey to the users.

2. *Discourse planning* which involves establishing the structure of the report i.e. structuring messages in a coherent way by choosing an appropriate text plan (cf. Appendix A).

3. *Sentence generation* which involves selecting text-based templates and filling in qualitative and quantitative values to produce explanations in natural language form in order to convey messages.

The explanations can help the DMs to concentrate on those aspects that are significant in the decision making process and therefore considerably reduce the time needed for parameter assessment [cf. e.g. Geldermann et al., 2007]. Further details about the generation of explanations as well as exemplar reports are given in Appendix A as well as in [Papamichail and French, 2003].

Figure 4.5 summarises the preference elicitation and evaluation processes in RODOS and Web-HIPRE. These processes are interactive and it is possible to iteratively correct the decision parameters in the case that the decision makers' preferences and value judgments are not accurately represented by the model. Contributing to the generation of an audit trail for the decision making process and to an enhancement of the confidence in the results of the decision analysis, Web-HIPRE including the explanation module seeks to improve the acceptability of the RODOS system as a whole [cf. e.g. Geldermann et al., 2007].

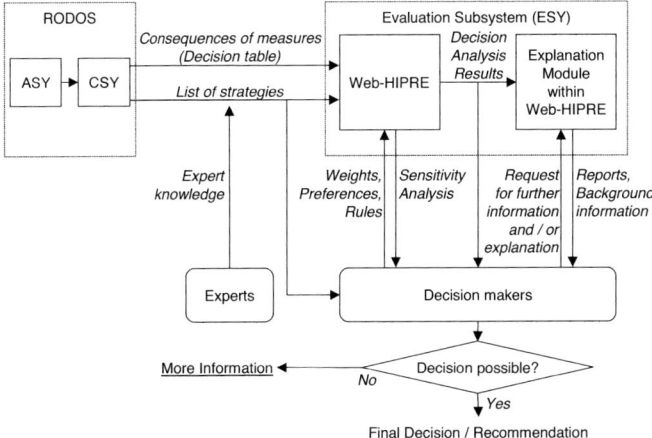

Figure 4.5: The Process of Preference Elicitation and Evaluation in RODOS and Web-HIPRE [adapted from French, 2000; Bertsch et al., 2006b]

It should be noted that the explanation module has been developed for deterministic multi-attribute decision analyses. This means that it is adjusted to the features of standard decision support as provided, for instance, by Web-HIPRE. Taking account of different types of uncertainty leads to additional information in the results which, so far, is not explained by the existing explanation facilities. Consequently, there is a need to add understandable explanations about the impact of the occurring uncertainties in order to increase the usability and acceptance of the more complex approaches that take uncertainties into consideration. This constitutes a challenging future research possibility in this area. Exemplarily, an extension of the explanation module towards explaining the results of multi-dimensional sensitivity analyses, i.e. an extension of the sensitivity analysis report, is proposed in Appendix A.

4.3   A Hypothetical Case Study

The hypothetical case study introduced in the following originally provided the basis to discuss agricultural countermeasure and remediation strategies within a moderated decision making workshop in Germany. The course of action of the workshop is described in Section 4.4. The data for this hypothetical case study was generated with the RODOS system. A low to intermediate contamination of a larger area with important food production (such as milk) was assumed to be caused by a serious accident at a nuclear power plant which triggered the immediate shutdown of the reactor. Starting four hours after the accident, radioactive material was released into the atmosphere over a period of three hours. Further emissions were not expected according to the plant operators. Another three hours later and thenceforward, all air monitoring stations in Germany reported normal levels of radioactivity in the atmosphere.

The historical weather conditions which were used for this hypothetical scenario indicated that the radioactive cloud mainly passed agricultural areas. Due to south-westerly winds, the radioactive cloud was blown in a north-easterly direction. Radioactive material from the cloud deposited onto the ground. While the cloud passed, heavy precipitation and even thunderstorms were observed resulting in local inhomogeneities of the ground contamination.

It was assumed that about 50 % of the plant inventory of radioactive noble gases and about 0.1 % of the plant inventory of iodine I-131 and radioactive aerosols were released during the accident (the iodine fully in elementary form). In the near range (up to 1 km from the nuclear power plant) the dose rate reached up to 1 000 μSv/h (micro Sievert[28] per hour), 200 μSv/h at a distance of 10 km and 50 μSv/h 25 km away. In all other affected areas at distances larger than 25 km the dose rate varied between 0.01 and 50 μSv/h, corresponding to ground concentrations of 1 to 3 000 kBq/m^2 (kilo Becquerel[29] per square meter) for iodine I-131 (see Figure 4.6) and aerosols and 0.1 to 300 kBq/m^2 for caesium Cs-137 (see Figure 4.7), when taking into account the actual nuclide spectrum [cf. e.g. Raskob et al., 2005a; Bertsch et al., 2006b; Geldermann et al., 2007].

With a physical half-life of 8 days, iodine I-131 is commonly used as reference nuclide for decisions on countermeasures in the short term (within the first week). In the longer

---

[28] Sievert (symbol Sv) is a unit of equivalent dose or effective dose (of radiation), and thus depends on the biological effects of radiation as opposed to the physical aspects, characterised by the absorbed dose (which is measured in gray).

[29] Becquerel (symbol Bq) is a unit of radioactivity, defined as the activity of a quantity of radioactive material in which one nucleus decays per second and is thus equivalent to s^{-1}.

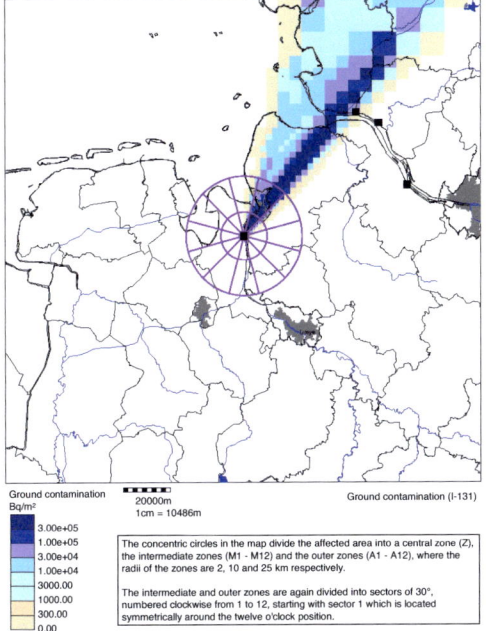

Ground contamination
Bq/m²

3.00e+05
1.00e+05
3.00e+04
1.00e+04
3000.00
1000.00
300.00
0.00

20000m
1cm = 10486m

Ground contamination (I-131)

The concentric circles in the map divide the affected area into a central zone (Z),
the intermediate zones (M1 - M12) and the outer zones (A1 - A12), where the
radii of the zones are 2, 10 and 25 km respectively.

The intermediate and outer zones are again divided into sectors of 30°,
numbered clockwise from 1 to 12, starting with sector 1 which is located
symmetrically around the twelve o'clock position.

Figure 4.6: Ground Contamination for Iodine I-131 in the Surrounding Area of the Nuclear Power Plant

term, caesium Cs-137 with a physical half-life of 30.23 years is often used as reference nuclide. While Figure 4.6 illustrates the ground contamination situation for iodine I-131 (as calculated by the ASY of RODOS) in the surrounding area of the nuclear power plant, Figure 4.7 shows the ground contamination for caesium Cs-137 for the accident scenario assumed within the case study.

Since the main focus of the workshop was the discussion of agricultural measures in the medium and long term rather than the discussion of emergency actions, it was assumed, after an analysis and forecast of the radiological situation, that the following immediate and early countermeasures (implemented before the radioactive release started) were initiated (see Figure 4.6 or Figure 4.7 for the location of the different zones):

- Evacuation of inhabitants from the central zone.

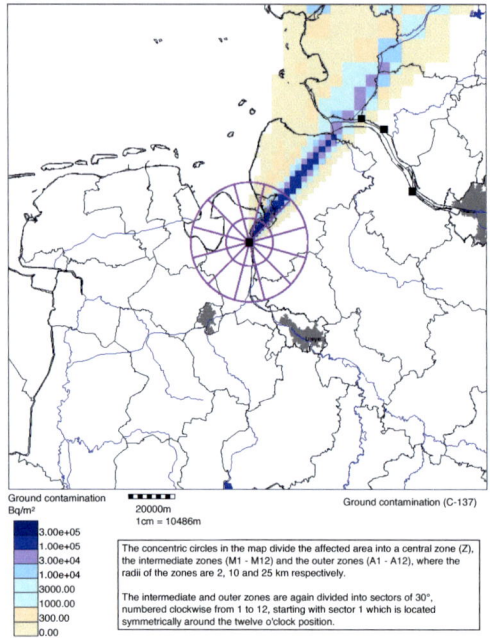

Figure 4.7: Ground Contamination for Caesium Cs-137 in the Surrounding Area of the Nuclear Power Plant

- Sheltering of inhabitants in the intermediate zones M1, M2, M3 and outer zones A1, A2, A3, until the morning after the accident.

- Distribution of iodine tablets to children in the intermediate zones M1, M2, and M3.

With respect to agriculture and food, the inhabitants in the affected districts received the following recommendations:

- Cover and/or close green houses and nurseries.

- Cover agricultural areas with vegetables, fruit and herbs.

- Cover open storages for animal feed and foodstuffs.

- Close animal stables and reduce ventilation.

The calculations for the potential countermeasure and remediation strategies were based on maximum permitted levels of radioactive contamination in foodstuffs and feedingstuffs that may be placed on the market following a nuclear accident or any other case of radiological emergency [cf. Regulation (Euratom) No 3954/87; Regulation (Euratom) No 944/89; Regulation (Euratom) No 770/90]. The countermeasures were calculated in those areas where the predicted contamination would exceed these limits.

4.4   A Moderated Workshop

A series of moderated decision making workshops focussing on the evaluation of counter-measure and remediation strategies in the event of a nuclear emergency with a release of radionuclides was organised across Europe. These workshops were inter alia aimed at investigating the applicability of the RODOS system with its various components and at familiarising the responsible persons with the MCDA tools and methods [Geldermann et al., 2005; Raskob et al., 2005a; Sinkko et al., 2005; Geldermann et al., 2007]. Another intention was to ensure that the developments meet the requirements of the potential users. Two workshops were organised in Germany, of which one was focussed on dis-cussing agricultural countermeasure and remediation strategies[30]. As mentioned above, the hypothetical case study introduced in Section 4.3 provided the basis for the discussion within the workshop. The group of participants included officials and politicians of re-gional, state and federal authorities as well as expert advisers for radiation protection and a number of stakeholder groups [cf. Bertsch et al., 2006b]. The decision making process within the workshop and, in particular, the process of preference elicitation was guided by a moderator/facilitator.

At the beginning of the workshop, the case study was introduced to the participants. The subsequent analysis and discussion focussed on the following eight countermeasure and remediation strategies for milk:

- **No Action:** No Action

- **Disp:** Disposal (of the produced milk)

- **Proc:** Processing (of milk)

- **Stor:** Storage

---

[30] The workshops in Germany were organised in collaboration with the Federal Office for Radiation Protection (BfS) in Freiburg, Germany.

- **Rmov,T=0:** Removal of cows from contaminated pastures at time T=0 feeding with uncontaminated feed

- **Rmov,T>0:** Removal of cows from contaminated pastures after two days (T>0), feeding with uncontaminated feed

- **Rduc,T=0:** Reduction of contaminated feed and substitution with uncontaminated or less contaminated feed

- **AddS+Proc:** Adding of sorbents to the food to reduce the activity concentration (of milk and meat) and subsequent processing

The strategy "No Action" is often considered for comparison purposes. However, under certain circumstances it can also be considered as an actual option. As the name suggests, "Disposal" does, in contrast to the subsequent strategies, not aim at reducing the activity concentration in milk in any way but simply at the disposal of the contaminated milk whose activity concentration exceeds the intervention levels.

The aim of the strategy "Processing" is to produce milk products with activity concentrations less than intervention levels from contaminated liquid milk which would subsequently be suitable for human consumption. Processing raw milk into butter or cheese may be used to reduce the activity concentrations of long-lived radionuclides such as caesium Cs-137 and strontium Sr-90 (i.e. starting with milk with activity concentrations in excess of the intervention levels, an activity concentration in the end product below these levels can be obtained). For short-lived radionuclides, such as iodine I-131, "Processing" may well be combined with a period of "Storage" because the activity concentration may quickly fall below the intervention levels due to the short physical half-life. Another aim of combining the strategies "Processing" and "Storage" can be the conversion of contaminated milk into a more stable end product for storage and subsequent disposal, additionally offering the responsible authorities more time to plan disposal options. For instance, a straightforward option is the processing of liquid milk into whole milk powder. However, it should be noted that "Processing" may nevertheless produce contaminated by-products [cf. Nisbet et al., 2006].

The "Removal" and "Reduction" strategies provide animals with less or uncontaminated feedstuffs. Target animals may be those grazing contaminated pastures or already housed animals which otherwise would be receiving contaminated food. Livestock may be housed in stables ("Removal") or fenced in enclosures to prevent grazing of contaminated pasture. The animals are then given nutritionally balanced diets comprising uncontaminated and/or less contaminated feed, i.e. the animals' uptake of radionuclides through ingestion is stopped or at least reduced. The final animal products thus have activity concentrations below the intervention levels [cf. Nisbet et al., 2006].

The strategy "Adding of sorbents and subsequent processing" is aimed at binding radio-caesium by adding special sorbents, such as ammonium iron hexacyanoferrate (AFCF, also called "Giese-salt"), to the animals' food. These sorbents reduce the gut uptake of radiocaesium by ruminants in agricultural and semi-natural environments. As for the "Processing", "Storage", "Removal" and "Reduction" strategies, the aim of this combined strategy is to decrease the activity concentration in the final animal products below the intervention levels [cf. Nisbet et al., 2006].

4.4.1 Problem Structuring

The accident scenario of the hypothetical case study was analysed and structured in a moderated discussion. At first, the workshop participants determined the relevant decision attributes from the list of available attributes in RODOS. Additional important attributes which are not provided by RODOS were identified by the experts and stakeholders on the regional, state and federal level via card inquiry. The selected attributes, their respective denotations and the units in which they can be measured are compiled in Table 4.2. The attributes which are measured on a 0–100 scale were estimated by the attending stakeholders and experts. It should be noted that the cost modelling functionality of RODOS, as described in Section 4.2.3, was not available at the time of the workshop, which is why the attribute *costs* is estimated on a 0–100 scale. However, this should not be seen as a drawback since the group of participants was able to provide good estimates as a result of their expertise and experience.

Collecting, structuring and assorting of information during the discussion provided deeper insight into the core of the problems under scrutiny and lead to a shared understanding amongst all participants [Bertsch et al., 2006b; Geldermann et al., 2007]. The structuring and modelling process of the decision problem resulted in an attribute tree (a hierarchy of criteria) which shows the overall goal "total utility" (of performing a countermeasure strategy) as the top criterion being split up into the criteria "radiological effectiveness", "resources", "impact" and "acceptance", each of which is split up again (see Figure 4.8). The higher level criteria, which were used to structure the selected attributes into a hierarchy of criteria (such as "resources" and "impact"), as well as their respective denotations are compiled in Table 4.3. Since they represent aggregated performance scores (on a 0–1 scale), no units are shown for the criteria in Table 4.3.

Table 4.2: Selected Decision Attributes and their Respective Meanings

Abbrevation	Meaning	Unit
avoided ind. dose adults	avoided individual dose (adults – 1 year)	[mSv]
avoided ind. dose children	avoided individual dose (children – 1 year)	[mSv]
avoided collective dose	avoided collective dose	[manSv]
received collective dose	received collective dose	[manSv]
max. ind. worker dose	maximum individual dose received by worker	[mSv]
collective worker dose	collective dose received by workers	[manSv]
no. of workers	necessary number of workers needed to conduct a measure	[#]
supplies	supplies (e.g. (agricultural) machinery) required to conduct a measure	[0 − 100]
total food above	total amount of food above the limit	[kg]
food above yr-1	amount of food above the limit after 1 year	[kg]
size of aff. area	size of affected area	[km^2]
costs	costs to conduct a measure	[0 − 100]
public	acceptance of a decision by the public	[0 − 100]
affected prod.	acceptance of a decision by the affected producers (e.g. agriculturists)	[0 − 100]
trade and ind.	acceptance of a decision by the trade and industry	[0 − 100]

Table 4.3: Higher Level Criteria and their Respective Meanings

Abbrevation	Meaning
total utility	total utility of a measure (with respect to milk)
rad. effectiveness	radiological effectiveness
population	radiological effectiveness with respect to the population
worker	radiological effectiveness with respect to the worker(s)
resources	necessary resources to conduct a measure
impact	impact of a measure
acceptance	acceptance of a decision

The consequences of the eight considered strategies with respect to the selected attributes are shown in Table 4.4 (page 113) and Table 4.5 (page 114). While Table 4.4 contains the values of the attributes whose consequences can be directly calculated by RODOS, the values of the attributes listed in Table 4.5 are those estimated by the attending stakeholders and experts. As indicated above, a fictitious scale ranging from 0 to 100 is

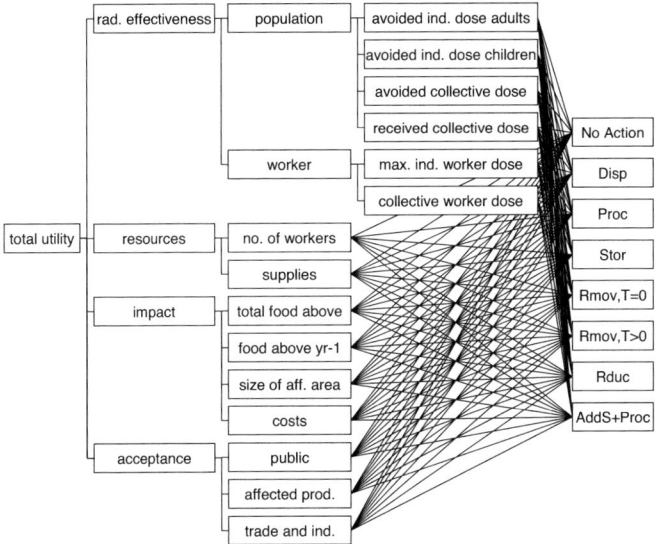

Figure 4.8: Attribute Tree for the Hypothetical Case Study

assumed for the latter, where 100 corresponds to the highest value (resp. utility) and 0 to the lowest. The data in Table 4.4 and Table 4.5 constitute the basis of the subsequent decision analysis within the workshop.

4.4.2   Preference Elicitation

At first, the weighting of the criteria of the attribute tree was carried out. The following inter-criteria preferences (weights) were elicited in a group discussion using direct and SWING weighting, where mostly qualitative results are reported since the aim of the workshop was the creation of awareness:

"radiological effectiveness" vs. "resources" vs. "impact" vs. "acceptance":
While formulating priorities in the workshop using the SWING method, the acceptance of a measure was given the highest rating (100 points). This choice was based on the premise that acceptance by the public, affected individuals and business have the highest relevance with respect to the specific decision, since together they form the critical foundation upon which future developments are built. The actual effects of a measure were

given the second highest rating, based on the magnitude of the decision (size of affected area) and the consequences of the measure (amount of waste above the threshold, cost etc.). The radiological effectiveness was weighted only lightly in fourth place since it only plays a superficial role for agricultural measures.

"population" vs. "worker": The maximum dose for the population is determined by estimating the intake of radioactivity through contaminated food. In this case the radiation dose for the workers is insignificant and additional exposure resulting from future measures is very low.

"avoided individual dose (adults – 1 year)" vs. "avoided individual dose (children – 1 year)" vs. "avoided collective dose" vs. "received collective dose": The different dose values are calculated based on the foodstuff milk under the assumption of 100 % local production and consumption. Since milk with contamination above a certain intervention limit is banned from the market, the maximum dose values calculated here are highly unlikely. Consequently the comparison of these values between measures with respect to radiological effectiveness can only be regarded as an indicator. As a result, the avoided collective dose for one year is the most important in the evaluation of the SWING method followed by the avoided individual dose for children within one year. The remaining doses receive only a minor weighting.

"max. individual dose received by worker" vs. "collective dose received by worker": In contrast to the calculated dose values for the population, the calculated dose values for the workers are directly related to the actual execution of the measure and thus contribute to the radiation exposure. This would indicate a strong weighting for the individual dose. However, since no significant radiation exposure during the implementation of the measure is expected, the maximum individual dose received by the worker and the collective dose are presumed equal.

"No. of workers" vs. "supplies": The two attributes "no. of workers" and "supplies" are required to estimate the required resources of a measure. They receive approximately the same weighting with slightly more importance assigned to the number of workers. In essence both are equally significant for judging the measure, but they have different dimensions of a required resource.

"total food above" vs. "food above yr-1" vs. "size of area" vs. "costs": The weighting within "impact" in order of importance was: size of area, total food above, cost and food above yr-1. Measures affecting agriculture are influenced to a very large degree by the size of the area involved. The less land involved, the easier decision making usually is. The total amount of waste produced also carries substantial importance due to its effects on judging the feasibility of a measure and on the criteria costs. Due to the long time period and the need for quick acceptance, the "food above the limit" values after one year plays only a minor role.

"public" vs. "affected producers" vs. "trade and industry": The highest weight within the category "acceptance" was given to the public, followed by industry and those affected by the measures. This ranking reflects the fact that the measures affect only a small area, with industry playing a larger role due to cooperation requirements. The public's large role is explained by the need for overall trust and consequently acceptance of future measures.

Subsequently, the value functions and their respective shapes were defined for each individual attribute using both linear and exponential functions. After the completion of the preference elicitation, the question was raised for discussion whether a fixed attribute tree, containing information about an initial set of relevant decision attributes and criteria as well as feasible countermeasure strategies identified by stakeholders and experts, was desirable or whether an attribute tree should always by developed spontaneously in the event of an emergency.

The selection and structuring of relevant strategies and attributes to be included in an attribute tree is a crucial part of the decision making process. The participants of the workshop noted that they need more guidance in order to cope with this task. Furthermore, they claimed that this can be a very time-consuming process which would be particularly problematic in real emergency situations involving stress etc. An approach to overcome this problem is the elaboration of a limited initial attribute tree, that can be "suggested" by the decision support system to have a starting point for the discussion. Other attributes, not included in such an initial tree but perceived to be relevant by the decision makers, could then be inserted into the tree in a second step.

The approach of using a limited initial tree as starting point in a MCDA cycle is discussed controversially. Besides the advantages as regards the guidance and ease in the problem structuring process provided by a limited initial tree and also the saving of time, a major drawback is seen in the influence of the (pre-defined) limited initial tree on the decision making process and the decision makers who should, from a purely methodological point of view, create a context-dependent attribute tree for the specific decision situation (under guidance of a moderator/facilitator). However, the use of pre-defined weights is strongly disadvised. The weights usually have a crucial impact on the final ranking of the strategies. In addition, the experiences from the workshops have shown that the elicitation of preferences, in the presence of a moderator/facilitator, is usually not as time-consuming as the problem structuring process when creating an attribute tree from scratch.

4.4.3   Selected Results

Following the preference elicitation, the aggregation and sensitivity analyses can be carried out and illustrated. The following illustrations have been generated with the MATLAB prototype which has been implemented within this thesis. The aggregated ranking in Figure 4.9 shows that "Rmov,T=0" is the most preferred alternative followed by "Disp". While "acceptance" provides a large contribution to the good overall performance of both of these alternatives, "impact" is the most important factor in differentiating between them. Since the weights assigned to "radiological effectiveness" and "resources" are comparatively small, the differences in the overall scores which would provide reasons to favor "Disp" over "Rmov,T=0", do not have a large effect on the results of the analysis [Geldermann et al., 2007].

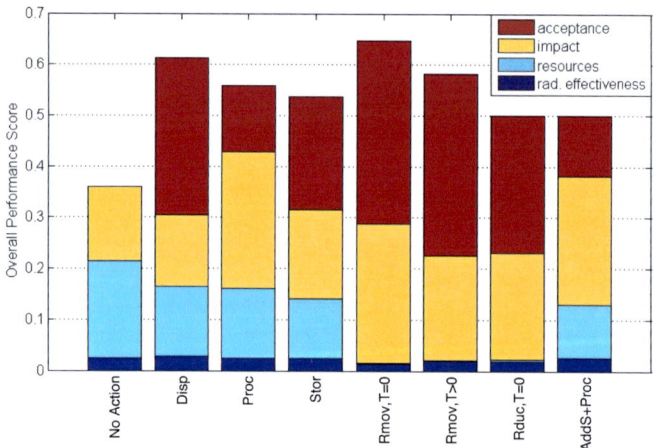

Figure 4.9: Results of Decision Analysis Illustrated as a Stacked-Bar Chart

In addition, a sensitivity analysis on "acceptance" (see Figure 4.10) allows the examination of the robustness of the choice of an alternative relative to changes of the weight assigned to "acceptance". Moreover, the sensitivity analysis graph shows the range of weights for "acceptance" for which an alternative is the most preferred. For the assumptions made within the workshop, the weight for "acceptance" can be changed by approximately 15 %

without changing the optimality of "Rmov,T=0". For a further reduction of the weight, "Proc" turns out to be the best choice.

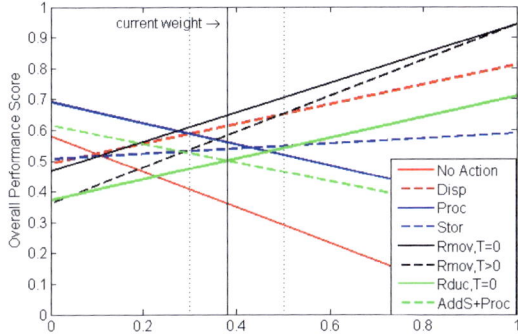

Figure 4.10: Sensitivity Analysis on the Weight of "acceptance"

Furthermore, Figure 4.11 shows the sensitivity of the ranking with respect to changes of the weight of "impact". The graph shows that the weight of "impact" can be increased arbitrarily without changing the optimality of "Rmov,T=0" but it can only be decreased by approximately 5 % without effectuating changes in the ranking. For a smaller weight, "Disp" receives the highest overall performance score.

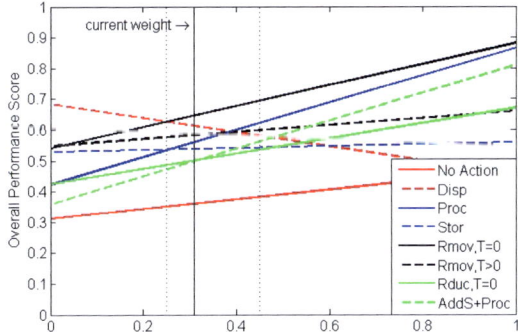

Figure 4.11: Sensitivity Analysis on the Weight of "impact"

Finally, the explanation module can be used to generate comparative reports as well as sensitivity analysis reports to provide the results of the decision analysis in natural language format. An extract of a comparative report for "Rmov,T=0" and "Disp" is shown in Figure 4.12, allowing to gain a deeper insight into the factors differentiating between the two alternatives [cf. e.g. Raskob et al., 2005a]. A further comparative report as well as a sensitivity analysis report for the case study can be found in Appendix A.

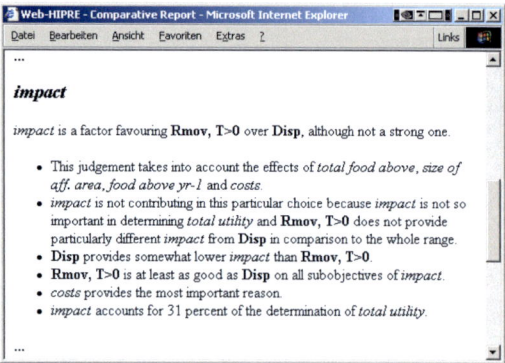

Figure 4.12: Extract of a Comparative Report

Table 4.4: Decision Table – Part 1 – Values Directly Calculated by RODOS

	No Action	Disp	Proc	Stor	Rmov, T=0	Rmov, T>0	Rduc, T=0	AddS+ Proc
avoided ind. ad. [mSv]	0	3.80E+0	1.28E-2	4.13E-5	7.18E-3	9.99E-4	3.51E-4	5.55E-1
avoided ind. chi. [mSv]	0	4.32E+1	2.71E-2	7.13E-4	1.01E-1	1.36E-2	5.14E-3	1.06E+0
avoided collect. [manSv]	0	1.86E+4	1.57E+3	1.24E+2	3.37E+3	2.75E+2	6.83E+2	8.02E+3
collective dose [manSv]	1.90E+4	3.33E+2	1.74E+4	1.89E+4	1.56E+4	1.87E+4	1.83E+4	1.10E+4
max. ind. work. [mSv]	0	0	0	0	3.09E-3	1.87E-3	1.93E-3	0
collect. worker [manSv]	0	0	0	0	2.25E+0	3.42E-1	3.43E-1	0
no. of workers [#]	0	0	0	0	435	329	329	0
total food above [kg]	1.50E+8	1.50E+8	1.17E+7	1.49E+8	1.07E+8	1.34E+8	1.46E+8	1.09E+7
food above yr-1 [kg]	3.41E+5	3.41E+5	1.21E+4	2.33E+5	2.33E+5	2.33E+5	2.33E+5	1.13E+4
size of aff. area [km²]	2.57E+3	2.57E+3	9.11E+2	2.57E+3	6.36E+2	2.56E+3	2.44E+3	9.11E+2

Table 4.5: Decision Table – Part 2 – Values Estimated by Experts and Stakeholders (On a Fictitious 0–100 Scale)

	No Action	Disp	Proc	Stor	Rmov, T=0	Rmov, T>0	Rduc, T=0	AddS+ Proc
supplies	0	10	10	20	40	40	30	80
costs	90	100	20	50	20	20	20	35
public	0	100	5	15	80	80	30	5
affected prod.	0	20	70	60	100	100	80	50
trade and ind.	0	40	5	50	80	80	60	5

4.5   Uncertainty Modelling for the Case Study

It has been pointed out before that results of any numerical model, such as the models within the RODOS model chain, are always afflicted with some uncertainty, which can be attributed to the uncertainty of the input data, to uncertain model parameters or to the general imperfection of the numerical model in describing physical processes. This makes the decision analysis more complex in comparison to the process as carried out in the workshop and described in Section 4.4. In order to cope with this task, the Monte Carlo approaches introduced in Chapter 3, allowing to consistently model, propagate and visualise different types of uncertainty in a decision making process, will be applied and demonstrated on the basis of the hypothetical case study. While the modelling of the uncertainties of the input data and their propagation through the RODOS model chain is described in Section 4.5.1, the modelling of the preferential uncertainties, introduced during the decision making process, is carried out in Section 4.5.2.

4.5.1   Data Uncertainty Modelling

The uncertainty in the input data can be considered by assigning probability distributions to the uncertain quantities. The uncertainties in the results are then assessed by propagating these probability distributions through the model. Uncertainties are also propagated in the model chain by feeding downstream models (i.e. models requiring input data produced by other models running earlier in the model chain) with resulting uncertainties of upstream models (i.e. models providing data as input to other models running later in the model chain). The main source of uncertainty for atmospheric dispersion modelling is the input data, here primarily the *source term* data, the effective release height and the *wind field* data [Bertsch et al., 2005; Gering, 2005]. Dispersion parameters and plume rise parameters also contribute to the uncertainty of dispersion results, but typically to a lower extent.

In this research, the uncertainty modelling of the input data exemplarily concentrates on two key variables for the dispersion model: *source term* and *wind direction*. A log-normal distribution is assigned to the source term, i.e. the quantity of released radioactive material, since a deviation of an order of magnitude is considered to be equiprobable in both directions. A normal distribution is assigned to the mean wind direction with a standard deviation of 30° [cf. Gering, 2005]. Propagating these initial uncertainties through the models of the RODOS model chain is a major challenge, especially for such high-dimensional, non-linear models. But a Monte Carlo approach, in which probability

distributions of variables are approximated by ensembles of values sampled according to
the probability distributions, is suitable to cope with this task. This means, that multiple
results (forming an ensemble) are calculated with the dispersion model, each based on
one sampled value for the source term and one for the mean wind direction as input data.
The values sampled for the source term and the mean wind direction – relative to the
deterministic values described in Section 4.4 – are listed in Table 4.6 for 10 samples as
used for this research.[31]

The multiple results from the atmospheric dispersion model are transferred to the next
model in the RODOS model chain, the deposition model, which calculates multiple results
each based on one possible input from the dispersion model. The influence of parameter
uncertainties in the ASY, for instance in the deposition model, is considered similarly by
sampling multiple sets of model parameters according to pre-defined probability distributions, e.g. for the deposition time (air–soil) or the transfer rates (soil–plants as well
as plants–animals), and applying one parameter set after the other when calculating the
multiple model results. In a similar way, the multiple results are propagated through the
food chain and dose model and the countermeasure simulation model, but without consideration of additional uncertainties arising from parameter uncertainties within these
models.

*Table 4.6: Sampled Values for Mean Wind Direction and Source Term Relative to Deterministic
Values*

Sample No.	Deviation of mean wind direction from deterministic mean wind direction	Deviation of source term from deterministic source term
1	$^+_-0°$	× 1.0
2	$^+_-0°$	× 0.01
3	+30°	× 1.0
4	$^+_-0°$	× 100
5	-29°	× 0.02
6	-40°	× 0.007
7	+6°	× 5.1
8	-24°	× 0.9
9	+48°	× 488
10	-4°	× 1.2

---

[31] In terms of a Monte Carlo simulation, 10 samples are not representative. However, in view of the high
computational effort of the RODOS simulations, a sample size of 10 is nevertheless considered to be
appropriate to exemplarily demonstrate the developed concept.

The multiple Monte Carlo runs of the ASY and CSY models lead to multiple results for the consequences of the countermeasures. Thus, the multi-attribute decision analysis is not based on one (deterministic) decision table but on a set of decision tables where each table corresponds to one sample (realisation/scenario) which are simultaneously evaluated. The complete set of decision tables can be found in Appendix B. Since the entries of Table 4.5 were assessed by the workshop participants and not calculated by RODOS, a justifiable uncertainty modelling would necessitate more workshops where the participants are explicitly asked to assess (possibly different) values for each scenario. Hence, within this research, these values remain deterministic and thus unchanged for the ten scenarios.

While from a theoretical point of view, probability is a unique way to represent uncertainty, the propagation of probability distributions through a complex model chain, such as in RODOS, is a highly challenging task in practice [O'Hagan and Oakley, 2004]. The original probability distributions of the high-dimensional input data (in this research, exemplarily the source term and the mean wind direction) are subject to a number of nonlinear transformations when being propagated through the model chain. In general, Monte Carlo simulation is an adequate method for such problems but it is nevertheless hardly possible to make a statement about the probability distributions of the simulated consequences in the decision table or about their relation to the original probability distributions of the input data. Statistical tests, however, allow to analyse whether the data in the set of decision tables follow certain probability distributions. For instance, the W test introduced by Shapiro and Wilk [1965] allows to test a set of data for normality. The procedure of the W test and its application to the set of decision tables of the case study is described in Appendix B. It shows that the hypothesis of normality can be rejected for most of the consequences. Taking the logarithm of the data and subsequently applying the test (i.e. investigating whether the data is log-normally distributed) leads to less rejections of the hypothesis but the hypothesis is still rejected for many consequences. Hence, it cannot be significantly concluded that the data in the set of decision tables are normally or log-normally distributed. Consequently, the corresponding expected utility calculations (cf. Section 2.3) will not be based on Equation 2.22, which presupposes normal distributions, but rather on Equation 2.25, which calculates the expected utility for a discrete empirical distribution. However, except for the procedure described at the end of Section 3.4.1, the methods introduced in Chapter 3 do not presume normally distributed data and are thus entirely applied to the data of the case study.

4.5.2   Preferential Uncertainty Modelling

The preferential uncertainties are modelled by replacing the deterministic preference parameters with intervals. Firstly, parameter intervals seem to model human preferences
more realistically than discrete values. Secondly, if a decision is not to be taken by a
single person but by a group, it will be easier for that group to agree on common parameter intervals than on discrete values. It will easily be possible to find out whether
or not the variation of certain preference parameters has an impact on the ranking of the
alternatives. Thus, disagreements which do not affect the results can be eliminated from
debate and the group can focus on discussing the differences that do matter in terms of
the results [French, 2003]. For the hypothetical case study, the capability of the methods
introduced in Section 3.3 is demonstrated for the n-dimensional triplet (w, ρ, x_{max}) (where
n is the number of considered attributes). The parameter x_{min} is not varied since, in the
case study, x_{min} is equal to zero for almost all considered attributes and negative values
do not make sense.

4.5.2.1   Modelling Inter-Criteria Preferential Uncertainties

Concerning the inter-criteria preference parameters, instead of assigning precise weights
to the attributes, it is sufficient to assign intervals. These intervals may differ in size
if appropriate. For the case study, weight intervals between 10 % and 20 % around the
discrete weights, which were used in the workshop, have been assigned. The exemplar
intervals (as used within this thesis) are compiled in Table 4.7. These intervals can also
be seen as representations of the linguistic imprecisions associated with the qualitative
weight elicitation results described in Section 4.4.2.

It should be emphasised that it is important to choose the weight intervals in such a way
that $C_w \cap H \neq \emptyset$ (cf. Section 3.3.1). For instance, a comparison of the ranges of the
assigned weight intervals and the ranges of the actually drawn weights (i.e. a comparison
of Table 4.7 and the first diagram in Figure 4.23 on page 131) can provide the basis for
such a consistency check.

Table 4.7: Assigned Weight Intervals

1st Level Criteria [Weight interval]	2nd Level Criteria [Weight interval]	3rd Level Criteria [Weight interval]
rad. effectiveness [0.10 − 0.25]	population [0.80 − 0.95]	avoided ind. dose adults [0.05 − 0.20] avoided ind. dose children [0.15 − 0.30] avoided collective dose [0.40 − 0.55] received collective dose [0.05 − 0.20]
	worker [0.05 − 0.20]	max. ind. worker dose [0.40 − 0.60] collective worker dose [0.40 − 0.60]
resources [0.15 − 0.30]	no. of workers [0.45 − 0.60] supplies [0.40 − 0.55]	
impact [0.25 − 0.45]	total food above [0.25 − 0.40] food above yr-1 [0.05 − 0.15] size of aff. area [0.35 − 0.50] costs [0.15 − 0.25]	
acceptance [0.30 − 0.50]	public [0.40 − 0.55] affected prod. [0.20 − 0.30] trade and ind. [0.25 − 0.35]	

4.5.2.2   Modelling Intra-Criteria Preferential Uncertainties

In order to support a group of decision makers in determining the shape(s) of the value function(s), they are allowed to assign intervals for the parameters ρ_i (which define the shapes) instead of precise values. To demonstrate the method, the parameters ρ_i for the 15 attributes are all varied between 0.5 and 10 for increasing preferences (or -10 and -0.5 for decreasing preferences respectively).

In addition to the value functions' curvatures, their domains' boundaries are varied. The upper boundaries of the value functions' domains are varied in an interval between the maximum of the occurring scores and the value augmented by 20 %.

4.6   Results for the Case Study

Besides the multi-attribute decision analysis, as carried out in the workshop and described in Section 4.4, additional analyses and graphical illustrations can provide an improved understanding of the importance of the different factors affecting a decision. Thus, in a first step, additional visualisations for the deterministic data and parameters, as used in the workshop, are presented in Section 4.6.1. Furthermore, sophisticated approaches for uncertainty handling, as introduced in Chapter 2.3 and Chapter 3, allow to gain a deeper insight into the robustness of decisions in the context of the case study. Consequently, the main focus of this section is on showing understandable visualisations of the uncertainties in the MADM results. While in Section 4.6.2, such visualisations are shown for data uncertainties whose modelling is described in Section 4.5.1, Section 4.6.3 deals with the visualisation of the uncertainties of the preference parameters as modelled in Section 4.5.2. Finally, Section 4.6.4 shows the results of a combined consideration of data and parameter uncertainties for the case study.

4.6.1   Visualisation of Results for Deterministic Values

As mentioned above, additional visualisation techniques for the deterministic results of the case study will be presented in this subsection with the objective of providing a deeper understanding of the importance of the different factors that affect a decision. For instance, a spider diagram can be used for the visual comparison of several alternatives with respect to the different attributes. Figure 4.13 shows the single-attribute performance scores of the eight alternatives with respect to the individual attributes considered in the case study. Each axis in the diagram corresponds to one attribute and the alternatives are represented by lines forming a polygonal traverse. Rather than presenting precise values, Figure 4.13 provides an overall impression of the decision problem. For the case study, the spider diagram shows for instance that the alternative "Disp" shows a very good performance with respect to the dose attributes (including worker doses) as well as the attributes "no. of workers" and "supplies" while "Rmov,T=0" performs better with respect to attributes such as "acceptance by affected producers", "acceptance by trade and industry" or "size of affected area".

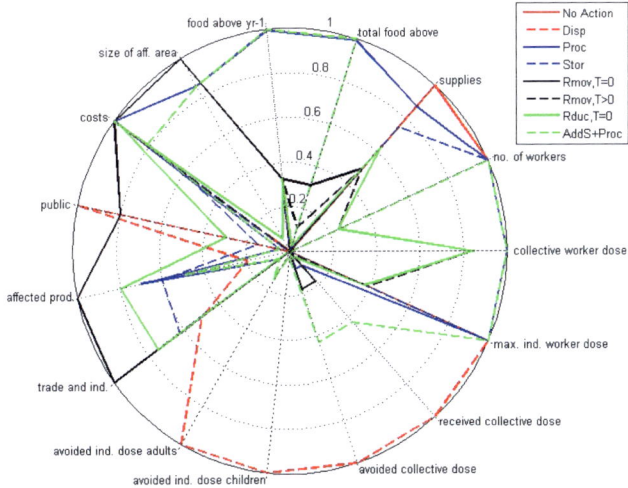

Figure 4.13: Spider Diagram for the Case Study

Since the general overview provided by spider diagrams becomes increasingly confusing with a growing number of attributes or alternatives, factor-analytic techniques, such as principal component analysis (PCA), can be helpful in providing a condensed impression of decision problems. Figure 4.14 shows the results projected on the PCA plane for the case study. The alternatives are plotted as triangles and the attributes are displayed as straight lines emanating from the origin.

In general, alternatives projected close together in the plane show similar characteristics. For instance, Figure 4.14 shows that the alternatives "Rmov,T=0", "Rmov,T>0" and "Rduc,T=0" possess similar properties. Furthermore, the alternatives "Proc" and "AddS+Proc" are plotted close to each other. However, the different groups of alternatives, show disparate characteristics. Additionally, the PCA diagram shows that the

alternatives "Rmov,T=0", "Rmov,T>0" and "Rduc,T=0" show good performance with
respect to the attributes grouped under the criteria "impact" and "acceptance" (in the
attribute tree) while "Disp" for instance performs better with respect to the attributes
grouped under the criteria "radiological effectiveness" and "resources".

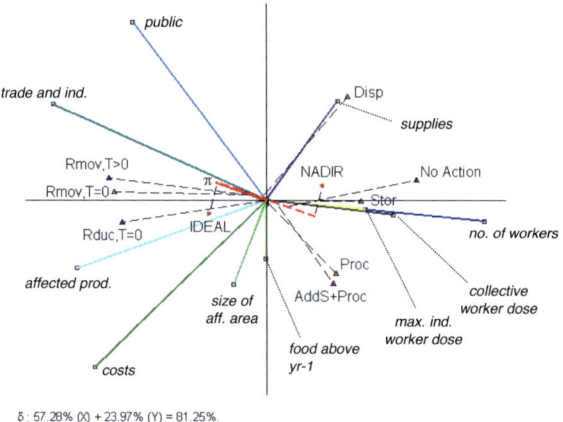

$\delta : 57.28\% \; (X) + 23.97\% \; (Y) = 81.25\%.$

Figure 4.14: PCA Plane for the Case Study

Concerning the projections of the attributes, their length is a measure of the influence
of the respective attribute on the decision problem, as described in Section 3.2.3. This
means, for instance, that the PCA diagram implies that the attributes "public acceptance", "acceptance by trade and industry" or "acceptance by the affected producers"
have a higher influence on the results than the attributes "max. individual worker dose"
or "food above yr-1". Moreover, the PCA plane of the case study shows that the selected
attributes can be said to be representative for the decision problem since they point in
all directions within the plane. Furthermore, the relative proportion of the variance represented in the PCA plane in comparison to the total variance can be calculated. Figure
4.14 shows that 81.25 % of the variance are preserved which is a very good result for a
projection from a 15-dimensional on a 2-dimensional space.

While a PCA diagram provides a valuable overview of the performance of the alternatives
relative to the different attributes, the information is usually represented unweighted.
Thus, the decision axis π (the projection of the normed weighting vector w) is displayed
in the diagram in Figure 4.14 in addition to the alternatives and attributes. In general,
π points in the direction of the preferred alternatives according to the preferences of the

decision makers. However, an exact aggregated ranking in the PCA plane can be obtained by projecting the alternatives orthogonally on the weighting vector (in the 15-dimensional original data space of the attributes) and by subsequently determining the order of the respective perpendiculars on w. The "projections of these projections" are shown as dashed lines in Figure 4.14. The intersections of these dashed lines with the decision axis $[-\pi, +\pi]$ allow to read off the ranking of the alternatives.

In addition to the eight considered alternatives, the two fictitious alternatives IDEAL and NADIR are displayed in Figure 4.14. These two points can provide valuable support in assessing the quality of the alternatives based on their relative positions in comparison to these points, i.e. alternatives projected close to the IDEAL, have high performance scores, while alternatives projected near the NADIR do not correspond to the preferences of the decision makers. The projections of the IDEAL and NADIR alternatives intersect the decision axis in $-\pi$ and π respectively (in the axis' ends).

Beyond the deterministic illustrations presented in Figure 4.13 and Figure 4.14, visualisations of the effect of the different types of uncertainty on the results of the case study are shown in the following. Starting from results of investigating the impact of data uncertainties (Section 4.5.1) and parameter uncertainties (Section 4.6.3) individually, results of a combined consideration of both types of uncertainty are presented in Section 4.6.4.

4.6.2   Results Taking Data Uncertainties into Account

As described in Section 2.3 and Section 3.2, there are different possibilities to illustrate the impact of data uncertainties on MADM results. One simple way to illustrate the results including data uncertainties is to visualise the expected utilities in the form of a bar chart. Figure 4.15 shows such a bar chart for $\kappa = 0.5$ (the risk attitude factor). As mentioned before, since there is no substantive evidence that the underlying data is normally distributed, the discrete empirical function of Equation 2.25 (page 36) is used for the calculation of the expected utilities.

In comparison to the deterministic results, the alternatives "Rmov,T=0" and "Disp" turn out to be almost equally preferable, followed by "Rmov,T>0", "Proc" and "Stor". In general, it can be noted that the alternatives' scores are closer together than in the deterministic case, i.e. it is more difficult to differentiate between the different alternatives. While the uncertainties in the results due to the uncertain input data are implicitly included in Figure 4.15, a drawback of the representation is that the ranges in which the results can vary in consequence of the underlying uncertainty are not visible.

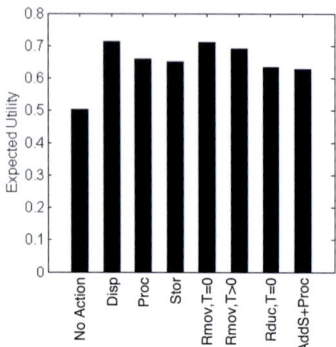

Figure 4.15: Expected Utilities for $\kappa = 0.5$ Visualised as Bar Chart

As described in Section 2.3, two types of sensitivity analyses can be shown besides the expected utilities. Firstly, the sensitivity of the expected utilities with respect to the parameter κ, reflecting the risk attitude, needs to be analysed. This is shown in Figure 4.16. While in general, the expected utilities decrease when κ increases, no rank reversals are observable when varying κ.

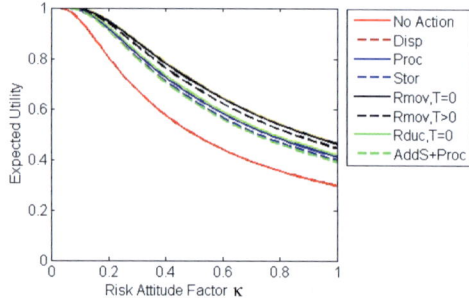

Figure 4.16: Sensitivity of Expected Utilities with Respect to κ

Secondly, it is important to analyse the sensitivity of the expected utilities with respect to weight changes. For instance, Figure 4.17 shows a sensitivity analysis for the weight of the criterion "acceptance". In contrast to the "standard sensitivity analysis" carried out in Section 4.4, the alternatives are not represented by straight lines but by curves.

However, these curves do not intersect twice for the case study, which is generally possible
as described in Section 2.3.

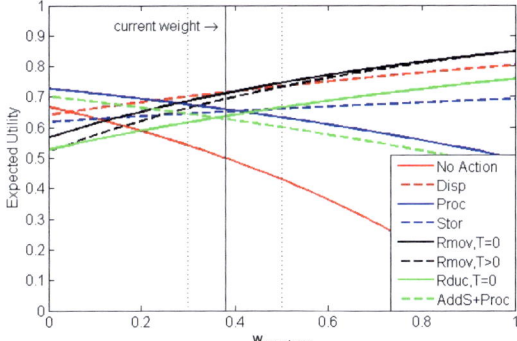

Figure 4.17: Sensitivity of Expected Utilities with Respect to the Weight of "acceptance" (for
   $\kappa = 0.5$)

Figure 4.17 shows that the alternatives "Rmov,T=0" and "Disp" perform more or less
equally well for the current weight of acceptance (approximately 38 %). For a higher
weight, "Rmov,T=0" receives the highest expected utility, for a weight between approximately 25 % and 38 %, "Disp" turns out to be the most preferred alternative and for a
weight smaller than 25 %, "Proc" receives the highest expected utility. In addition, the
dashed vertical lines in Figure 4.17 show the limits of the weight interval assigned to the
criterion "acceptance" (cf. Table 4.7) which allows to investigate whether or not changes
in the ranking occur when varying the weight of "acceptance" within these limits. While
the performance scores of "Rmov,T=0" and "Disp" are very similar, Figure 4.17 does
show that these two alternatives dominate the others within the assigned weight limits.
The simulation based approach to simultaneously vary this weight and the weights of the
other criteria within the respective intervals is demonstrated in Section 4.6.3.

While Figure 4.15 provides an aggregated overview, it disguises the fact that changes in the
ranking can occur in consequence of the underlying data uncertainty, i.e. that different
alternatives may be most preferable in the different scenarios. Figure 4.18 shows the
overall performance scores of all alternatives in all scenarios, sorted in ascending order
of the performance score of "Rmov,T=0". While Figure 4.15 shows a slightly higher
expected utility for "Disp" in comparison to "Rmov,T=0", Figure 4.18 shows that, when
carrying out deterministic analyses for each scenario in parallel, "Rmov,T=0" receives
the highest score in five, "Disp" in four and "Rmov,T>0" in one of the ten scenarios.

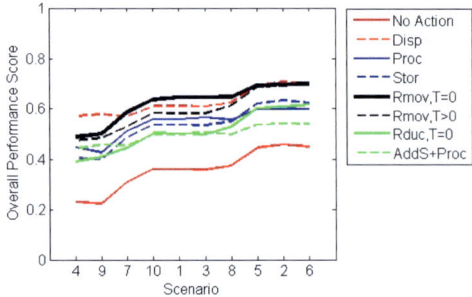

Figure 4.18: Overall Performance Scores for the Different Scenarios

Thus, since the ranking of the alternatives can obviously change as a result of the underlying uncertainty, the focus of the rest of the section is on visualisation techniques that are aimed at explicitly illustrating and communicating the uncertainties associated with the results of the decision analysis while seeking to not cause an information overload.

In addition to the information provided by Figure 4.18, it would be supportive to obtain information about the respective contributions of the individual criteria to the results and to the uncertainties in the results. In order to achieve this goal, an illustration by means of a stacked-bar chart, as proposed in Section 3.2, can be useful (see Figure 4.19).

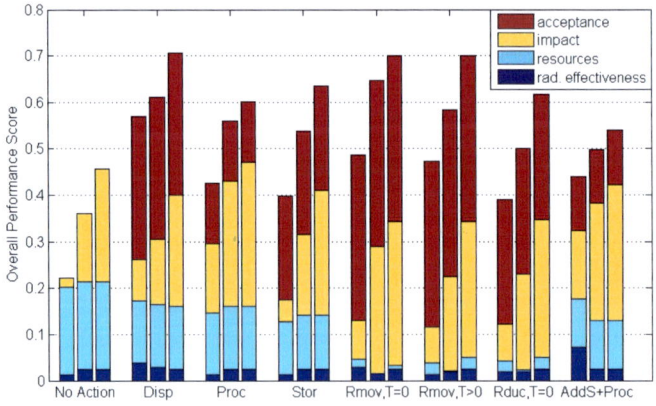

Figure 4.19: Visualisation of Uncertainties in Results Using a Stacked-Bar Chart

In order to illustrate the *uncertainty ranges*, the simultaneously calculated results are not all visualised but the results of the scenarios corresponding to the 5 %- and 95 %-quantiles (of the overall performance score) are shown alongside the results of the most probable scenario in Figure 4.19. As stated in Section 3.2, these scenarios will be referred to as *worst case* and *best case* scenarios respectively.

Figure 4.19 contains important information for the decision makers. Using a stacked-bar chart for the visualisation of the results does not only allow to investigate the *uncertainty ranges* of the overall goal but also to explore which of the considered criteria are subject to uncertainties and shows the *uncertainty ranges* of the individual criteria as well as their contribution to the uncertainties in the overall ranking. Furthermore, the proposed stacked-bar chart allows to analyse the distinguishability of the alternatives. For the considered case study, it is hard to distinguish between the alternatives "Disp", "Rmov,T=0" and "Rmov,T>0" in consequence of their very similar performance scores.

In addition to Figure 4.19, the application of PCA provides a good overview on the effect of the data uncertainties and allows to graphically explore the distinguishability of the alternatives in the PCA plane (see Figure 4.20). Such a visualisation allows to explore whether or not the different alternatives can be evaluated meaningfully based on the considered attributes and the uncertainties afflicted with the data in the decision tables of the different scenarios.

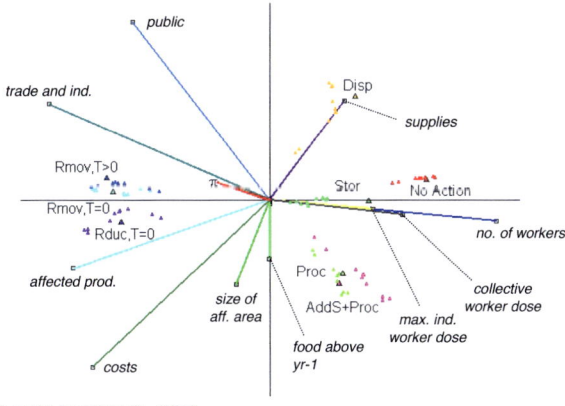

Figure 4.20: PCA Visualising the Uncertainty of the Data in the Different Scenarios

The range of variation of an alternative due to the underlying data uncertainty is represented by the complete set of points in the plane corresponding to this alternative. For instance, Figure 4.20 shows that the alternatives "Rmov,T=0", "Rmov,T>0" and "Rduc,T=0" are not clearly distinguishable as a result of the uncertainties. Furthermore, the sets of points corresponding to the alternatives "Proc" and "AddS+Proc" overlap to a large extent. However, considering the overlapping alternatives as groups of alternatives respectively, it can be said that the different groups are clearly distinguishable from each other.

4.6.3   Results Taking Preferential Uncertainties into Account

Besides analysing the impact of data uncertainties on the decision analysis' results, it is very important to investigate the stability of the results with respect to variations of the subjective preference parameters. Especially in the late phase of a nuclear emergency, the integration of reliable measurements into the model calculations can reduce the magnitude of the data uncertainties. However, the uncertainties associated with the preference parameters can nevertheless have a substantial impact on the results.

While classical one-dimensional sensitivity analyses, as described in Section 4.4, can help to assess the robustness of a decision with respect to weight changes, the major drawback of the procedure is that it is limited to varying one weight at a time. The focus of this section is on considering the impact of simultaneous variations of the inter-criteria as well as the intra-criteria preference parameters in the context of the case study by allowing the assignment of parameter intervals instead of precise parameters.

Concerning the inter-criteria preference parameters, results for 1000 samples (of w) are shown in Figure 4.21. The left diagram shows the spread of the overall performance scores as a results of the preferential uncertainties. Using intervals for preference modelling, most of the alternatives in the case study are not clearly distinguishable from each other. But the results in the left diagram do show that, even in the "worst cases", the alternatives "Rmov,T=0" and "Disp" have a higher performance score than the alternative "No Action" in the "best case" which means that the latter option is dominated by the first two. While the left diagram provides a good overview on the impact of the uncertainties of the inter-criteria preferential information, it is not possible to read off information about the relative frequency of the performance scores of the different alternatives (i.e. performance scores at the lower and upper bound of the shown ranges will usually occur less frequently than those in the middle of the ranges). However, such information is provided in the right diagram. As already stated in Section 3.3, the illustration by means of plotting the performance scores versus the cumulative percentage has also been proposed by Butler et al. [1997]. This visualisation provides detailed information of the complete distribution of the results.

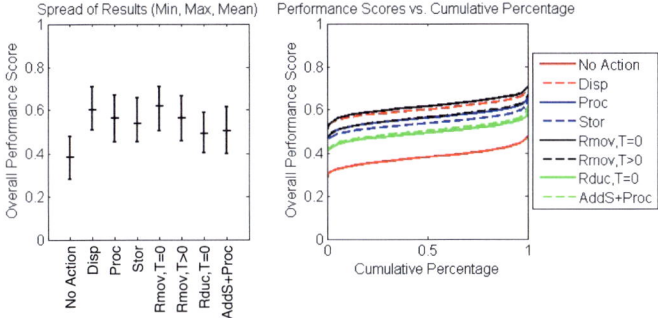

Figure 4.21: Impact of Inter-Criteria Preferential Uncertainties on the Results

It is important to note that the performance scores of the different alternatives at an imaginary "perpendicular cut" through the diagram of the cumulative percentages (right diagram in Figure 4.21) do not necessarily belong to only one weight combination. Thus, information about the exact percentage at which a certain alternative is ranked first cannot be read off from this diagram immediately. This means, for instance, that it cannot be concluded from the right diagram in Figure 4.21 that the alternative "Rmov,T=0" receives the highest overall performance score for all drawn weight combinations. However, an illustration as in Figure 4.22 (where "Rmov,T=0" is visualised as in Figure 4.21 but the other strategies are sorted in such a way that their scores at an imaginary "perpendicular cut" do belong to the same weight combination) or an analytical evaluation can be helpful to provide such accurate information. For the considered case study, "Rmov,T=0" is ranked first for 63 % of the drawn weight combinations while the alternatives "Disp" and "Proc" receive the highest overall performance score for 34 % and 3 % of the parameters samples respectively. Additionally, a visualisation as in Figure 4.22 can provide insight into potential correlations between the different alternatives. For example, Figure 4.22 indicates a correlation between the alternatives "Rmov,T=0", "Rmov,T>0" and "Rduc,T=0". This observation is in accordance with the PCA plot in Figure 4.14.

Furthermore, a "backwards calculation" can help to investigate the origin of potential differences in the results (see Figure 4.23). In addition to the information provided in Figures 4.21 and 4.22, an exploration which weight combinations result in which preferred alterna-

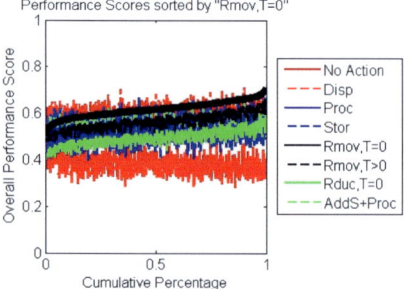

Figure 4.22: Impact of Inter-Criteria Preferential Uncertainties on the Results Sorted in As-
*   cending Order of "Rmov,T=0"*

tive is helpful for a decision making group. Figure 4.23 offers such information in an easily
understandable way. The upper diagram shows the range of all drawn weight combinations. The second diagram only shows those weight combinations for which "Rmov,T=0"
has the highest overall performance score. While the third diagram shows the weight intervals for which "Disp" turns out to be the most preferred alternative, the fourth diagram
shows those intervals for which "Proc" becomes most preferred.

While the intervals in the diagrams seem to be more or less the same for many attributes,
differences between the first and the second diagram can be seen for the attribute "no. of
workers". While the assigned interval approximately allows the weight to vary between
0.08 and 0.18, the weight of "no. of workers" for which "Rmov,T=0" turns out to be the
most preferred alternative is not higher than 0.12 (indicated by the loop in the second
diagram). Differences between the first and the third diagram can be detected for the
attribute "size of affected area". Weight combinations for which "Disp" receives the
highest overall performance score do not exceed a weight of 0.18 on "size of affected
area" as indicated by the loop in the third diagram. Comparing the first and the fourth
diagram, differences can be observed for the attributes "total food above", "size of affected
area", "acceptance by public", "acceptance by trade and industry" as well as "avoided
collective dose" (see the five loops in the fourth diagram). Especially, the weight intervals
corresponding to the acceptance by the public and by trade and industry and resulting in
"Proc" as the most preferred alternative are only small sections at the lower boundaries
of the total weight ranges of the respective attributes. However, while the information
offered by Figures 4.21 and 4.22 is useful for a group of decision makers to reduce the
set of reasonable alternatives, the information offered by Figure 4.23 can be very helpful
to the group when choosing an alternative from the reduced set by providing support to

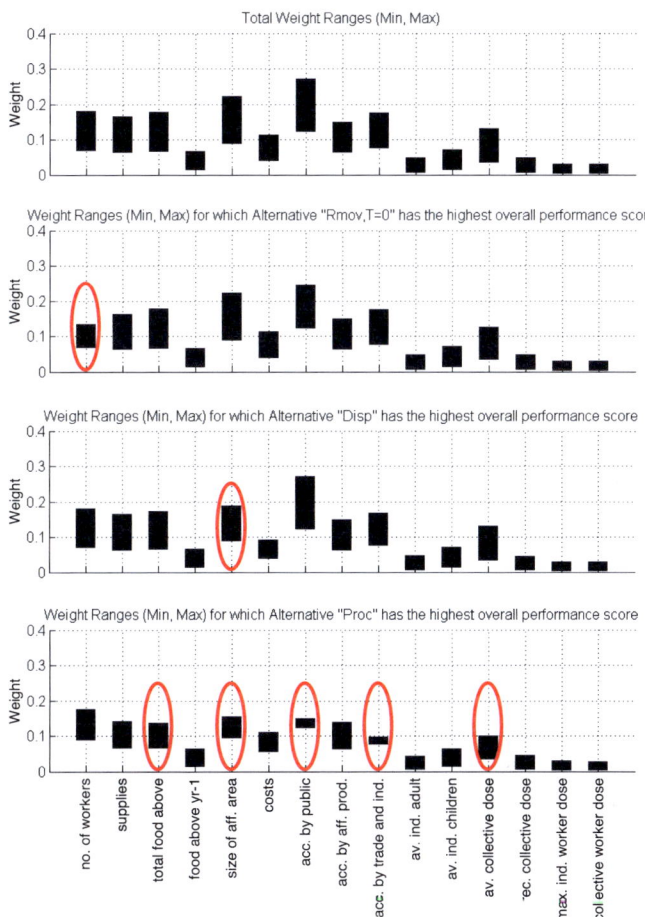

Figure 4.23: Backwards Calculation Concerning Inter-Criteria Preference Parameters

focus on the most important weight parameters in terms of their respective impacts on the results.

Concerning the intra-criteria preference parameters, similar results can be generated and visualised. The resulting scores for 1000 samples of (ρ, x_{max}) are shown in Figure 4.24 (as mentioned above, x_{min} is not varied in this case study since x_{min} is equal to zero for almost all considered attributes and negative values do not make sense). Again, the left diagram shows the spread of the overall performance scores as a result of the preferential uncertainties. Most of the alternatives are not clearly distinguishable from each other. But the left diagram does show that, even in the "best case", the alternative "No Action" has a lower performance score than all other alternatives in the "worst cases" which means that the alternative "No Action" is dominated by the others. Furthermore, the left diagram shows for example that the alternative "Rmov,T=0" has the "highest worst performance score", i.e. following a *maximin* strategy [cf. e.g. Bamberg and Coenenberg, 1994; Laux, 2005], the decision makers would choose this alternative. Contrarily, following a *maximax* strategy, they would prefer the alternative "Proc". In addition to the good general overview of the impact of the intra-criteria preferential uncertainties provided by the left diagram, the right diagram offers information about the relative frequency of the performance scores of the different alternatives. Providing detailed information about the complete distribution of the results, the performance scores are again plotted against the cumulative percentage as proposed by Butler et al. [1997]. An additional analytical evaluation shows that, for variations of the intra-criteria preference parameters, the alternative "Rmov,T=0" is only ranked first for 40 %, while "Disp" and "Proc" receive the highest score for 53 % and 7 % of the drawn parameter combinations respectively.

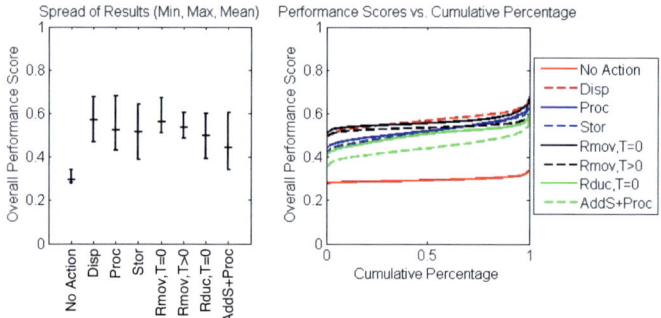

Figure 4.24: Impact of Intra-Criteria Preferential Uncertainties on the Results

As for the inter-criteria preference parameters, a "backwards calculation" can help to investigate which intra-criteria parameter combinations result in which preferred alternative. Figure 4.25 visualises such a backwards calculation. The upper diagram shows the intervals of all drawn samples of the value function parameter ρ. The second diagram only shows those parameter combinations for which "Rmov,T=0" has the highest over-

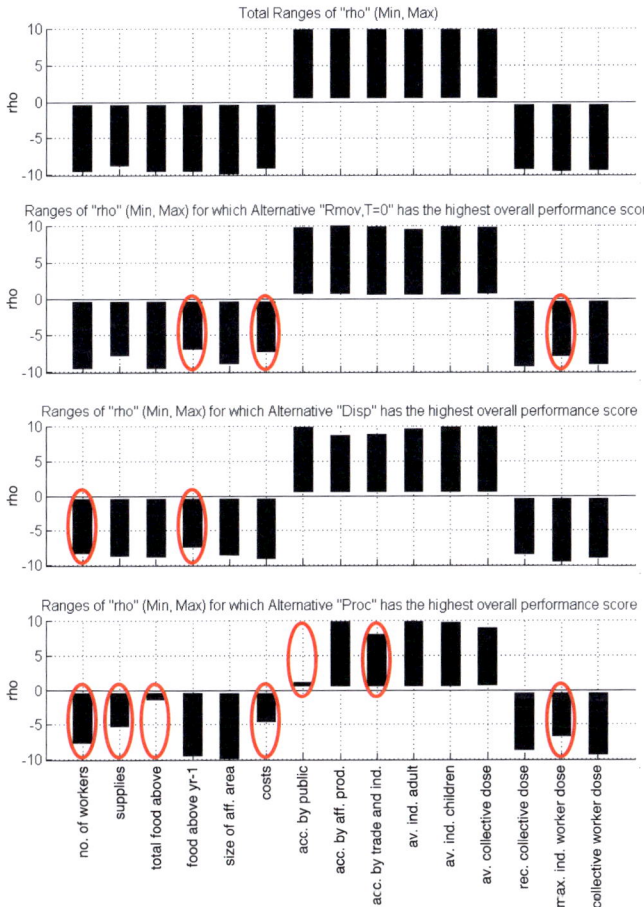

Figure 4.25: Backwards Calculation Concerning Intra-Criteria Preference Parameters

all performance score. While the third diagram shows the parameter intervals for which "Disp" turns out to be the most preferred alternative, the fourth diagram shows those intervals for which "Proc" becomes most preferred.

The intervals in the diagrams seem to be more or less the same for many attributes. Small differences between the first and the second diagram can be seen for the attributes "food above yr-1", "costs" and "max. individual worker dose". While the assigned intervals allow ρ_i to vary between -10.0 and -0.5 for each of the attributes, the ρ_i for which "Rmov,T=0" turns out to be the most preferred alternative is not smaller than approximately -7.0 for these three attributes (indicated by the loops in the second diagram). For decreasing preferences, negative ρ_i close to zero represent strongly curved convex value functions. Thus, the second diagram in Figure 4.25 implies that such curved convex value functions for the attributes "food above yr-1", "costs" and "max. individual worker dose" lead to high performance scores of "Rmov,T=0" while for rather linear value functions for these attributes, "Rmov,T=0" does not turn out to be the most preferred alternative. Similar conclusions for the alternative "Disp" can be drawn from comparing the first and the third diagram. Comparing the first and the fourth diagram, differences can be observed for the attributes "no. of workers", "supplies", "total food above", "costs", "acceptance by public", "acceptance by trade and industry" as well as "max. individual worker dose" (see the seven loops in the fourth diagram). Especially, the intervals corresponding to the attributes "total food above" and "acceptance by public" are very small and close to zero implying that only very strong curvatures of the corresponding value functions lead to "Proc" being the most preferred alternative. Again, the information offered by such a backwards calculation can help a group of decision makers to focus on the most important intra-criteria preference parameters in terms of their respective impacts on the results.

Considering the inter-criteria and intra-criteria preferential uncertainties simultaneously, increases the indistinguishability of the alternatives (from a preferential perspective). The results for 1000 samples of the random triplet (w, ρ, x_{max}) are shown in Figure 4.26.

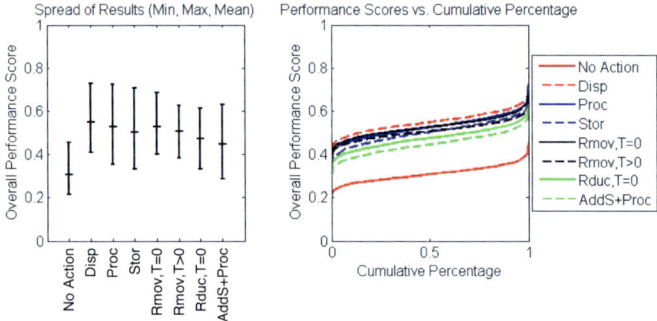

Figure 4.26: Impact of all Preferential Uncertainties on the Results

The left diagram in Figure 4.26 shows the spread of the overall performance scores as a result of the complete preferential uncertainty. In this case, no dominated or dominating alternatives can be observed. In addition, plotting the overall performance scores against the cumulative percentage, the right diagram illustrates the relative frequency of the performance scores of the different alternatives.

Figure 4.27 shows the same results sorted by "Rmov,T=0", i.e. "Rmov,T=0" is visualised as in Figure 4.26 but the other strategies are sorted in such a way that their scores at an imaginary "perpendicular cut" through the diagram do belong to the same parameter combination. Hence, Figure 4.27 provides information about the percentage at which an alternative is ranked first. Alternatively, the results can be evaluated analytically. When varying all preference parameters simultaneously within the afore assigned intervals (cf. Section 4.5.2), the alternative "Rmov,T=0" is only ranked first for 25 %, while "Disp" and "Proc" receive the highest score for 52 % and 23 % of the drawn parameter combinations respectively.

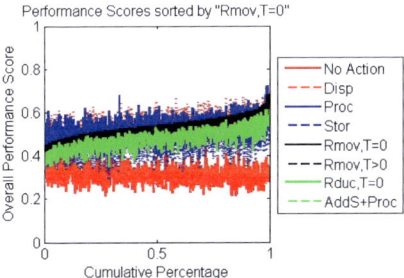

Figure 4.27: Impact of all Preferential Uncertainties on the Results Sorted in Ascending Order of "Rmov, T=0"

In addition, Figure 4.27 provides insight into potential correlations between the different alternatives. Similar to the observation when varying the inter-criteria preferential parameters only, a correlation between the alternatives "Rmov,T=0", "Rmov,T>0" and "Rduc,T=0" can for instance be detected. This result can also be observed in the PCA plot in Figure 4.28. Furthermore, in addition to the above visualisations, Figure 4.28 provides an alternative overview on the effect of the preferential uncertainties and allows to graphically explore the distinguishability of the alternatives in the PCA plane from a preferential perspective.

The range of variation of an alternative due to the intra-criteria preferential uncertainty is represented by the complete set of points in the plane corresponding to this alternative.

Consequently, Figure 4.28 allows to explore whether or not the different alternatives can be evaluated meaningfully based on the considered attributes and the uncertainties afflicted with the intra-criteria preference parameters. For instance, Figure 4.28 shows that the alternatives "Rmov,T=0", "Rmov,T>0" and "Rduc,T=0" are not clearly distinguishable as a result of the intra-criteria uncertainties. Furthermore, the sets of points corresponding to the alternatives "Proc" and "AddS+Proc" overlap to a small extent as well as those corresponding to the alternatives "Disp" and "Stor".

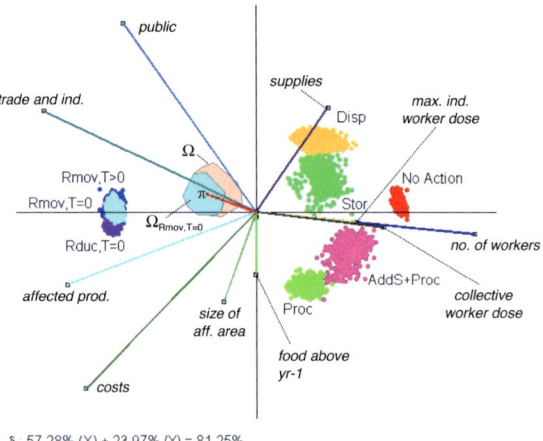

δ : 57.28% (X) + 23.97% (Y) = 81.25%.

Figure 4.28: Complete Overview of the Impact of Preferential Uncertainties in the PCA Plane

However, considering the overlapping alternatives as groups of alternatives respectively, it can be said that the different groups are clearly distinguishable from each other. In addition to the intra-criteria preferential uncertainties (i.e. the uncertainties associated with the shapes and domains' boundaries of the value functions), the weight space is projected onto the PCA plane as illustrated in Figure 4.28. The projection of the complete weight space or, more precisely, its convex hull Ω, marks the range in which the projection π of the weighting vector can move when varying the weights within the defined weight interval limits. The position of Ω relative to the origin in the plane gives a general impression of the magnitude of the impact of the inter-criteria preferential uncertainties. In this case study, Ω does not include the origin, implying that all valid weight combinations point at least in a similar direction. Consequently, the alternatives lying in this direction, such as "Rmov,T=0" for instance, perform well in general.

As argued in Section 3.3.4 already, an exact determination of the effects of varying the weights within their intervals based on the projected weight space Ω and the decision axis π is problematic. Thus, the results of the backwards calculation (see Figure 4.23) are additionally made available in the PCA plane, i.e. besides the complete weight space, the weight combinations for which a certain alternative is the most preferred can be projected separately onto the plane. For instance, the *preference region* of the alternative "Rmov,T=0", denoted $\Omega_{Rmov,T=0}$, is shown in Figure 4.28.

4.6.4 Combined Analysis of Data and Parameter Uncertainties in the Context of the Case Study

As pointed out in Section 3.1, a large advantage of using Monte Carlo analysis for uncertainty handling in MADM is the straightforward possibility to simultaneously consider different types of uncertainty in an understandable and transparent way. From a methodological perspective, two possibilities to simultaneously consider and visualise data and parameter uncertainties have been introduced in Section 3.4: Firstly, the incorporation of the simulation based approaches for preferential uncertainty handling into the framework of utility theory and, secondly, the simultaneous analysis of data and parameter uncertainties in the PCA plane. Both approaches will be demonstrated in the context of the case study.

For the integration of the multi-dimensional sensitivity analysis approaches into expected utility theory, the newly introduced visualisations shown in Figures 4.22 and 4.27, providing insight into potential correlations between the different alternatives, have been chosen. In Figure 4.29, the expected utilities are plotted against the cumulative percentage for $\kappa = 0.5$ (where κ is the risk attitude factor). While in the left diagram, the results are sorted by "Rmov,T=0", the results in the right diagram are sorted by "Disp", i.e. the other strategies are sorted in such a way that their scores at an imaginary "perpendicular cut" do belong to the same parameter combination (in both diagrams). An analytical evaluation based on the information provided in Figure 4.29 indicates that the alternative "Rmov,T=0" achieves the highest expected utility for 25 %, while "Disp" achieves the highest expected utility for 75 % of the drawn parameter combinations.

While in Figure 4.29, the effect of the data uncertainties on the results is only implicitly represented (the data uncertainties are incorporated in the expected utilities), the aim of simultaneously considering data and parameter uncertainties in the PCA plane is to explicitly illustrate the ranges in which the results can vary due to the different types of uncertainty. As pointed out in Section 3.4.2 already, the combined exploration of

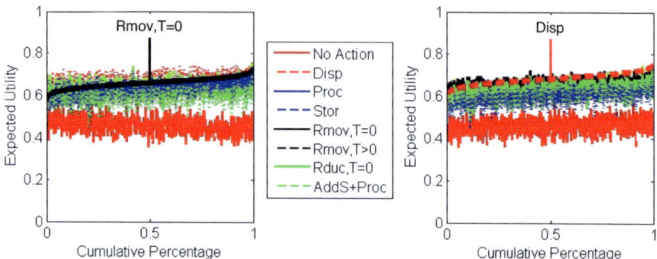

Figure 4.29: Expected Utilities Versus Cumulative Percentage Sorted by "Rmov,T=0" (Left) and "Disp" (Right)

the impact of data and parameter uncertainties in the PCA plane is very similar to the simultaneous consideration of intra-criteria and inter-criteria preferential uncertainties in the PCA plane.

While the uncertainties of the inter-criteria preference parameters are visualised in the PCA plane in the form of the projected weight space Ω, the uncertainties of the intra-criteria preference parameters and the data uncertainties both affect the position of the alternatives' projections in the plane. The latter two types of uncertainty are both visualised as scatter plots. Simultaneously considering data and parameter uncertainties instead of considering each type individually means that each of the $\tau = 1\,000$ drawn parameter combinations is associated with each of the $\nu = 10$ scenarios resulting in $\nu \cdot \tau = 10\,000$ projections per alternative. As for the data uncertainties (cf. Section 4.6.2), they are shown in the form of triangles in the plane (see Figure 4.30).

Again, the spread of the projections corresponding to a certain alternative represents the range of variation and it can be graphically explored whether or not the different alternatives are distinguishable from each other in the light of the underlying uncertainty. In consequence of the occurring interferences between the effects of the data and the parameter uncertainties when being simultaneously considered, the spread of each alternative is larger than the corresponding spread when considering data and parameter uncertainties separately (cf. Figures 4.20 and 4.28). The distinguishability decreases accordingly. For example, Figure 4.30 shows that the alternatives "Rmov,T=0", "Rmov,T>0" and "Rduc,T=0" are no longer distinguishable as a result of the uncertainties. Furthermore, the projections corresponding to the alternatives "Proc" and "AddS+Proc" as well as those corresponding to the alternatives "Disp" and "Stor" are not clearly distinguishable. The different groups of alternatives, however, are still distinguishable from each other.

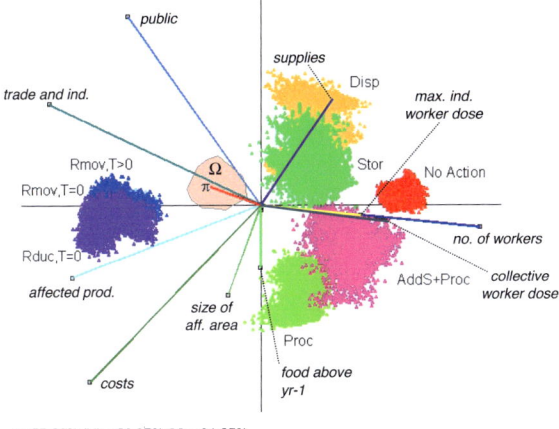

$\delta : 57.28\% \ (X) + 23.97\% \ (Y) = 81.25\%.$

Figure 4.30: Combined Illustration of the Impact of Data and Parameter Uncertainties in the PCA Plane

Showing the projected weight space Ω as well as the scatter plots, representing the data and the intra-criteria preferential uncertainties, the PCA plane in Figure 4.30 provides a complete graphical impression of the impact of the different types of uncertainty on the MADM results.

4.7 Summarising Discussion of the Case Study

The developed and implemented multi-attribute decision support methods have been applied to an exemplar case study in the context of industrial risk management. Within the large field of industrial risk management, nuclear emergency and remediation management is an important and challenging area. Besides the resulting severe and far-reaching consequences of a potential emergency, risk management and emergency planning are very relevant in nuclear power generation due to the fact that a large part of electricity is generated from nuclear energy – in Europe as well as world-wide. Energy supply is a very important part of critical infrastructure and an area-wide, secure electricity supply is essential for the functioning of a modern society. Thus, crisis situations in the energy sector constitute a special challenge in comparison to emergency preparedness and management in many other areas which often involve contingency plans or checklists that can been prepared in advance and used in emergency exercises.

For an integrated approach to industrial risk management, multidisciplinary and multi-scale approaches are needed taking various, at least partially conflicting objectives into account. Besides the purely economic factors, health and safety aspects, the environmental impact and the technical feasibility need to be considered for example. Additionally, decision situations in the event of a nuclear or radiological emergency involve different stakeholder and expert groups with diverse background knowledge and different views, responsibilities and interests. With the rising demand for information by the mass media and the public, methods are needed to assess how such decision situations are resolved [cf. Renn, 2001; Wybo, 2006]. Contributing to transparency and traceability of decisions and allowing to take political and socio-psychological aspects into account, multi-attribute decision analysis contributes to improve the communication and justification of the results of decision making processes and can be helpful in forming an audit trail. Such a decision analytical approach to industrial risk management is essential in addition to the economic and technical modelling in order to enhance public confidence and understanding in relation to the corresponding decision processes.

The uncertainties occurring in the context of the case study require an adequate modelling and visualisation. The applicability of the newly developed and implemented approaches for uncertainty handling in multi-attribute decision support has been demonstrated on the basis of the case study. Especially the presented multi-dimensional sensitivity analysis approach can contribute to facilitate the consensus building within a group. It is likely that different members of a group argue for different preference parameters. The described methods can provide valuable insights into the robustness of a decision and also allow to explore trade-offs between conflicting objectives (such as radiological effectiveness and resources for instance).

From the uncertainty analyses carried out for the case study, it can be concluded that either the alternative "Disposal" or the alternative "Rmov,T=0" is ranked first. The proposed approach to multi-dimensional sensitivity analysis allows to explore which parameter constellations result in which of these two alternatives as the most preferred.

The knowledge acquired by conducting such comprehensive uncertainty analyses in the context of the case study can also be used for countermeasure planning purposes, and can consequently contribute to an improved emergency preparedness. In particular, concerning the planning of long-term measures, the time horizon for their implementation may vary between a few months and several years. In this way, the developed methods provide valuable support for strategic planning in relation to industrial risk management.

Some points need further discussion. For instance, a "deterministic uncertainty analysis" (i.e. basically, carrying out deterministic evaluations for the different scenarios and subsequently comparing the results), as carried out in Section 4.6.2 and illustrated in Figure 4.18, shows that the alternative "Rmov,T=0" receives the highest score in five, "Disp" in four and "Rmov,T>0" in one of the ten scenarios. Contrariwise, calculating the expected utilities results in a slightly higher expected utility for "Disp" in comparison to "Rmov,T=0" (see Figure 4.15 in Section 4.6.2). Kirkwood [1992], for instance, argues that deterministic uncertainty analysis approaches tend to overestimate the impact of the uncertainties. However, it is important to note that the possibility that changes in the ranking are possible in consequence of the underlying uncertainties, is often disguised by expected utility based approaches. In practical applications it is thus important to analyse if the underlying uncertainties have a significant effect on the results. Especially, the effect of the uncertainties introduced during the multi-attribute analysis (i.e. the uncertainties of the preference parameters) is often substantial.

However, concerning the countermeasure and remediation strategies considered within the case study, discussions evolved within the workshop, whether or not such measures are acceptable and implementable at all, i.e. whether or not it is possible to bring food to the market in which the contamination has been reduced below the respective intervention level by carrying out one of the discussed measures. The answer to this question certainly depends on the availability of non-contaminated food and thus on the dimension of the emergency. But since the acceptance of consuming contaminated food at all, even lowly contaminated food (below the intervention level), is assumed to be very low in general, a rethinking recently began. Especially for regionally bordered events, the different stakeholders and experts in the workshop estimate that non-contaminated food from non-affected areas will be made available instead of bringing lowly contaminated food to the market. Consequently, discussions recently emerged, for instance in Germany, on shifting the decision context from deciding between different agricultural countermeasure and remediation strategies towards deciding between different waste disposal options [cf. e.g. Kaulard et al., 2006]. However, this decision situation is not less challenging and MADA can again be used to design transparent decision making processes in this context.

Chapter 5

Conclusions and Outlook

The complexity of contemporary industrial, economic, environmental and social infrastructure networks requires an integrated, multidisciplinary and multiscale approach to industrial risk management, i.e. many scientific disciplines need to be involved in a comprehensive analysis of industrial risks. However, these various disciplines have developed their risk and vulnerability models mostly independently from each other so far.

The combination of various scientific approaches leads to an enriched insight into a realistic modelling, taking the needs of real world decision making and disaster resilience into account. One approach that provides an integrated picture of decision situations in industrial risk management by allowing to simultaneously consider technical, economic, environmental as well as socio-psychological and political factors is multi-criteria decision analysis.

In this thesis, a concept has been developed to support the resolution of complex decision situations which occur when handling the risks arising from emergency situations in the nuclear power generation sector. The focus of this section is to derive conclusions and to point out how the findings can be extended and transfered to other industrial systems and emergencies. Additionally, possibilities for methodological extensions of the proposed and applied multi-criteria approach are identified.

5.1   Conclusions for Industrial Risk Management

Failures in industrial operating procedures and the potentially arising emergency situations can differ in many ways. For instance, concerning their causes, they may be induced internally (i.e. they emanate from the production process itself or rather from losing control over the production process) or externally (i.e. they emanate for instance from a natural disaster). The respective dimensions of the emergency situations' impact on the economy, the environment and the society as a whole may differ considerably, too.

Since today's industrial systems are characterised by a continuous interchange of information, goods or services amongst the systems' components (i.e. they are *tightly coupled*) and by unfamiliar or unplanned interactions between the various components, which may not immediately be visible or comprehensible, such systems confront us with the problem of "managing the unexpected" in the event of a technical failure due to the unpredictable nature of the interactions. The occurrence of an emergency within a system may not only affect the industrial system itself, but also the community in which it is embedded, for instance by causing economic losses, environmental damages or disruptions of electricity and water supply. Consequently, the risk arising from such an emergency can be regarded as affecting multiple members, parts or components of the system and propagating quickly among the individual parts or components of the network.

In order to support a structured analysis of risk in such complex systems, methods from the area of operations research have been applied. While the application of operations research methods is standard in the area of production planning, they have not yet been well adapted to planning problems in the context of unexpected events. Recently, their application in the context of managing risks in supply chains is for instance addressed in Vahrenkamp and Siepermann [2007] but the discussion is primarily focussed on exercise and merchandising risk. Special emphasis within this thesis has been placed on providing support for the evaluation of countermeasure and remediation strategies in the aftermath of an unexpected event in an industrial system. Thereby, special focus has been put on analysing the consequences of a nuclear or radiological emergency and different countermeasure and remediation strategies for the society and the environment in the light of various types of uncertainty.

The knowledge acquired by such analyses enables a better understanding of industrial risks. This leads to a better understanding of strategic countermeasure planning problems and can thus contribute to an improved risk awareness and emergency preparedness.

The consequence assessment constitutes an important part of any planning problem in the context of emergency preparedness. Within the scope of nuclear emergency management, the RODOS system can be used to assess the consequences of different countermeasure and remediation strategies. In view of the high efforts for the development of a system such as RODOS, the question arises, in which other contexts such a decision support system can be used to support the resolution of complex decision situations. Besides internally-induced emergencies at nuclear power plants, nuclear or radiological emergencies due to acts of terrorism – may they pertain to a nuclear power plant or to a "dirty bomb" – are recently discussed. In both cases, RODOS is straightforwardly applicable.

Furthermore, non-nuclear emergency situations may require coherent and structured decision support. Both, natural or other industrial emergencies can have a significant impact on the environment as well as the society and may thus necessitate the implementation of countermeasure or remediation strategies. While in RODOS, a Gaussian model is used to calculate the atmospheric dispersion of the radioactivity, several other approaches for meteorological dispersion modelling are discussed in literature [cf. e.g. Sennewald, 1996]. However, thinking about accidents in chemical industry for instance (such as Seveso (1976), Bhopal (1984), Schweizerhalle/Basel (1986) or Jilin/Harbin (2005)), the availability of model forecasts concerning the dispersion/propagation of gas or water pollutions is very important in order to be able to implement adequate emergency actions – at least in areas at a certain distance from the accident site. Moreover, information about potentially affected areas, as provided by RODOS for nuclear or radiological events, supports decisions on where to implement which countermeasures.

In analogy to nuclear or radiological emergencies, the protection of human lives and health has the highest priority in the early phase after any industrial emergency. In the long term, however, when discussing the efficiency of different remediation strategies, the decision situations become more complex, in nuclear as well as in non-nuclear emergencies. Consequently, methods are needed that support a transparent resolution of such complex decision situations.

5.2   Conclusions Concerning the Multi-Criteria Approach

Besides providing geographic information about the areas being impacted in the event of an industrial emergency, a major challenge in the context of industrial risk management is the evaluation of different countermeasure and remediation strategies taking into account their respective strengths and weaknesses according to their technical, economic, environmental and socio-psychological performance. However, there will usually not be one single alternative performing best with respect to all relevant decision criteria. Thus, incomparabilities occur, i.e. one alternative may be better with respect to one criterion while another one may be better with respect to another criterion. Multi-attribute decision analysis (MADA) aims at reducing such incomparabilities by explicitly incorporating preferential information of the responsible decision makers. In this way, MADA helps to compile a ranking of the different alternatives. Additionally, MADA is suitable to summarise the findings of the various disciplines involved in industrial risk management and to incorporate the respective results in common guidelines and recommendations.

Furthermore, contributing to transparency and traceability of decisions, MADA is helpful to satisfy the increasing demand for information by the mass media and the public. The communication and justification of the results of decision making processes is an important part of any decision support system in the context of industrial risk management, since, without such trust building components, the corresponding decisions are likely not be accepted by the general public.

In this thesis, multi-attribute value and utility theory (MAVT/MAUT) have been used to support the evaluation of different countermeasure and remediation strategies in the context of handling the risks emerging from technical failures in industry. Reasons for choosing MAVT/MAUT include their transparent nature and the already proved successful application in the context of emergency management. Additionally, the International Commission on Radiological Protection (ICRP) recommends the use of MAVT in the context of radiation protection.

Since decision making processes in industrial risk management are subject to various different types of uncertainty, a framework to classify and handle the arising uncertainties has been elaborated. This framework reflects the various sources of uncertainty and their respective implications for the risk management process. Providing an appropriate framework to address the different occurring types of uncertainty (e.g. data and preferential uncertainties) in an understandable and transparent way, a decision making approach based on Monte Carlo analysis has been proposed in this thesis. This approach is accompanied by a number of graphical representations to support the visualisation and communication of the ranges in which the results can vary in consequence of the underlying uncertainties.

Besides the comprehensive visualisation techniques proposed to support the communication of the MADM results, a valuable benefit of the developed multi-dimensional Monte Carlo sensitivity analysis framework is the approach for backwards calculation. The corresponding illustrations provide valuable insights into the robustness of decisions by allowing to graphically explore which parameter combinations result in which preferred alternative. These benefits are particularly helpful for consensus building within a group.

5.3   Outlook

The proposed framework for decision support in industrial risk management can be enhanced and extended in several ways. For instance, in order to increase the usability and acceptance of the developed framework for uncertainty handling, the explanation module (cf. Section 4.2.5) needs to be extended, i.e. explanations about the uncertainties in the results need to be added (cf. Appendix A). Furthermore, it should be emphasised that the proposed methods are universally applicable and can thus be applied in any context where MADA is used to support the resolution of a complex decision situation. For instance, within the nuclear sector, the problem of nuclear waste management constitutes a typical MCDA problem. Even though this has already been subject to a large number of research studies [cf. e.g. Keeney, 1987; Merkhofer and Keeney, 1987; Keeney and von Winterfeldt, 1994; Taji et al., 2005; CoRWM, 2006], research potential does exist because the final storage is yet an unsolved problem and the design of transparent decision processes under participation of the public and thus the need of structured and understandable communication becomes increasingly relevant [McDaniels et al., 1999; Walker, 2000]. Moreover, MCDA could for instance be used to support the choice between different power generation alternatives, which is likely to represent a problem of rising importance in future since it affects the long-term development of the power generation mix within a country. Two additional particularly important needs for future research are pointed out in detail in the remainder of this section.

5.3.1   Sequential Decision Making

One of the essential tasks of decision makers before, during and after an emergency is the spatial and temporal assignment of available resources to different operation areas. To find solutions for such a complex task, information about early warning data, damages and victims, available resources, etc., is needed as well as temporally varying information about the evolution of the emergency situation.

While MADA constitutes a valuable contribution to the transparency of decision processes, the existing methods are not able to reflect the sequential and iterative process of decision making in real life. Decisions are usually not taken at one single point as it is often assumed for reasons of simplicity. In reality, in the event of an industrial emergency, decisions are rather nested in a series of decisions which are related to each other [French and Ríos-Insua, 2000]. Moreover, up-to-date data – if available – would be included for each new decision, such as the atmospheric dispersion of the radioactive plume in the context of the case study. This sequential character of decision problems is often represented by illustrations such as influence diagrams and decision trees (see Figure 5.1). In such an influence diagram, the following labelling is often used [cf. e.g. Clemen and Reilly, 2001]: Rectangles (or squares) represent decision nodes, ellipses (or circles) represent chance nodes and diamonds as well as rounded rectangles represent value nodes which are sometimes also called consequence nodes. While rounded rectangles represent values of individual attributes/criteria within an attribute tree (such as the attribute tree of the case study in Figure 4.8), diamonds are used for the values of the overall goal. The respective nodes are thus also called terminal nodes.

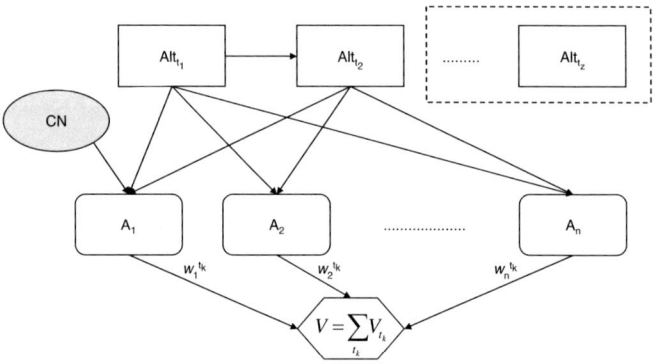

Figure 5.1: Influence Diagram for Multiple Time Steps and Multiple Attributes

For instance, Alt_{t_k} denotes a set of alternatives available at time step t_k (with $1 \leq k \leq z$) in the influence diagram in Figure 5.1. The different available alternatives at each time step will usually show different performances with respect to the different attributes $A_1, ..., A_n$. In addition, one or several chance nodes "CN" representing the uncertain environment, e.g. meteorological conditions, can effect the outcome of one or several alternative(s) with respect to one or several attribute(s). The values of the individual criteria can then be weighted with the weights $w_1^{t_k}, ..., w_n^{t_k}$, which may be time-variant, and finally the overall value V is obtained which is to be maximised.

In the context of the case study discussed in Chapter 4, for example, decisions on whether or not removing cows from contaminated pasture would be taken immediately whereas decisions on the processing of milk would be discussed at a later date. This means that the following concrete alternatives can for instance be assigned to the sets of alternatives

Alt_{t_k} in this context: $Alt_{t_1} = \{$"No Action", "Disp", "Rmov,T=0", "Rduc,T=0"$\}$, Alt_{t_2} $= \{$"No Action", "Disp", "Proc", "Stor", "Rmov,T>0", "AddS+Proc"$\}$.

The labelling used for influence diagrams can also be used for decision trees. An interesting fact is that a decision tree corresponds to each influence diagram and can be derived from it (but not the other way round). A decision tree that corresponds to the influence diagram in Figure 5.1 is shown in Figure 5.2. While an influence diagram emphasises the influences and the conditionality and provides a good overview and representation of the structure of a decision problem, a decision tree clearly displays the temporal interrelationships between the individual decisions and chance nodes (external influences and/or random events). Both representations complement each other and provide a broad range of perspectives concerning a sequential decision problem.

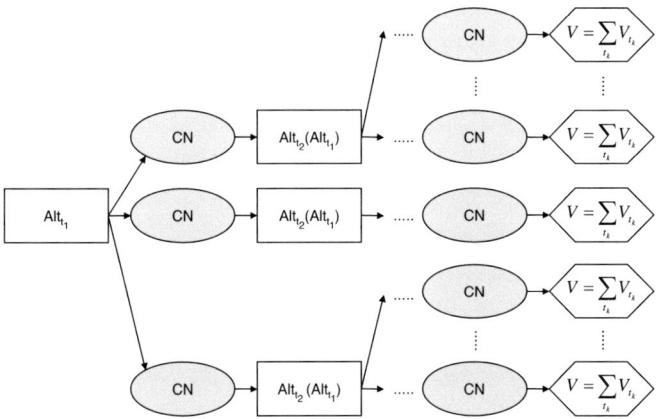

Figure 5.2: Decision Tree Corresponding to the Influence Diagram in Figure 5.1

Each decision node in the tree represents a MAVT analysis where the set of alternatives can vary and not only depends on the time but also on the decisions taken at the previous time steps. For example, the set Alt_{t_2} of available alternatives at time step t_2 depends on the decision taken at time step t_1. In Figure 5.2, only one arrow starts from each chance node. In a real emergency, it is hard to quantify any probabilities for arbitrary chance nodes right from the beginning and to assign discrete probabilities to the arrows in a justifiable way. Concerning the context of the case study, it is assumed that the "chance factor" can be related to the data assimilation modules of RODOS. Taking into account up-to-date monitoring data (e.g. measurement results) at each time step, the data assimilation modules improve the results of the calculations of the system. Thus, they reflect the external influence on the decision making process at each time step.

A decision tree such as in Figure 5.2 can be resolved by the so-called "roll back" method (also called backward recursion) which is based on Bellman's principle of optimality [cf. e.g. Bellman, 1957]. The aim is the determination of an optimal solution (an optimal sequence of decisions, i.e. the path in the decision tree that leads to the highest total value in the terminal node). Bellman's principle of optimality says that each partial path of an optimal path is again optimal concerning the starting node. Thus, it is possible to reduce the resolution of a multi-level decision problem to the solution of a single-step decision problem. Following this principle, one "moves backwards" through the decision tree starting at the terminal node on the right side and ending at the root node on the left side of the tree. The entire planning problem is divided into single-step decision problems and "rolled up" from the back [cf. e.g. Laux, 2005].

A general advantage of decision trees is the straightforward possibility to conjointly consider sequential aspects and uncertainties in decision problems through the chance nodes. For instance, Göbelt [2001] makes use of this property, using decision trees to consider uncertainties in continuous investment planning problems in the energy supply sector.

However, a problematic aspect for the application of decision trees in the context of the case study is the (a priori) determination of the different time steps, i.e. decision phases, and their respective lengths. An additional challenge is constituted by the high uncertainty of the dynamically evolving external environment in reality and the corresponding interdependencies within industrial systems, the economy and the society as a whole which needs to be taken into account for a reliable consequence assessment. Furthermore, decision trees rapidly become very large [French and Ríos-Insua, 2000]. The suitability of such a concept for industrial risk management and the understandability for decision makers in the event of a real emergency thus needs to be further investigated. It is often noted that decision makers would never use decision analysis methods themselves anyway, but even if they had advisers (decision analysis experts), it would be very complicated to elicit the necessary information from the decision makers. More information on these topics can for instance be found in Bellman [1957]; DeGroot [1970]; Berger [1985]; Oliver and Smith [1990]; French and Ríos-Insua [2000].

5.3.2   Indirect Consequence Assessment and Cascading Effects

Modern industrial production, providing goods and services for society, implicates global, hierarchically structured supply chain networks. The analysis of the vulnerability of such complex networks when they are affected by internally or externally induced extreme events constitutes a challenging task. A general estimation of the structural and the functional vulnerability of different industry branches including their critical infrastructures as well as adequate models to simulate indirect losses as a function of the economic vulnerability of supply chain networks do not yet exist.

As pointed out in Section 4.2.3, the model for economic consequence assessment in RODOS is very elementary. It gives a course overview of the incurring direct costs by calculating unit costs of decontamination techniques in inhabited areas as well as agricultural countermeasures while indirect costs are not considered at all. Consequently, the suitability of the cost model within RODOS for a profound economic impact assessment of an emergency is limited. In order to enhance the assessment of economic consequences within RODOS, quantitative methods for the modelling of the direct as well as the indirect losses are needed. For instance, a promising approach is proposed by van der Veen and Logtmeijer [2005] who discuss the transfer of standard approaches in economics, such as input-output analysis, to the area of analysing the effects of an emergency within industrial production networks and the economy as a whole.

However, due to a lack of risk awareness, the industry is not well prepared to cope with unexpected emergencies. The high complexity of investigating the vulnerability of industrial supply chain networks originates inter alia from the global interlacement, the hierarchical structure and the dynamic evolution of the external environment. Classical approaches of supply chain management are focused on the coordination of demand and supply, but research of unexpected deviations from normal enterprise resource planning has not yet been performed.

In order to be prepared for a disaster, the knowledge of the possibly affected industrial assets and functions is important. For instance, besides the radiological consequences, a nuclear emergency can cause disruptions of electricity supply. Even more severely, from the perspective of the security of supply, a strong storm could cut down the electricity supply in a whole region in Germany (as it happened in Westphalia in 2005). As a consequence, both economy (for example industry branches heavily depending on electricity like telecommunication or aluminium production companies and their subsequent business partners) and society (e.g. people dependent on the functioning of normal processes of supply like old or ill people) could be affected. Furthermore, the cold chain in the food industry could be disrupted resulting in putrefying foodstuffs, which then would need to be disposed and/or processed. If the possible damage within the whole supply chain network could be estimated, then acceptable expenses for risk mitigation could be judged at the different levels of companies and economy/society. Likewise, insurances could estimate the possible damage in a more appropriate way [cf. e.g. Merz et al., 2007; Geldermann et al., 2008].

Chapter 6

Summary

The complexity of today's industrial production networks constitutes a new challenge for industrial risk and safety management. A single company, complete industrial production systems as well as the society as a whole are exposed to various different types of risk every day. In order to handle potential risks in industry and their respective impact on mankind and the environment, an integrated approach to risk management and industrial environmental policy is needed, since complex decision situations need to be resolved in a wide variety of circumstances.

Understanding the risks emanating from technical failures in industrial operating procedures and the potentially arising emergency situations is very important for a sustainable development. Special attention must be paid when the individual production processes are coupled and when their respective time and length scales within a production network are strongly disparate. The modelling and handling of risks arising from such processes necessitates integrated, interdisciplinary and multiscale approaches.

The complex decision situations which need to be resolved in the context of industrial risk management require the consideration of various conflicting criteria. In particular, aspects of health and safety, the technical feasibility and the environmental impact need to be considered besides the purely economic factors. An explicit examination of the trade-offs between these conflicting objectives plays an important role in providing a sound understanding of a decision situation. Furthermore, different scientific expert groups are usually involved with heterogeneous technical background knowledge in different disciplines. Know-how from economic, ecological, engineering and natural sciences must be brought together, taking account of political as well as socio-psychological factors.

Providing the basis for the evaluation of conflicting criteria and for bringing together existing knowledge from different disciplines, Multi-Criteria Decision Analysis (MCDA) is helpful to resolve the complexity of the occurring decision situations. Furthermore, seeking to facilitate the communication of decisions and contributing to form an audit trail, MCDA provides valuable support in explaining how decisions are taken, which is important in the light of the rising demand from the mass media and the public for information and justification from authorities.

Within the field of MCDA, the approaches Multi-Attribute Value Theory (MAVT) and Multi-Attribute Utility Theory (MAUT) have been described in detail because of their understandable nature and their suitability to support decision making in relation to industrial risk management. Contributing to transparency and traceability of decision making, MAVT provides a basis for participatory processes and group decisions in the context of the case study.

In order to address the various types of uncertainty, which may arise in a decision making process in industrial risk management, a framework for uncertainty handling has been proposed. On the basis of a structured uncertainty classification, methods based on Monte Carlo simulation can be used for a consistent modelling, propagation and visualisation of the different types of uncertainty. Special focus has been put on approaches that allow to explicitly illustrate the spread, i.e. the ranges in which the Multi-Attribute Decision Making (MADM) results can vary in consequence of the uncertainties.

The added value of the developed methods particularly lies in the proposed framework for multi-dimensional sensitivity analysis which allows to explore the robustness of the MADM results with respect to simultaneous variations of the subjective preference parameters. Additionally, they contribute to facilitate the preference elicitation and consensus building in decision making groups. The elaborated approaches provide valuable insights into the robustness of decisions and also allow to investigate trade-offs between the different conflicting criteria. Thus, these different analyses lead to a deeper understanding of decision problems. Especially, a comprehensive approach for value function sensitivity analysis (i.e. the analysis of the intra-criteria preferential uncertainties), including an investigation of the impact of varying the boundaries of the value functions' domains, has not previously been mentioned in literature. Furthermore, the introduced approaches to perform backwards calculations and the corresponding graphical visualisations are particularly valuable allowing to consistently and transparently link the uncertainties in the results to the uncertainties in the MADM input data and parameters. Finally, the integration of the proposed multi-dimensional sensitivity analyses into the framework of expected utility theory allows, for the first time, to investigate the sensitivity of MAUT results with respect to simultaneous variations of different decision parameters.

The developed methods have been implemented in a software prototype in MATLAB in order to demonstrate their capabilities in the context of a case study from industrial risk management. Within the large field of industrial risk management, nuclear emergency and remediation management is an important and challenging area because, firstly, the resulting consequences of a potential emergency are severe and far-reaching and, secondly, electricity supply is a very relevant part of critical infrastructure. Since a large part of electricity is generated by nuclear energy and an area-wide, secure electricity supply is essential for the functioning of modern industrial production networks as well as the society in general, the creation of awareness of the possibility of technical failure and an improved preparedness to deal with the risks and to cope with emergencies are indispensable.

Multi-attribute decision analysis constitutes an important contribution to transparently resolving complex decision situations in the context of the case study. The modelling of the different types of uncertainty occurring in such decision situations has been dealt with in detail. The developed Monte Carlo framework allows a consistent modelling of the uncertainties of the empirical input data and their propagation through the model chain of the Real-time Online Decision Support System for Nuclear Emergency Management (RODOS). Additionally, the different types of uncertainty can be simultaneously considered and visualised. In particular, the proposed sensitivity analyses provide valuable support in analysing the robustness of decisions in emergency management and also allow to explore trade-offs between conflicting objectives such as, for instance, radiological effectiveness and resources.

Finally, potential for future research has been pointed out. Especially, a methodological extension of the decision making framework in order to reflect the sequential character of decision problems in practice as well as an improvement of the models for economic consequence assessment have been emphasised.

From applying the developed methods to the case study, it can be concluded that the total set of decision alternatives could be significantly reduced by analysing the impact of the data uncertainties. Subsequently, the multi-dimensional sensitivity analyses allow to explore which parameter combinations result in which of the remaining alternatives as the most preferred. The knowledge acquired by conducting such uncertainty analyses within the scope of the case study can be transferred to strategic countermeasure planning problems, and can consequently contribute to an improved risk awareness and emergency preparedness.

In this thesis, a framework has been developed for an integrated handling of risks emanating from emergency situations arising from technical failures in industrial production. Providing an integrated picture of decision situations by allowing the simultaneous consideration of technical, economic, environmental as well as socio-psychological and political aspects, the application of multi-criteria decision analysis has been demonstrated in the scope of a case study from emergency and remediation management in the nuclear power generation sector. Additionally, being suitable to integrate knowledge and experiences from various scientific approaches, MCDA leads to an enriched insight into the modelling of real world decision problems. A comprehensive uncertainty analysis, allowing to simultaneously consider and visualise the various types of uncertainty that can arise in any decision process, has not been mentioned in literature so far. Making use of the new multi-dimensional sensitivity analysis techniques and of the combination of Monte Carlo simulation and principal component analysis to support the visualisation, provides a deeper understanding of the effects of the data and parameter uncertainties on the overall results in the process of evaluating decision alternatives.

Bibliography

A. Arbel. Approximate articulation of preference and priority derivation. *European Journal of Operational Research*, 43:317–326, 1989.

V. Arnold, N. Clark, P. A. Collier, S. A. Leech, and S. G. Sutton. The Differential Use and Effect of Knowledge-Based System Explanations in Novice and Expert Judgement Decisions. *MIS Quarterly*, 30(1):79–97, 2006.

G. Bamberg and A. G. Coenenberg. *Betriebswirtschaftliche Entscheidungslehre*. Verlag Vahlen, München, 1994.

F. H. Barron and B. E. Barret. Decision Quality Used Ranked Attribute Weights. *Management Science*, 42:1515–1523, 1996.

F. H. Barron, D. v. Winterfeldt, and G. W. Fischer. Empirical and Theoretical Relationships between Value and Utility Functions. *Acta Psychologica*, 56:233–244, 1984.

L. Basson. *Context, Compensation and Uncertainty in Environmental Decision Making*. PhD thesis, Department of Chemical Engineering, University of Sydney, Australia, 2004.

L. Basson and J. G. Petrie. An Integrated Approach for the Consideration of Uncertainty in Decision Making Supported by Life Cycle Assessment. *Environmental Modelling & Software*, 22(2):167–176, 2007.

T. Bedford and R. M. Cooke. *Probabilistic Risk Analysis: Foundations and Methods*. Cambridge University Press, Cambridge, 2001.

T. C. Beierle and J. Cayford. *Democracy in Practice: Public Participation in Environmental Decisions*. Resources for the Future Press, Washington, DC, 2002.

R. E. Bellman. *Dynamic Programming*. Princeton University Press, Princeton, New Jersey, 1957.

R. E. Bellman and L. H. Zadeh. Decision-Making in a Fuzzy Environment. *Management Science*, 17(4):141–164, 1970.

V. Belton and T. Stewart. DEA and MCDA: Competing or Complementary Approaches. In N. Meskens and M. Roubens, editors, *Advances in Decision Analysis*, chapter 6, pages 87–104. Kluwer Academic Publishers, Boston, 1999.

V. Belton and T. Stewart. *Multiple Criteria Decision Analysis - An integrated approach*. Kluwer Academic Press, Boston, 2002.

V. Belton and S. Vickers. Use of a simple multi-attribute value function incorporating visual interactive sensitivity analysis for multiple criteria decision making. In B. e Costa, editor, *Readings in Multiple Criteria Decision Aid*, pages 319–334. Springer, Heidelberg, 1990.

J. O. Berger. *Statistical Decision Theory and Bayesian Analysis*. Springer, New York, 1985.

T. Bernold, editor. *Industrial Risk Management: A Life-Cycle Engineering Approach - Proceedings of the International Conference*, Zürich, Switzerland, 1989.

D. Bernoulli. Specimen theoriae novae de mensura sortis. In *Comentarii Academiae Scientiarum Imperiales Petropolitanae*, chapter 5, pages 175–192. (Translated into English by L. Sommer. Exposition of a new theory on the measurement of risk. Econometrica 22(1):23-36, 1954.), 1738.

V. Bertsch, J. Geldermann, and O. Rentz. Multidimensional Monte Carlo Sensitivity Analysis in Multi-Criteria Decision Support. In F. Mayer and J. Stahre, editors, *Proceedings of the 9th IFAC Symposium on Automated Systems Based on Human Skill And Knowledge*, Nancy, France, 2006a.

V. Bertsch, J. Geldermann, and O. Rentz. Preference Sensitivity Analyses for Multi-Attribute Decision Support. In K.-H. Waldmann and U. M. Stocker, editors, *Operations Research Proceedings 2006*, pages 411–416. Springer, 2007a.

V. Bertsch, J. Geldermann, O. Rentz, and W. Raskob. Multi-Criteria Decision Support and Stakeholder Involvement in Emergency Management. *International Journal of Emergency Management*, 3(2/3):114–130, 2006b.

V. Bertsch, F. Gering, J. Geldermann, and O. Rentz. Modelling, Propagation and Visualisation of Uncertainties in the Real-time On-line Decision Support System RODOS.

In *International Conference on Monitoring, Assessments and Uncertainties for Nuclear and Radiological Emergency Response*, Rio de Janeiro, Brazil, 2005.

V. Bertsch, O. Rentz, and J. Geldermann. Preference Elicitation and Sensitivity Analysis in Multi-Criteria Group Decision Support for Nuclear Remediation Management. In B. van de Walle, P. Burghardt, and K. Nieuwenhuis, editors, *Proceedings of ISCRAM 2007 – 4th International Conference on Information Systems for Crisis Response and Management*, pages 395–404, Delft, The Netherlands, 2007b. VUBPRESS, Brussels.

V. Bertsch, M. Treitz, J. Geldermann, and O. Rentz. Sensitivity Analyses in Multi-Attribute Decision Support for Off-Site Nuclear Emergency and Recovery Management. *International Journal of Energy Sector Management*, 1(4):342–365, 2007c.

A. Beutelspacher. *Lineare Algebra*. Vieweg, Wiesbaden, 1995.

R. Blong. Volcanic hazards risk assessment. In R. Scarpa and R. I. Tilling, editors, *Monitoring and Mitigation of Volcano Hazards*, pages 675–698. Springer, 1996.

H. Büning. *Robuste und adaptive Tests*. Walter de Gruyter, Berlin, 1991.

C. G. E. Boender, J. G. de Graan, and F. A. Lootsma. Multi-criteria decision analysis with fuzzy pairwise comparisons. *Fuzzy Sets and Systems*, 29:133–143, 1989.

E. J. Bonano. Decision Making under Uncertainty and Risk Assessment. In R. L. Deshotels and R. D. Zimmerman, editors, *Cost-Effective Risk Assessment for Process Design*. McGraw-Hill, New York, 1995.

D. Borst, D. Jung, S. M. Murshed, and U. Werner. Development of a methodology to assess man-made risks in Germany. *Natural Hazards and Earth System Sciences*, 6: 779–802, 2006.

U. Bose, A. M. Davey, and D. L. Olson. Multi-attribute utility methods in group decision making: past applications and potential for inclusion in GDSS. *OMEGA - The International Journal of Management Science*, 25(6):691–706, 1997.

J.-P. Brans and B. Mareschal. The PROMCALC and GAIA decision support system for Multi-criteria decision aid. *Decision Support System*, 12:297–310, 1994.

J.-P. Brans and B. Mareschal. The PROMETHEE VI procedure: How to differentiate hard from soft multicriteria problems. *Journal of Decision Systems*, 4:213–223, 1995.

J.-P. Brans and B. Mareschal. PROMETHEE Methods. In J. Figueira, S. Greco, and M. Ehrgott, editors, *Multiple Criteria Decision Analysis - State of the Art Surveys*, pages 163–195. Springer, New York, 2005.

J.-P. Brans, B. Mareschal, and P. Vincke. PROMETHEE: a new family of outranking methods in multicriteria analysis. In *Operational Research, IFORS 84*, pages 477–490, Amsterdam, 1984. North-Holland.

J.-P. Brans and P. Vincke. A Preference Ranking Organisation Method: The PROMETHEE Method for Multi-Criteria Decision Making. *Management Science*, 31: 647–656, 1985.

R. J. Brent. *Applied cost-benefit analysis*. Edward Elgar, Cheltenham, 1996.

J. Brown, K. Mortimer, K. Andersson, T. Duranova, A. Mrskova, R. Hänninen, T. Ikäheimonen, G. Kirchner, V. Bertsch, F. Gallay, N. Reales, D. Hammond, and P. Kwakman. Generic Handbook for Assisting in the Management of Contaminated Inhabited Areas in Europe Following a Radiological Emergency. Report within the EURANOS Project (Integrated Project FI6R-CT-2004-508843, see: http://www.euranos.fzk.de), European Commission (EC), 2007.

J. J. Buckley. Fuzzy hierarchical analysis. *Fuzzy Sets and Systems*, 17:233–247, 1985.

J. Butler, J. Jia, and J. Dyer. Simulation techniques for the sensitivity analysis of multi-criteria decision models. *European Journal of Operational Research*, 103:531–546, 1997.

G. Caminada, S. French, K. Politis, and J. Q. Smith. Uncertainty in RODOS. RODOS Report RODOS(B)-RP(94)-05, 2000.

C. Carlsson and R. Fullér. Fuzzy multiple criteria decision making: recent developments. *Fuzzy Sets and Systems*, 78:139–153, 1996.

E. Carter. *Nuclear Emergency Management Procedures Across Europe*. PhD thesis, The University of Manchester, 2005.

J.-C. Charpentier. Four main objectives for the future of chemical and process engineering mainly concerned by the science and technologies of new materials production. *Chemical Engineering Journal*, 107:3–17, 2005.

J. L. Chevalier and J. F. L. Téno. Life Cycle Analysis with Ill-Defined Data and Its Application to Building Products. *International Journal of Life Cycle Assessment*, 1 (2):90–96, 1996.

R. T. Clemen and T. Reilly. *Making hard decisions with DecisionTools*. Duxbury Thomson Learning, Pacific Grove, CA, 2001.

H. Cochrane. Economic loss: myth and measurement. *Disaster Prevention and Management*, 13(4):290–296, 2004.

R. N. Collender and J. A. Chalfant. An Alternative Approach to Decisions under Uncertainty Using the Empirical Moment-Generating Function. *American Journal of Agricultural Economics*, 68(3):727–731, 1986.

CoRWM. The long-term management of radioactive waste: the work of the Committee on Radioactive Waste Management (CoRWM). Report, 2006.

D. Crichton. The Risk Triangle. In J. Ingleton, editor, *Natural Disaster Management*, pages 102–103. Tudor Rose, Leicester, 1999.

B. de Baets, B. V. de Walle, and E. E. Kerre. Fuzzy preference structures and their characterization. *Journal of Fuzzy Mathematics*, 3:373–381, 1995.

M. de Nooij, C. Bijovoet, and C. Koopmans. The Demand for Supply Security. In *Research Symposium European Electricity Markets*, The Hague, 2003.

M. H. DeGroot. *Optimal Statistical Decisions*. McGraw-Hill, New York, 1970.

KonTraG, 1998. *Gesetz zur Kontrolle und Transparenz im Unternehmensbereich (KonTraG), verkündet im Bundesgesetzblatt 1998 Teil I Nr. 24, ausgegeben zu Bonn am 30. April 1998*. Deutscher Bundestag.

J. S. Dhaliwal and I. Benbasat. The use and effects of knowledge-based system explanations: Theoretical foundations and a framework for empirical evaluation. *Information Systems Research*, 7:342–362, 1996.

W. Dinkelbach. *Sensitivitätsanalysen und parametrische Programmierung*. Springer, Berlin, 1969.

J. H. Dorfman. *Bayesian Economics Through Numerical Methods: A Guide to Econometrics and Decision-Making with Prior Information*. Springer, New York, 1997.

J. S. Dyer and R. K. Sarin. Relative Risk Aversion. *Management Science*, 28(8):875–886, 1982.

H.-J. Ebeling and T. Böhmer. *Blackouts, Netzmanagement, Kraftwerksinvestitionen*. Vwew Energieverlag, Frankfurt am Main, 2005.

A. W. F. Edwards. *Likelihood.* Cambridge University Press, Cambridge, 1972.

W. Edwards. How to use Multiattribute Utility Measurement for Social Decision Making. *IEEE Transactions on Systems, Man, and Cybernetics*, SMC-7:326–340, 1977.

W. Edwards and F. H. Barron. SMARTS and SMARTER: Improved Simple Methods for Multiattribute Utility Measurement. *Organizational Behaviour and Human Decision Processes*, 60:306–325, 1994.

J. Ehrhardt, J. Präsler-Sauer, O. Schüle, G. Benz, M. Rafat, and J. Richter. Development of RODOS, a Comprehensive Decision Support System for Nuclear Emergencies in Europe - an Overview. *Radiation Protection Dosimetry*, 1993.

J. Ehrhardt and A. Weiss. *RODOS: Decision Support for Off-Site Nuclear Emergency Management in Europe. EUR 19144 EN.* Luxembourg, European Community, 2000.

J.-L. Esquivié and J.-L. Wybo. 11/9: a historical perspective. *International Journal of Emergency Management*, 1(3):290–297, 2003.

Regulation (Euratom) No 770/90. *Commission Regulation (Euratom) No 770/90 of 29 March 1990 laying down maximum permitted levels of radioactive contamination of feedingstuffs following a nuclear accident or any other case of radiological emergency.* European Atomic Energy Community (Euratom).

Regulation (Euratom) No 944/89. *Commission Regulation (Euratom) No 944/89 of 12 April 1989 laying down maximum permitted levels of radioactive contamination in minor foodstuffs following a nuclear accident or any other case of radiological emergency.* European Atomic Energy Community (Euratom).

Regulation (Euratom) No 3954/87. *Council Regulation (Euratom) No 3954/87 of 22 December 1987 laying down maximum permitted levels of radioactive contamination of foodstuffs and of feedingstuffs following a nuclear accident or any other case of radiological emergency.* European Atomic Energy Community (Euratom).

ATEX Directive 94/9/EC. *ATEX Directive 94/9/EC of the European Council of 23 March 1994 concerning equipment and protective systems intended for use in potentially explosive atmospheres.* European Commission (EC).

IPPC Directive 96/61/EC. *Council Directive 96/61/EC of 24 September 1996 concerning integrated pollution prevention and control (IPPC).* European Commission (EC).

Directive 2006/121/EC. *Directive 2006/121/EC of the European Parliament and of the Council of 18 December 2006 amending Council Directive 67/548/EEC on the approximation of laws, regulations and administrative provisions relating to the classification, packaging and labelling of dangerous substances in order to adapt it to Regulation (EC) No 1907/2006 concerning the Registration, Evaluation, Authorisation and Restriction of Chemicals (REACH) and establishing a European Chemicals Agency.* European Commission (EC).

Directive 2006/48/EC. *Directive 2006/48/EC of the European Parliament and of the Council of 14 June 2006 relating to the taking up and pursuit of the business of credit institutions (recast).* European Commission (EC).

Directive 2006/49/EC. *Directive 2006/49/EC of the European Parliament and of the Council of 14 June 2006 on the capital adequacy of investment firms and credit institutions (recast).* European Commission (EC).

COM (2005) 576 final. *Green Paper on a European Programme for Critical Infrastructure Protection (EPCIP).* European Commission (EC).

Regulation (EC) No 1907/2006. *Regulation (EC) No 1907/2006 of the European Parliament and of the Council of 18 December 2006 concerning the Registration, Evaluation, Authorisation and Restriction of Chemicals (REACH), establishing a European Chemicals Agency, amending Directive 1999/45/EC and repealing Council Regulation (EEC) No 793/93 and Commission Regulation (EC) No 1488/94 as well as Council Directive 76/769/EEC and Commission Directives 91/155/EEC, 93/67/EEC, 93/105/EC and 2000/21/EC.* European Commission (EC).

Seveso II Directive 96/82/EC. *Seveso II Directive 96/82/EC of the European Council of 9 December 1996 on the control of major accidents hazards involving dangerous substances.* European Commission (EC).

Eurostat. Handbook for EU Agricultural Price Statistics. Luxembourg, 2002.

G. Evensen. Sequential data assimilation with a nonlinear quasi-geostrophic model using Monte-Carlo methods to forecast error statistics. *Journal of Geophysical Research*, 99 (C5):10143–10162, 1994.

S. E. Fienberg. When did Baysian Inference become "Bayesian"? *Bayesian Analysis*, 1 (1):1–40, 2006.

J. Figueira, S. Greco, and M. Ehrgott. *Multiple Criteria Decision Analysis - State of the Art Surveys.* Springer, New York, 2005.

P. C. Fishburn. Retrospective on the Utility Theory of von Neumann and Morgenstern. *Journal of Risk and Uncertainty*, 2:127–158, 1989.

G. Fishman. *Monte Carlo - Concepts, Algorithms, and Application*. Springer Series in Operation Research. Springer, New York, Berlin, Heidelberg, 1996.

C. Flaherty. 3D tactics: an advanced warfare concept in critical infrastructure protection. *International Journal of Emergency Management*, 4(1):33–44, 2007.

A. Fleury. *Eine Nachhaltigkeitsstrategie für den Energieversorgungssektor - dargestellt am Beispiel der Stromversorgung in Frankreich*. Universität Karlsruhe (TH), Karlsruhe, 2005.

S. French. *Decision Theory - an introduction to the mathematics of rationality*. Ellis Horwood Ltd., 1986.

S. French. Uncertainty and imprecision: Modelling and Analysis. *Journal of the Operational Research Society*, 46:70–79, 1995.

S. French. Multi-attribute decision support in the event of a nuclear accident. *Journal of Multi Criteria Decision Analysis*, 5:39–57, 1996.

S. French. Decision Support, Data Assimilation and Uncertainty Handling within RODOS. In J. Ehrhardt and A. Weiss, editors, *RODOS: Decision Support System for Off-Site Nuclear Emergency Management in Europe*, chapter 3.6. EUR 19144 EN, Luxemburg, European Commission, Office for Official Publications of the European Communities, 2000.

S. French. Modelling, making inferences and making decisions: the roles of sensitivity analysis. *TOP*, 11(2):229–251, 2003.

S. French, J. Bartzis, J. Ehrhardt, J. Lochard, M. Morrey, N. Papamichail, K. Sinkko, and A. Sohier. RODOS: Decision support for nuclear emergencies. In S. H. Zanakis, G. Doukidis, and G. Zopounidis, editors, *Recent Developments and Applications in Decision Making*, pages 379–394. Kluwer Academic Publishers, Dordrecht, 2000.

S. French, T. Bedford, and E. Atherton. Supporting ALARP decision-making by Cost Benefit Analysis and Multi-Attribute Utility Theory. *Journal of Risk Research*, 8(3): 207–223, 2005.

S. French and J. Geldermann. The varied contexts of environmental decision problems and their implications for decision support. *Environmental Policy and Science*, 8(4): 378–391, 2005.

S. French, J. Maule, and K. N. Papamichail. *Decision Behaviour, Analysis and Support: Decision making and how analysis and information systems may support this.* Manuscript to be published by Cambridge University Press, 2007.

S. French and C. Niculae. Believe in the Model: Mishandle the Emergency. *Journal of Homeland Security and Emergency Management,* 2(1):1–16, 2005.

S. French and D. Ríos-Insua. *Statistical Decision Theory.* Edward Arnold, London, 2000.

S. French and J. Q. Smith. *The Practice of Bayesian Analysis.* Arnold, London, 1997.

H. C. Frey and G. Nießen. *Monte-Carlo-Simulation - Quantitative Risikoanalyse für die Versicherungsindustrie.* Murmann, Hamburg, 2001.

M. Göbelt. *Entwicklung eines Modells für die Investitions- und Produktionsprogrammplanung von Energieversorgungsunternehmen im liberalisierten Markt.* PhD thesis, University of Karlsruhe (TH), 2001.

A. Gelb. *Applied Optimal Estimation.* MIT Press, Boston, 1974.

J. Geldermann. *Entwicklung eines multikriteriellen Entscheidungsunterstützungssystems zur integrierten Technikbewertung.* Fortschrittsberichte VDI, Reihe 16, Nr. 105. VDI Verlag, Düsseldorf, 1999.

J. Geldermann, V. Bertsch, and O. Rentz. Multi-Criteria Decision Support and Uncertainty Handling, Propagation and Visualisation for Emergency and Remediation Management. In H.-D. Haasis, H. Kopfer, and J. Schönberger, editors, *Operations Research Proceedings 2005,* pages 755–760. Springer, 2006.

J. Geldermann, V. Bertsch, M. Treitz, S. French, K. N. Papamichail, and R. P. Hamalainen. Multi-criteria Decision Support and Evaluation of Strategies for Nuclear Remediation Management. *OMEGA – The International Journal of Management Science (in press),* 2007.

J. Geldermann, C. Jahn, T. Spengler, and O. Rentz. Proposal for an Integrated Approach for the Assessment of Cross-Media Aspects Relevant for the Determination of "Best Available Techniques" BAT in the European Union. *International Journal of Life Cycle Assessment,* 4(2):94–106, 1999.

J. Geldermann, M. Merz, V. Bertsch, M. Hiete, O. Rentz, I. Seifert, A. H. Thieken, D. Borst, and U. Werner. The Reference Installation Approach for the Estimation of Industrial Assets at Risk. *European Journal of Industrial Engineering,* 2(1):73–93, 2008.

J. Geldermann and O. Rentz. Environmental Decisions and Electronic Democracy. *Journal of Multi-criteria Analysis*, 12(2-3):77–92, 2004.

J. Geldermann, T. Spengler, and O. Rentz. Fuzzy Outranking for Environmental Assessment, Case Study: Iron and Steel Making Industry. *Fuzzy Sets and Systems*, 115(1): 45–65, 2000.

J. Geldermann, M. Treitz, V. Bertsch, and O. Rentz. Moderated Decision Support and Countermeasure Planning for off-site Emergency Management. In R. Loulou, J.-P. Waaub, and G. Zaccour, editors, *Energy and Environment: Modeling and Analysis*, pages 63–80. Springer, 2005.

F. Gering. *Data assimilation methods for improving the prognoses of radionuclide deposition from radioecological models with measurements*. PhD thesis, Leopold-Franzens-Universität Innsbruck, 2005.

A. Geyer-Schulz. *Unscharfe Mengen im Operations-Research*. VWGÖ, Wien, 1986.

M. Ghil and P. Malanotte-Rizzoli. Data assimilation in meteorology and oceanography. *Advances in Geophysics*, 33:141–266, 1991.

I. Gilboa, A. Postlewaite, and D. Schmeidler. Rationality of Belief Or: Why Savage's Axioms are Neither Necessary nor Sufficient for Rationality, Second Version. Report, 2007.

K. Granger, T. Jones, M. Leiba, and G. Scott. Community risk in cairns: A multi-hazard risk assessment. agso (australian geological survey organisation) cities project, department of industry, science and resources, australia., 1999.

S. Gregor and I. Benbasat. Explanations from intelligent systems: Theoretical foundations and implications for practice. *MIS Quarterly*, 23:497–530, 1999.

C. M. Grinstead and J. L. Snell. *Introduction to Probability*. AMS, 1997.

D. Hahn and G. Laßmann. *Produktionswirtschaft, Controlling industrieller Produktion, Bd.1/2*, volume Band 1/2. Physika-Verlag, Heidelberg, 1999.

P. Helm. Integrated risk management for natural and technological disasters. *Tephra*, 15 (1):4–13, 1996.

J. C. Helton. Uncertainty and sensitivity analysis techniques for use in performance assessment for radioactive waste disposal. *Reliability Engineering & System Safety*, 42 (2-3):327–367, 1993.

J. C. Helton. Probability, conditional probability and complementary cumulative distribution functions in performance assessment for radioactive waste disposal. *Reliability Engineering and System Safety*, 54:145–163, 1996.

J. C. Helton and F. J. Davis. Latin Hypercube Sampling and the Propagation of Uncertainty in Analyses of Complex Systems. Report, 2002.

N. Henze. *Stochastik für Einsteiger*. Vieweg, Wiesbaden, 2006.

R. P. Hämäläinen, M. Lindstedt, and K. Sinkko. Multi-Attribute Risk Analysis in Nuclear Emergency Management. *Risk Analysis*, 20(4):455–468, 2000.

R. P. Hämäläinen and J. Mustajoki. Web-HIPRE – Java Applet for Value Tree and AHP Analysis. *Computer software, Systems Analysis Laboratory, Helsinki University of Technology*, 1998.

R. P. Hämäläinen, K. Sinkko, M. Lindstedt, M. Ammann, and A. Salo. RODOS and decision conferencing on early phase protective actions in Finland. Report, 1998.

J. Hodgkin, V. Belton, and A. Koulouri. Supporting the intelligent MCDA user: A case study in multi-person multi-criteria decision support. *European Journal of Operational Research*, 160(1):172–189, 2005.

W. Härdle and L. Simar. *Applied Multivariate Statistical Analysis*. Springer-Verlag, Berlin; Heidelberg, 2003.

C. L. Hwang and K. Yoon. *Multiple Attribute Decision Making: Methods and Applications; A State-of-the-Art Survey*. Springer, Heidelberg, 1981.

K. Hyde, H. R. Maier, and C. Colby. Incorporating Uncertainty in the PROMETHEE MCDA Method. *Journal of Multi-Criteria Decision Analysis*, 12:245–259, 2003.

IAEA. The International Nuclear Event Scale (INES). Report, 1999.

ICRP. ICRP Publication 55: Optimization and Decision-Making in Radiological Protection. *Annals of the ICRP*, 20(1), 1989.

R. L. Iman, J. M. Davenport, and D. K. Zeigler. Latin Hypercube Sampling (Program User's Guide). Report, 1980.

A. Jiménez, A. Mateos, and S. Ríos-Insua. Monte Carlo Simulation Techniques in a Decision Support System for Group Decision Making. *Group Decision and Negotiation*, 14(2):109–130, 2005.

D. Kahneman, P. Slovic, and A. Tversky. *Judgment under uncertainty: Heuristics and biases.* Cambridge University Press, Cambridge, 1982.

R. E. Kalman. A new approach to linear filtering and prediction problems. *Journal of Basic Engineering (ASME)*, 82(D):35–45, 1960.

J. Kaulard, E. Mergel, and W. Pfeffer. Ergebnisprotokoll zum Workshop "Interventions-maßnahmen bei Nahrungsmitteln nach kerntechnischen Unfällen – Entsorgung von Abfällen nach kerntechnischen Unfällen". Protocol of a Workshop organised by the "Gesellschaft für Anlagen- und Reaktorsicherheit (GRS)" on 01 March 2006 in Cologne, Germany, 2006.

R. L. Keeney. An Analysis of the Portfolio of Sites to Characterize for Selecting a Nuclear Repository. *Risk Analysis*, 7(2):195–218, 1987.

R. L. Keeney. *Value-Focused Thinking: A Path to Creative Decision Making.* Harvard University Press, 1992.

R. L. Keeney and H. Raiffa. *Decisions with multiple objectives: Preferences and value tradeoffs.* John Wiley, New York, 1976.

R. L. Keeney and D. von Winterfeldt. Managing Nuclear Waste from Power Plants. *Risk Analysis*, 14(1):107–130, 1994.

G. A. Kiker, T. S. Bridges, A. Varghese, T. P. Seager, and I. Linkov. Application of Multi-criteria Decision Analysis in Environmental Decision Making. *Integrated Environmental Assessment and Management*, 1(2):95–108, 2005.

J. P. Kincaid, J. Donovan, and B. Pettitt. Simulation techniques for training emergency response. *International Journal of Emergency Management*, 1(3):238–246, 2003.

C. W. Kirkwood. An overview of methods for applied decision analysis. *Interfaces*, 22(6): 28–39, 1992.

C. W. Kirkwood. *Strategic Decision Making – Multiobjective Decision Analysis with Spreadsheets.* Duxbury Press, Belmont, 1997.

D. A. Klein. *Decision-Analytic Intelligent Systems: Automated Explanation and Knowl-edge Acquisition.* Lawrence Erlbaum Associates, New Jersey, 1994.

T. C. Koopmans. Analysis of Production as an Efficient Combination of Activities. In T. C. Koopmans, editor, *Activity Analysis of Production and Allocation*, pages 33–97. John Wiley and Sons, New York, 1951.

R. Krzysztofowicz. Strength of preference and risk attitude in utility measurement. *Organizational Behavior and Human Performance*, 31(1):88–113, 1983.

T. Kötter. Prevention of Environmental Disasters by Spatial Planning and Land Management. In *2nd Regional Conference of the International Federation of Surveyors (FIG)*, 2003.

R. Lahdelma and P. Salminen. SMAA-2: Stochastik Multicriteria Acceptability Analysis for Group Decision Making. *Operations Research*, 49(3):444–454, 2001.

H. Laux. *Entscheidungstheorie*. Springer, Heidelberg, 2005.

R. Layard. *Cost Benefit Analysis*. Penguin Books, Harmondsworth, 1972.

E. Lindauer. Welche Bedeutung haben Betriebsstörungen und Störfälle in Kernkraftwerken? www.energie-fakten.de, 2005.

I. Linkov, A. Varghese, and S. Jamil. Multi-criteria decision analysis: A framework for structuring remedial decisions at contaminated sites. In I. Linkov and A. B. Ramadan, editors, *Comparative Risk Assessment and Environmental Decision Making*, pages 15–54. Kluwer Academic Publishers, 2004.

J. Y. Mao and I. Benbasat. The use of explanations in knowledge-based systems: Cognitive perspectives and a process-tracing analysis. *Journal of Management Information Systems*, 17:153–179, 2000.

B. Mareschal. Weight stability intervals in multicriteria decision aid. *European Journal of Operational Research*, 33:54–64, 1998.

A. Mateos, A. Jiménez, and S. Ríos-Insua. Monte Carlo simulation techniques for group decision making with incomplete information. *European Journal of Operational Research*, 174:1842–1864, 2006.

G. Mavrotas and P. Trifillis. Multicriteria decision analysis with minimum information: combining DEA with MAVT. *Computers and Operations Research*, 33:2083–2098, 2006.

T. L. McDaniels, R. S. Gregory, and D. Fields. Democratizing Risk Management: Successful Public Involvement in Local Water Management Decisions. *Risk Analysis*, 19 (3):497–510, 1999.

M. W. Merkhofer and R. L. Keeney. A Multiattribute Utility Analysis of Alternative Sites for the Disposal of Nuclear Waste. *Risk Analysis*, 7(2):173–194, 1987.

M. Merz, V. Bertsch, O. Rentz, and J. Geldermann. Assessment of Industrial Asset Values at Risk. In B. van de Walle, P. Burghardt, and C. Nieuwenhuis, editors, *Proceedings of ISCRAM 2007 – 4th International Conference on Information Systems for Crisis Response and Management*, pages 235–244, Delft, The Netherlands, 2007. VUBPRESS, Brussels.

T. Mikkelsen, S. Thykier-Nielsen, P. Astrup, J. M. Santabárbara, J. H. Sørensen, A. Rasmussen, S. Deme, and R. Martens. An operational real-time model chain for now- and forecasting of radioactive atmospheric releases on the local scale. In S.-E. Gryning and N. Chaumerliac, editors, *22. NATO/CCMS international technical meeting, June 1997*, Clermont-Ferrand, France, 1998. Plenum Press, New York.

M. G. Morgan and M. Henrion. *Uncertainty: A Guide to Dealing with Uncertainty in Quantitative Risk and Policy Analysis*. Cambridge University Press, New York, 1990.

G. Munda. NAIADE Manual & Tutorial. Joint Research Center of the European Commission, Ispra, Italy, 1996.

J. Mustajoki and R. P. Hämäläinen. Web-HIPRE: Global Decision Support by Value Tree and AHP Analysis. *INFOR*, 38(3):208–220, 2000.

J. Mustajoki, R. P. Hämäläinen, and M. R. K. Lindstedt. Using intervals for Global Sensitivity and Worst Case Analyses in Multiattribute Value Trees. *European Journal of Operational Research*, 174:278–292, 2006.

J. Mustajoki, R. P. Hämäläinen, and A. Salo. Decision Support by Interval SMART/SWING – Incorporating Imprecision in the SMART and SWING Methods. *Decision Sciences*, 36(2):317–339, 2005.

A. Nisbet, H. Rice, A. Jones, T. Jullien, V. Pupin, H. Ollagnon, F. Hardeman, B. Carlé, C. Turcanu, C. Papachristodoulou, K. Ioannides, R. Hänninen, A. Rantavaara, D. Solatie, E. Kostiainen, and D. Oughton. Generic handbook for assisting in the management of contaminated food productions systems in Europe following a radiological emergency. Report within the EURANOS Project (Integrated Project FI6R-CT-2004-508843, see: http://www.euranos.fzk.de), European Commission (EC), 2006.

Nuclear Power World Report 2006. *atw – International Journal for Nuclear Power*, 52 (4):273–277, 2007.

C. Oder. *Entwicklung eines auf der Theorie der unscharfen Mengen basierenden Energie-Emissions-Modells*. PhD thesis, University of Karlsruhe (TH), 1994.

A. O'Hagan and J. E. Oakley. Probability is perfect, but we can't elicit it perfectly. *Reliability Engineering & System Safety*, 85(1-3):239–248, 2004.

R. M. Oliver and J. Q. Smith. *Influence Diagrams, Belief Nets and Decision Analysis*. John Wiley, New York, 1990.

K. N. Papamichail. *Intelligent decision support fur nuclear emergencies*. PhD thesis, The University of Manchester, 2000.

K. N. Papamichail and S. French. Decision support in nuclear emergencies. *Journal of Hazardous Materials*, 71:321–342, 2000.

K. N. Papamichail and S. French. Explaining and Justifying the Advice of a Decision Support System: a Natural Language Generation Approach. *Expert Systems with Applications*, 24(1):35–48, 2003.

M. E. Paté-Cornell. Uncertainties in risk analysis: Six levels of treatment. *Reliability Engineering and System Safety*, 54:95–111, 1996.

D. W. Pearce and C. A. Nash. *The Social Appraisal of Projects: A text in Cost-Benefit Analysis*. Macmillan, London, 1981.

L. D. Phillips. A Theory of Requisite Decision Models. *Acta Psychologica*, 56:29–48, 1984.

J. W. Pratt, H. Raiffa, and R. Schlaifer. The Foundations of Decision Under Uncertainty: An Elementary Exposition. *Journal of the American Statistical Association*, 59(306): 353–375, 1964.

L. G. Proll, D. R. Insua, and A. Salhi. Mathematical programming and the sensitivity of multi-criteria decisions. *Annals of Operations Research*, 43:109–122, 1993.

M. Pöyhönen, H. Vrolijk, and R. P. Hämäläinen. Behavioral and procedural consequences of structural variation in value trees. *European Journal of Operational Research*, 134: 216–227, 2001.

R. B. D'Agostino and M. A. Stephens. *Goodness-of-fit Techniques*. Marcel Dekker, New York, 1986.

W. Raskob, V. Bertsch, J. Geldermann, S. Baig, and F. Gering. Demands to and experience with the Decision Support System RODOS for off-site emergency management in the decision making process in Germany. In B. van de Walle and B. Carlé, editors, *Proceedings of the Second International Conference on Information Systems for Crisis Response and Management*, pages 269–278, Brussels, Belgium, 2005a.

W. Raskob, J. Ehrhardt, and M. Rafat. Status of the RODOS system for off-site emergency management after nuclear and radiological accidents. In *International Conference on Monitoring, Assessments and Uncertainties for Nuclear and Radiological Emergency Response*, Rio de Janeiro, Brazil, 2005b.

E. Reiter and R. Dale. *Building Applied Natural Language Generation Systems*. Cambridge University Press, Cambridge, UK, 2000.

O. Renn. The Role of Risk Communication and Public Dialogue for Improving Risk Management. In S. Gerrard, R. K. Turner, and I. J. Bateman, editors, *Environmental Risk Planning*, pages 312–337. Edward Elgar Publishing House, Cheltenham, 2001.

O. Renn. The Challenge of Integrating Deliberation and Expertise: Participation and Discourse in Risk Management. In T. L. McDaniels and M. J. Small, editors, *Risk Analysis and Society: An Interdisciplinary Characterization of the Field*, pages 289–366. Cambridge University Press, Cambridge, 2004.

O. Rentz. Operations research and environmental policy. In H.-D. Haasis and T. Spengler, editors, *Produktion und Umwelt*, pages 1–26. Springer, Heidelberg, 2004.

R. A. Ribeiro. Fuzzy multiple attribute decision making: a review and new preference elicitation techniques. *Fuzzy Sets and Systems*, 78:155–181, 1996.

H. W. Richardson, P. Gordon, and J. E. M. II. *The Economic Impacts of Terrorist Attacks*. Edward Elgar Publishing, 2006.

C. Rojas-Palma, H. Madsen, F. Gering, R. Puch, and et al. Data assimilation in the decision support system RODOS. *Radiation Protection Dosimetry*, 104(1):31–40, 2003.

H. Rommelfanger. *Fuzzy Decision Support-Systeme - Entscheiden bei Unschärfe*. Springer, Berlin, 1994.

D. Ríos-Insua and S. French. A framework for sensitivity analysis in discrete multi-objective decision making. *European Journal of Operational Research*, 54:176–190, 1991.

D. Ríos-Insua and F. Ruggeri. *Robust Bayesian Analysis*. Lecture Notes in Statistics. Springer, New York, 2000.

S. Ríos-Insua, A. Jiménez, and A. Mateos. Sensitivity Analysis in a Generic Multi-Attribute Decision Support System. In K. J. Engemann and G. E. Lasker, editors, *Advances in Decision Technology and Intelligent Information Systems, Vol. IV*, pages 31–35. The International Institute for Advanced Studies in Systems Research and Cybernetics, Canada, 2003.

J. Rosenhead and J. Mingers. *Rational Analysis for a Problematic World Revisited*. John Wiley and Sons, Chichester, 2001.

G. G. Roussas. *A first course in mathematical statistics*. Addison-Wesley, Massachusetts, 1973.

B. Roy. *Multi-Criteria Modelling for Decision Aiding*. Kluwer, Dordrecht, 1996.

B. Roy and D. Bouyssou. *Aide multicritère à la décision*. Economica, Paris, 1993.

S. Thykier-Nielsen and S. Deme and E. Láng. Calculation Method for Gamma-dose Rates from Gaussian Puffs. Risø-R-775 (EN), 1995.

T. L. Saaty. *The Analytic Hierarchy Process*. McGraw Hill, New York, 1980.

T. L. Saaty and L. G. Vargas. Uncertainty and rank order in the analytic hierarchy process. *European Journal of Operational Research*, 32:107–117, 1987.

A. Salo and R. P. Hämäläinen. Preference Programming through Approximate Ratio Comparisons. *European Journal of Operational Research*, 82:458–475, 1995.

A. Salo and R. P. Hämäläinen. On the measurement of preferences in the analytical hierarchly process (with discussion). *Journal of Multi Criteria Decision Analysis*, 1997.

A. A. Salo. Interactive decision aiding for group decision support. *European Journal of Operational Research*, 84(1):134–149, 1995.

A. Saltelli, K. Chan, and E. M. Scott. *Sensitivity Analysis*. John Wiley and Sons, Chichester, 2000.

L. J. Savage. *The Foundations of Statistics*. Wiley, New York, 1954.

C. Schieber and C. Benhamou. Estimation of the unit cost of decontamination techniques. RODOS Report RODOS(WG3)-TN(99)-32, 1999a.

C. Schieber and C. Benhamou. Unit costs to be used for the evaluation of the long term agricultural countermeasures. RODOS Report RODOS(WG3)-TN(99)-30, 1999b.

H. Schollenberger. *Analyse und Verbesserung der Arbeitsabläufe in Betrieben der Reparaturlackierung*. Dissertation, University of Karlsruhe (available online at: http://www.uvka.de/univerlag/volltexte/2006/108/). Karlsruhe University Press, Karlsruhe, 2006.

J. W. Seifert. *Visualization, Presentation, Moderation*. Wiley-VCH, Weinheim, 2002.

E. Sennewald. *Modellierung von Immissionsverteilungen – Modelle zur Ozonprognose und zur flächendeckenden Abschätzung von Immissionskonzentrationen: Theoretische Grundlagen und praktische Anwendungen.* PhD thesis, University of Karlsruhe (TH), 1996.

S. S. Shapiro and M. B. Wilk. An analysis of variance test for normality (complete samples). *Biometrika*, 52(3/4):591–611, 1965.

D. Shaw, M. Westcombe, J. Hodgkin, and G. Montibeller. Problem structuring methods for large group interventions. *Journal of the Operational Research Society*, 55:453–463, 2004.

K. Sinkko. *Nuclear Emergency Response Planning based on Participatory Decision Analytic Approaches.* PhD thesis, Helsinki University of Technology, 2004.

K. Sinkko, M. Ammann, R. P. Hämäläinen, and J. Mustajoki. Facilitated workshop on clean-up actions in inhabited areas in Finland after an accidental release of radionuclides. Report, 2005.

A. Smidts. The Relationship between Risk Attitude and Strength of Preference: A Test of Intrinsic Risk Attitude. *Management Science*, 43(3):357–370, 1997.

K. Smith. *Environmental Hazards: Assessing Risk and Reducing Disaster.* Routledge, 1996.

J. T. Stewart and F. B. Losa. Towards reconciling outranking and value measurement practice. *European Journal of Operational Research*, 145:645–659, 2003.

T. J. Stewart. A Descriptive Approach to Multiple-Criteria Decision Making. *The Journal of the Operational Research Society*, 32(1):45–53, 1981.

T. Mikkelsen and S. Thykier-Nielsen and P. Astrup and J. M. Santabárbara and J. H. Sørensen and A. Rasmussen and L. Robertson and A. Ullerstig and S. Deme and R. Martens and J. G. Bartzis and J. Päsler-Sauer. MET-RODOS: A Comprehensive Atmospheric Dispersion Module. *Radiation Protection Dosimetry*, 73(1-4):45–56, 1997.

K. Taji, J. K. Levy, J. Hartmann, M. L. Bell, R. M. Anderson, B. F. Hobbs, and T. Feglar. Identifying potential repositories for radioactive waste : multiple criteria decision analysis and critical infrastructure systems. *International Journal of Critical Infrastructures*, 1(4):404–422, 2005.

S. Tilmes. *Verfahren zur Analyse von Messungen atmosphärischer Spurengase mit dem Ziel der Assimilation in Chemie-Transportmodellen.* Deutscher Wetterdienst, Offenbach am Main, 1999.

N. H. Timm. *Applied multivariate analysis.* Springer, New York, 2002.

M. Treitz. *Production Process Design Using Multi-Criteria Analysis.* Dissertation, University of Karlsruhe (available online at: http://www.uvka.de/univerlag/volltexte/2006/178/). Karlsruhe University Press, Karlsruhe, 2006.

M. Treitz, H. Schollenberger, V. Bertsch, J. Geldermann, and O. Rentz. Process Design based on Operations Research: A Metric for Resource Efficiency. In *Clean Environment for All: 2nd International Conference on Environmental Concerns: Innovative Technologies and Management Options*, pages 842–853, Xiamen, P.R.China, 2004.

TSCA 15 U.S.C. S/S 2601 et seq. 1976. *Toxic Substances Control Act (TSCA) of 1976, enacted by the Congress of the USA, US Code: Title 15, Chapter 53.*

A. Tversky and D. Kahneman. The framing of decisions and the psychology of choice. *Science*, 211:453–458, 1981.

A. Tversky and D. Kahneman. Rational Choice and the Framing of Decisions. *The Journal of Business*, 59(4):251–278, 1986.

UNISDR. Natural Disasters and Sustainable Development: Understanding the links between development, environment and natural disasters. Background Paper No. 5 for the World Summit on Sustainable Development, submitted by the United Nations International Strategy for Disaster Reduction (UNISDR), 2002.

UNSCEAR. Sources and Effects of Ionizing Radiation. Report, 2000.

R. Vahrenkamp and C. Siepermann. *Risikomanagement in Supply Chains.* Erich Schmidt Verlag, Berlin, 2007.

B. van de Walle and B. K. E. E. de Baets. Fuzzy multi-criteria analysis of cutting techniques in a nuclear reactor dismantling project. *Fuzzy Sets and Systems*, 74:115–126, 1995.

A. van der Veen. Disasters and economic damage: macro, meso and micro approaches. *Disaster Prevention and Management*, 13(4):274–279, 2004.

A. van der Veen and C. Logtmeijer. Economic Hotspots: Visualizing Vulnerability to Flooding. *Natural Hazards*, 36:65–80, 2005.

P. J. M. van Laarhoven and W. Pedrycz. A fuzzy extension of Saaty's priority theory. *Fuzzy Sets and Systems*, 11:229–241, 1983.

R. Vetschera. MCView: An integrated graphical system to support multi-attribute decisions. *Decision Support Systems*, 11:363–371, 1994a.

R. Vetschera. Visualisierungstechniken in Entscheidungsproblemen bei mehrfacher Zielsetzung. *OR Spektrum*, 16:227–241, 1994b.

J. von Neumann and O. Morgenstern. *Theory of Games and Economic Behavior*. Princeton University Press, Princeton, NJ, 1947.

D. von Winterfeldt and W. Edwards. *Decision Analysis and Behavioral Research*. Cambridge University Press, Cambridge, 1986.

W. E. Walker. Policy Analysis: A Systematic Approach to Supporting Policymaking in the Public Sector. *Journal of Multi-Criteria Decision Analysis*, 9:11–27, 2000.

M. Weber and K. Borcherding. Behavioural problems in weight judgements. *European Journal of Operational Research*, 67:1–12, 1993.

W. Wergen. Datenassimilation – ein Überblick. *promet*, 27(3/4):142–149, 2002.

U. Werner and C. Lechtenbörger. Phänomen Terrorismus. Die institutionelle Bearbeitung dieser Bedrohung in Deutschland. *Homeland Security: Das Medium für Innere Sicherheit und Bevölkerungsschutz*, 1(2):16–22, 2004.

U. Werner, C. Lechtenbörger, and D. Borst. Project Man-Made Hazards (CEDIM) – First Results. In D. Malzahn and T. Plapp, editors, *Disasters and Society – From Hazard Assessment to Risk Reduction*, pages 399–406. Logos Verlag, Berlin, 2004.

J.-L. Wybo. Editorial. *International Journal of Emergency Management*, 3(2/3):99–100, 2006.

L. A. Zadeh. Fuzzy Sets. *Information and Control*, 8:338–353, 1965.

L. A. Zadeh. Fuzzy Sets as a Basis for a Theory of Possibility. *Fuzzy Sets and Systems*, 1:3–28, 1978.

K. Zhang. *Entwicklung eines integrierten multikriteriellen Gruppenentscheidungsunterstützungssystems (MGDSS)*. Dissertation, University of Karlsruhe. Shaker Publishing, Aachen, 2004.

Appendix A

The Explanation Module

As described in Section 4.2.5, the language generation process of the explanation module involves the three stages *content determination, discourse planning* and *sentence generation* [cf. Papamichail, 2000]. This process is graphically illustrated in Figure A.1.

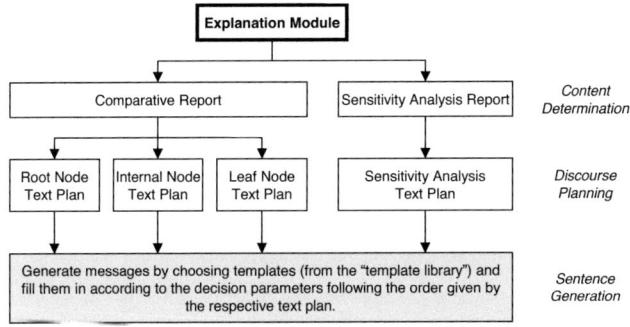

Figure A.1: The General Structure of the Explanation Module

Each of these steps is shortly described in the following (Sections A.1-A.3). Subsequently, a possible extension of the existing language generation methods is proposed in Section A.4. The aim of this extension is to explain the results of a multi-dimensional sensitivity analysis and thus to increase the usability and acceptance of the new approaches for uncertainty handling.

A.1 Content Determination

In the content determination step, the users of the explanation module can decide whether a comparative report or a sensitivity analysis report shall be generated. The aim of the comparative report is to compare two alternatives to each other by determining how much better one alternative is over another, by arguing for or against a choice, by identifying whether or not an objective differentiates between two alternatives and by detecting the most significant factors in the ranking of alternatives. A sensitivity analysis report explains the sensitivity analysis graph, i.e. it describes the effects of varying the weight of a criterion on the MADM results.

A.2 Discourse Planning

Once the users have decided whether a comparative report or a sensitivity analysis report shall be generated, the individual messages of the report need to be structured in a coherent way. If a comparative report is to be generated, the users need to choose two alternatives and one or several attribute(s) or objective(s) with respect to which the two alternatives shall be compared. The content of the messages generated by the comparative report depends on the type of the selected objective(s), i.e. their respective position in the attribute tree. Explanations referring to the root node objective (such as "total utility" in the attribute tree of the considered case study, see Figure 4.8 on page 107) are rather general, while explanations referring to internal node objectives (such as "impact" in Figure 4.8) and leaf node objectives (such as "total food above" in the case study) are more detailed and specific [cf. e.g. Papamichail, 2000; Papamichail and French, 2003].

Thus, in the discourse planning step, different text plans are associated with the different types of objectives (see Figure A.2). For the messages of the sensitivity analysis report there is a fourth text plan (see Figure A.3). The general aim of discourse planning is to organise and structure the messages in order to compose a coherent report according to the respective text plan(s).

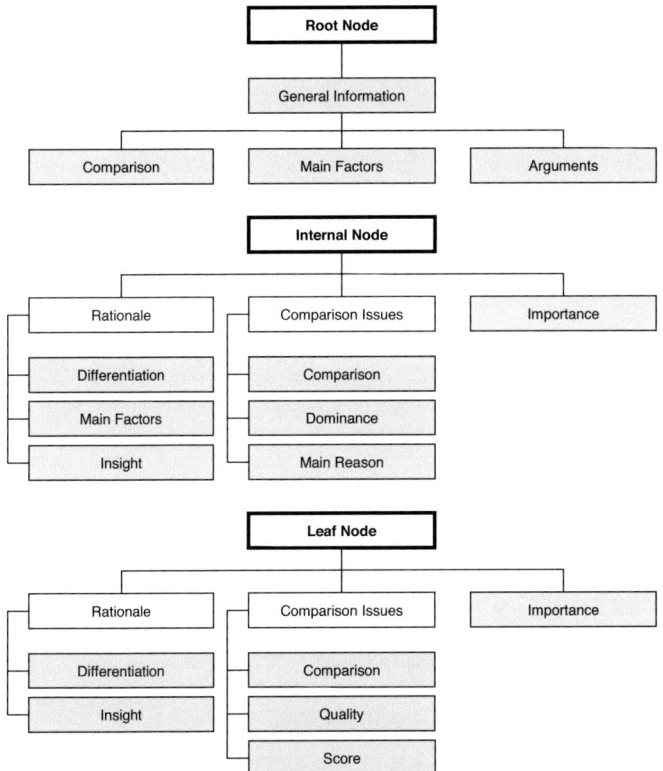

Figure A.2: Text Plans for the Comparative Report

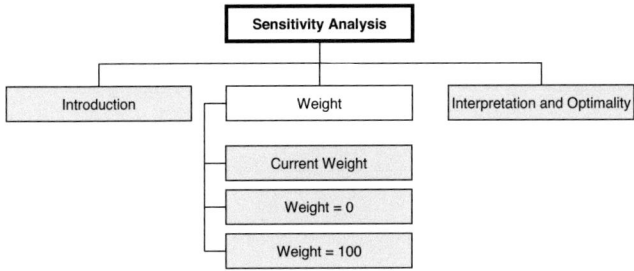

Figure A.3: Text Plan for the Sensitivity Analysis Report

A.3   Sentence Generation

In the sentence generation step, message templates are selected from the "template library", where each leaf node of a text plan is associated with an individual message. Subsequently, the templates are filled in according to the decision parameters following the order given by the respective text plan. As indicated by Figure A.2 and Figure A.3, fifteen different templates are used for the generation of explanations: ten for the comparative report and five for the sensitivity analysis report. In the order of appearance in the text plans, the messages' titles are: Comparison, Main Factors, Arguments, Differentiation, Insight, Dominance, Main Reason, Importance, Quality, Score, Introduction, Current Weight, Weight $= 0$, Weight $= 100$, Interpretation and Optimality. These message templates can be grouped into the five categories *Knowledge Representation*, *Model Parameters*, *Statistical Comparisons*, *Reasoning* and *Sensitivity Analysis* as follows:

- Knowledge Representation

    Main Factors

- Model Parameters

    Importance

    Score

- Statistical Comparisons

    Comparison

    Quality

- Reasoning

    Arguments

    Differentiation

    Insight

    Dominance

    Main Reason

- Sensitivity Analysis

    Introduction

    Current Weight

    Weight $= 0$

Weight = 100

Interpretation and Optimality

The structure of each of these templates and the generation of the corresponding messages is described in detail in Papamichail [2000]; Papamichail and French [2003]; Geldermann et al. [2007]. Exemplarily, the categories *statistical comparisons* and *sensitivity analysis* are described in the following.

A.3.1 Statistical Comparisons

Statistical comparisons focus on determining those decision parameters that are significant or important in the ranking of the alternatives. They are based on statistical interpretations of the decision model [cf. Klein, 1994]. Decision parameters that influence the final ranking are attribute weights, performance scores of alternatives and absolute differences between the alternatives' scores. For instance, the template "Quality", requiring one alternative and one objective as input, is used to generate a message showing how good a selected alternative is relative to the chosen objective [cf. Papamichail, 2000]:

<alternative> performs <semantic quantifier> on <objective> in the context of all available alternatives.

A *semantic quantifier* (SQ) is a verbal expression (such as "substantially better", "slightly worse", "significant" or "very good", "neither very good nor very poor", "very poor") that describes the quality of a parameter and can be determined in the following way. Given an objective, the mean μ and the standard deviation σ of the scores of all available alternatives relative to this objective can be calculated. Assuming that the score of an alternative (e.g. "Rmov,T=0" in the case study) is $s = 5$ on a scale from 0 to 100, the quality of the alternative can be described by mapping s (i.e. the score of the alternative) to a discrete set of semantic quantifiers as follows (where λ is a positive user-defined constant):

$$\text{if} \left\{ \begin{array}{c} s > \mu + \lambda\sigma \\ \mu - \lambda\sigma \leq s \leq \mu + \lambda\sigma \\ s < \mu - \lambda\sigma \end{array} \right\} \rightarrow \text{SQ} = \left\{ \begin{array}{c} \text{``very good''} \\ \text{``neither very good nor very poor''} \\ \text{``very poor''} \end{array} \right\} \quad (A.1)$$

In the context of the case study, a message generated by the explanation module can be:

Rmov,T=0 performs very poor on *avoided collective dose* in the context of all available alternatives.

Statistical explanations help decision makers to concentrate on those aspects that are significant in the decision process [cf. Klein, 1994]. Therefore, they contribute to considerably reduce the time needed for parameter assessment. An illustrative comparative report for the alternatives "Rmov,T=0" and "Disp" in the case study is shown in Figure A.4, allowing to gain deeper insight into the factors differentiating between the two alternatives.

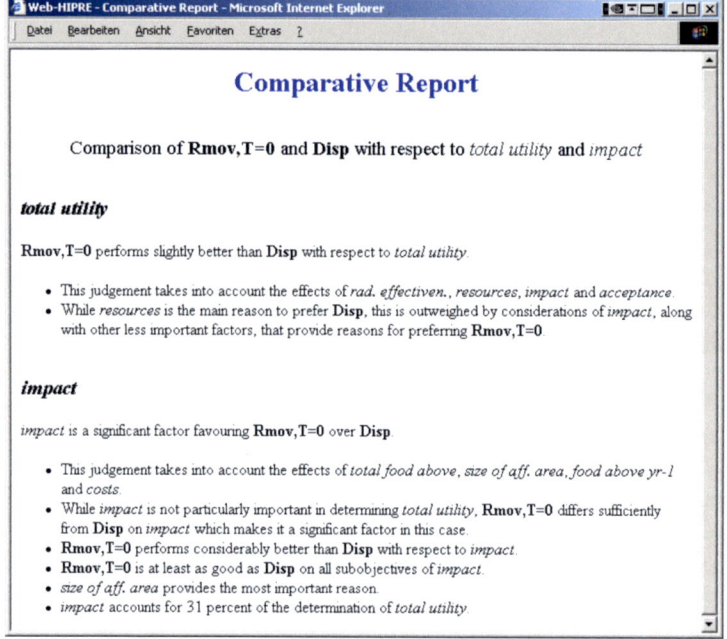

Figure A.4: An Illustrative Comparative Report

A.3.2   Sensitivity Analysis

The messages generated for the sensitivity analysis report communicate information in the form of text and tables. They are aimed at explaining the general purpose of a sensitivity analysis and why it is valuable. Furthermore, they seek to interpret the sensitivity analysis graph, i.e. the optimality of alternatives, when varying the weight of a chosen (sub-) criterion, is discussed [Papamichail, 2000].

In the following, the individual messages of a sensitivity analysis report will be shortly described. The template for the message "Introduction", mainly consisting of so-called canned text, is:

> This analysis examines how robust the choice of an alternative is to changes of the weight of <objective>.

The message "Current Weight" includes additional information about the goal of a sensitivity analysis. Subsequently, this message indicates the status quo, i.e. the current weight of the chosen objective and a table that shows the overall scores of all alternatives corresponding to this current weight. The associated template is:

> The lines in the graph of the sensitivity analysis, each associated with one alternative, show the weighted scores of the (associated) alternatives when the weight of <objective> is varied from 0 % to 100 %. The vertical line at <current weight of objective>% represents the status quo. The overall scores of the alternatives are:
> <table>

The messages "Weight = 0" and "Weight = 100" describe the situation of the overall scores of the alternatives if the weight of <objective> was zero or one hundred respectively. In other words, these two messages explain the situation at the left and the right border of the sensitivity analysis graph.

The message "Interpretation and Optimality" involves two tasks:

- Firstly, it identifies the weight ranges of <objective> for which an alternative is most preferred (relative to <objective>).

- Secondly, it indicates how much the weight of <objective> can be changed without changing the optimality of the most preferred alternative for the current weight of <objective>.

The aim of the two parts of the message "Interpretation and Optimality" is to help decision makers focus on the most critical factors in the decision-making process. For instance, if two or more decision makers disagree on the exact value of a weight of an objective, but they do agree on a weight range for which only one alternative is the most preferred, they can focus on other issues that might have more influence on the outcome of the decision analysis [cf. e.g. Papamichail, 2000; Geldermann et al., 2007]. The template associated with "Interpretation and Optimality" is:

The ranges of the weights of <objective> for which an alternative is the most preferred are:

<table>

The percentage on <objective> can be changed by as much as <calculated weight>% without changing the optimality of <alternative>.

For the context of the case study, an illustrative sensitivity analysis report for the weight of "impact" is shown in Figure A.5. The corresponding messages generated by the explanation module provide an improved understanding of robustness of the MADM results with respect to weight changes of the criterion "impact".

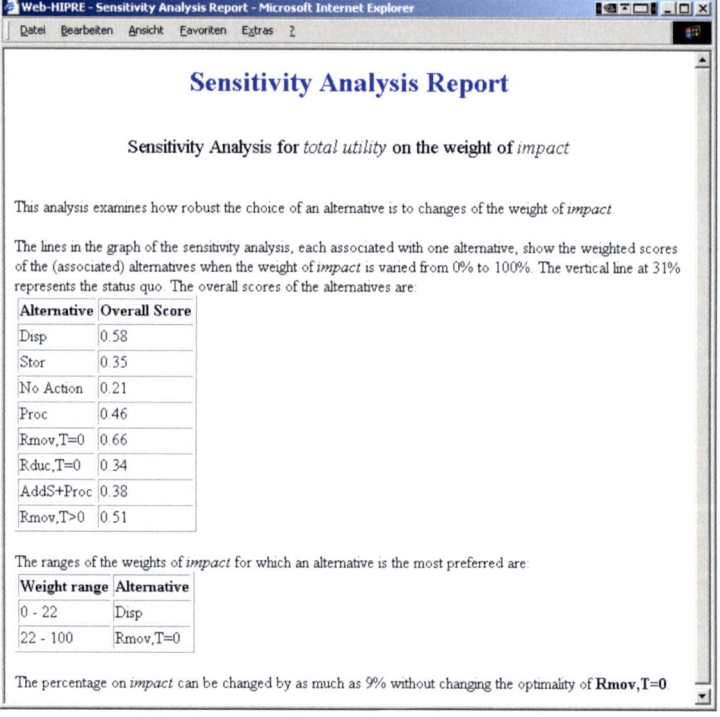

Figure A.5: Extract of an Illustrative Sensitivity Analysis Report

As already mentioned in Section 4.2.5, the explanation module has been developed for deterministic multi-attribute decision analyses. Taking account of different types of uncertainty leads to additional information in the results which, so far, is not explained by the existing explanation facilities. Thus, there is a need to add understandable explanations about the arising uncertainties. Exemplarily, an extension of the sensitivity analysis report is proposed in the following section.

A.4   A Step Towards Explaining the Results of Multi-Dimensional Sensitivity Analysis

In order to increase the usability and acceptance of the new approaches for uncertainty handling developed within this thesis, understandable messages about the occurring uncertainties and their respective impact on the results can be added to the explanation module. The generation of messages to explain the uncertainties in MADM results constitutes a challenging future research possibility which has not been mentioned in literature so far. Thus, it is important to transfer the knowledge and experience obtained during the development, implementation and use of the existing language generation methods to the field of explaining uncertainties in MADM. An extension towards explaining multi-dimensional sensitivity analyses is exemplarily proposed in the following.

The general process of generating reports, as illustrated in Figure A.1, remains unchanged when explaining the uncertainties, i.e. it involves the three stages content determination, discourse planning and sentence generation. Concerning the content determination, it is assumed in this section, that a report explaining the multi-dimensional sensitivity analysis shall be generated.

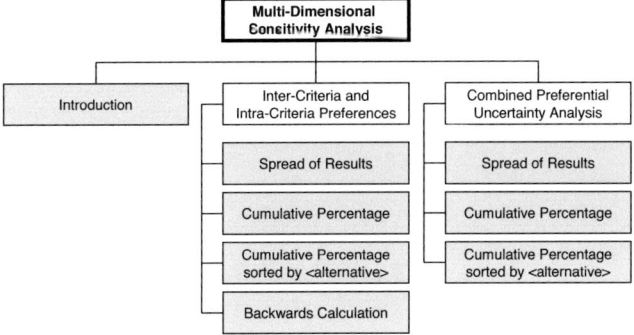

Figure A.6: Proposed Text Plan for a Multi-Dimensional Sensitivity Analysis Report

The discourse planning step differs from that of the one-dimensional sensitivity analysis since more than one diagram needs to interpreted. In order to organise and structure the generation of messages explaining figures 4.21–4.27 in a coherent way, a text plan as shown in Figure A.6 is proposed.

Each leaf node of the text plan shown in Figure A.6 can be associated with a message template. Concerning the sentence generation of a multi-dimensional sensitivity analysis report, templates need to selected from an extended "template library". As indicated in Figure A.6, five different templates are needed for the generation of the new explanations: Introduction, Spread of Results, Cumulative Percentage, Cumulative Percentage sorted by <alternative> and Backwards Calculation. For instance, the following template is proposed for the message "Introduction" (purely consisting of canned text):

> This analysis examines the robustness of the choice of an alternative with respect to simultaneous variations of the inter-criteria and intra-criteria preference parameters within the afore assigned intervals. The aim is to identify the most relevant preferential uncertainties, to explore their respective impact on the results and to examine whether or not the alternatives are distinguishable from each other in the light of the preferential uncertainties.

The generation of the remaining messages is much more complex. For example, in order to generate the message "Cumulative Percentage sorted by <alternative>", the following template, consisting of three main parts, is suggested:

> The lines in the diagram of the multi-dimensional sensitivity analysis, each associated with one alternative, show the overall performance scores of the (associated) alternatives in ascending order of the score of <alternative>. This means that the performance score of <alternative> is plotted versus the cumulative percentage and the other alternatives are sorted in such a way that their scores at an imaginary "perpendicular cut" through the diagram belong to the same sampled parameter combination.
> <alternative> is ranked first for <determined percentage>% of the drawn parameter combinations.
> Additionally, the diagram indicates a correlation between <alternative> and <correlated alternative>.

It should be noted that the third part of the above template is only needed in the event that a correlation is detected. However, in the context of the case study, a corresponding message generated by the explanation module in order to explain Figure 4.27 (see page 135) could be:

> The lines in the diagram of the multi-dimensional sensitivity analysis, each associated with one alternative, show the overall performance scores of the (associated) alternatives in ascending order of the score of **Rmov,T=0**. This means that the performance score of **Rmov,T=0** is plotted versus the cumulative percentage and the other alternatives are sorted in such a way that their scores at an imaginary "perpendicular cut" through the diagram belong to the same sampled parameter combination.
>
> **Rmov,T=0** is ranked first for 25 % of the drawn parameter combinations. Additionally, the diagram indicates a correlation between **Rmov,T=0**, **Rmov,T>0** and **Rduc,T=0**.

Templates for the messages "Spread of Results", "Cumulative Percentage" and "Backwards Calculation" can be defined analogously. Recapitulating, multi-dimensional sensitivity analysis reports seek to help decision makers in concentrating on the most relevant decision parameters and the most significant preferential uncertainties in terms of the results. Consequently, they can contribute to facilitate the preference elicitation process and offer valuable support for consensus finding within decision making groups.

Appendix B

Additional Data and Statistical Tests for the Case Study

The aim of this appendix is twofold: Firstly, the complete set of decision tables is presented in Section B.1, containing detailed information about the underlying data uncertainty in the case study. Secondly, a statistical procedure, allowing to test a set of data for normality, is described and applied to the set of decision tables of the case study (Section B.2).

B.1 Data Uncertainty Underlying the Calculations of the Case Study

As already described in Section 4.5, when taking data uncertainties into account within the scope of the case study, the multi-attribute decision analysis is not based on one (deterministic) decision table but on a set of decision tables since the multiple Monte Carlo runs of the ASY and CSY models within the RODOS system lead to multiple results for the consequences of the countermeasures. The tables B.1–B.10 constitute the complete set of decision tables, i.e. they represent the data uncertainty underlying the calculations of the case study. However, the entries of Table 4.5 (see page 114) were assessed by the workshop participants and not calculated by RODOS. Since a justifiable uncertainty modelling for the latter would necessitate more workshops where the participants are explicitly asked to assess values for each scenario, these values remain unchanged for the ten scenarios within this research.

Table B.1: Decision Table – Part 1 – Scenario 1

	No Action	Disp	Proc	Stor	Rmov, T=0	Rmov, T>0	Rduc, T=0	AddS+ Proc
avoided ind. ad. [mSv]	0	3.80E+0	1.28E-2	4.13E-5	7.18E-3	9.99E-4	3.51E-4	5.55E-1
avoided ind. chi. [mSv]	0	4.32E+1	2.71E-2	7.13E-4	1.01E-1	1.36E-2	5.14E-3	1.06E+0
avoided collect. [manSv]	0	1.86E+4	1.57E+3	1.24E+2	3.37E+3	2.75E+2	6.83E+2	8.02E+3
collective dose [manSv]	1.90E+4	3.33E+2	1.74E+4	1.89E+4	1.56E+4	1.87E+4	1.83E+4	1.10E+4
max. ind. work. [mSv]	0	0	0	0	3.09E-3	1.87E-3	1.93E-3	0
collect. worker [manSv]	0	0	0	0	2.25E+0	3.42E-1	3.43E-1	0
no. of workers [#]	0	0	0	0	435	329	329	0
total food above [kg]	1.50E+8	1.50E+8	1.17E+7	1.49E+8	1.07E+8	1.34E+8	1.46E+8	1.09E+7
food above yr-1 [kg]	3.41E+5	3.41E+5	1.21E+4	2.33E+5	2.33E+5	2.33E+5	2.33E+5	1.13E+4
size of aff. area [km²]	2.57E+3	2.57E+3	9.11E+2	2.57E+3	6.36E+2	2.56E+3	2.44E+3	9.11E+2

Table B.2: Decision Table – Part 1 – Scenario 2

	No Action	Disp	Proc	Stor	Rmov, T=0	Rmov, T>0	Rduc, T=0	AddS+ Proc
avoided ind. ad. [mSv]	0	3.80E-2	1.12E-2	3.04E-5	9.66E-3	7.19E-4	2.53E-4	1.29E-2
avoided ind. chi. [mSv]	0	4.32E-1	2.40E-2	5.50E-4	1.40E-1	9.84E-3	3.74E-3	2.75E-2
avoided collect. [manSv]	0	1.59E+2	6.42E+1	5.42E+0	1.13E+2	8.83E+0	7.99E+0	8.20E+1
collective dose [manSv]	1.71E+2	1.24E+2	1.07E+2	1.66E+2	5.87E+1	1.63E+2	1.63E+2	8.94E+1
max. ind. work. [mSv]	0	0	0	0	4.26E-5	3.79E-5	2.62E-5	0
collect. worker [manSv]	0	0	0	0	2.48E-2	6.42E-3	5.06E-3	0
no. of workers [#]	0	0	0	0	213	165	165	0
total food above [kg]	4.07E+6	4.07E+6	2.03E+5	3.92E+6	1.83E+6	3.30E+6	3.69E+6	1.96E+5
food above yr-1 [kg]	8.70E+3	8.70E+3	0	8.00E+3	8.01E+3	8.63E+3	8.63E+3	0
size of aff. area [km²]	2.12E+2	2.12E+2	3.59E+1	2.12E+2	2.65E+1	1.87E+2	1.44E+2	3.59E+1

Table B.3: Decision Table – Part 1 – Scenario 3

	No Action	Disp	Proc	Stor	Rmov, T=0	Rmov, T>0	Rduc, T=0	AddS+ Proc
avoided ind. ad. [mSv]	0	3.27E+0	1.37E-2	1.80E-5	4.69E-3	6.69E-4	2.18E-4	5.56E-1
avoided ind. chi. [mSv]	0	3.26E+1	3.14E-2	2.89E-4	4.95E-2	6.21E-3	2.29E-3	1.06E+0
avoided collect. [manSv]	0	1.67E+4	1.61E+3	1.06E+2	2.87E+3	2.43E+2	5.66E+2	7.72E+3
collective dose [manSv]	1.71E+4	3.50E+2	1.54E+4	1.70E+4	1.42E+4	1.68E+4	1.65E+4	9.34E+3
max. ind. work. [mSv]	0	0	0	0	4.53E-3	1.60E-3	1.75E-3	0
collect. worker [manSv]	0	0	0	0	2.70E+0	4.18E-1	4.68E-1	0
no. of workers [#]	0	0	0	0	478	390	411	0
total food above [kg]	1.80E+8	1.80E+8	1.41E+7	1.79E+8	1.42E+8	1.62E+8	1.76E+8	1.28E+7
food above yr-1 [kg]	2.69E+5	2.69E+5	2.10E+4	2.14E+5	2.14E+5	2.14E+5	2.14E+5	2.02E+4
size of aff. area [km^2]	2.67E+3	2.67E+3	7.64E+2	2.67E+3	6.04E+2	2.53E+3	2.49E+3	7.64E+2

Table B.4: Decision Table – Part 1 – Scenario 4

	No Action	Disp	Proc	Stor	Rmov, T=0	Rmov, T>0	Rduc, T=0	AddS+ Proc
avoided ind. ad. [mSv]	0	3.27E+2	1.42E-2	4.55E-5	3.88E-3	6.57E-4	2.30E-4	1.40E+2
avoided ind. chi. [mSv]	0	3.26E+3	3.12E-2	8.34E-4	4.04E-2	8.70E-3	3.31E-3	2.68E+2
avoided collect. [manSv]	0	1.85E+6	9.26E+3	2.19E+2	2.32E+5	4.68E+1	5.78E+4	7.99E+5
collective dose [manSv]	1.85E+6	5.82E+1	1.84E+6	1.85E+6	1.62E+6	1.85E+6	1.79E+6	1.05E+6
max. ind. work. [mSv]	0	0	0	0	3.97E-3	7.53E-4	8.24E-4	0
collect. worker [manSv]	0	0	0	0	3.97E-3	7.53E-4	8.24E-4	0
no. of workers [#]	0	0	0	0	110	91	97	0
total food above [kg]	5.24E+9	5.24E+9	7.30E+8	5.24E+9	5.23E+9	5.24E+9	5.24E+9	7.00E+8
food above yr-1 [kg]	1.18E+6	1.18E+6	4.99E+5	1.17E+6	1.17E+6	1.17E+6	1.17E+6	4.54E+5
size of aff. area [km²]	3.85E+3	3.85E+3	3.59E+3	3.85E+3	3.57E+3	3.85E+3	3.82E+3	3.59E+3

Table B.5: Decision Table – Part 1 – Scenario 5

	No Action	Disp	Proc	Stor	Rmov, T=0	Rmov, T>0	Rduc, T=0	AddS+ Proc
avoided ind. ad. [mSv]	0	6.03E-2	8.46E-3	5.75E-5	1.56E-2	9.96E-4	3.49E-4	1.23E-2
avoided ind. chi. [mSv]	0	6.02E-1	1.84E-2	1.06E-3	2.19E-1	1.31E-2	5.00E-3	2.62E-2
avoided collect. [manSv]	0	5.08E+2	2.04E+2	1.18E+1	3.52E+2	2.46E+1	2.45E+1	2.67E+2
collective dose [manSv]	5.37E+2	2.95E+1	3.33E+2	5.25E+2	1.85E+2	5.12E+2	5.13E+2	2.70E+2
max. ind. work. [mSv]	0	0	0	0	1.10E-4	6.92E-5	7.60E-5	0
collect. worker [manSv]	0	0	0	0	8.75E-2	1.22E-2	1.73E-2	0
no. of workers [#]	0	0	0	0	225	114	132	0
total food above [kg]	1.10E+7	1.10E+7	6.40E+5	1.09E+7	5.35E+6	9.51E+6	1.06E+7	6.21E+5
food above yr-1 [kg]	2.49E+4	2.49E+4	8.47E+1	2.46E+4	2.49E+4	2.49E+4	2.49E+4	8.47E+1
size of aff. area [km²]	4.93E+2	4.93E+2	9.36E+1	4.93E+2	7.49E+1	4.93E+2	3.37E+2	9.36E+1

Table B.6: Decision Table – Part 1 – Scenario 6

	No Action	Disp	Proc	Stor	Rmov, T=0	Rmov, T>0	Rduc, T=0	AddS+ Proc
avoided ind. ad. [mSv]	0	2.29E-2	8.09E-3	6.99E-5	6.21E-3	9.70E-4	3.37E-4	9.24E-3
avoided ind. chi. [mSv]	0	2.29E-1	1.75E-2	1.30E-3	8.69E-2	1.24E-2	4.70E-3	2.00E-2
avoided collect. [manSv]	0	2.28E+2	1.02E+2	6.51E+0	1.63E+2	1.50E+1	1.24E+1	1.26E+2
collective dose [manSv]	2.41E+2	1.24E+1	1.39E+2	2.34E+2	7.73E+1	2.26E+2	2.28E+2	1.15E+2
max. ind. work. [mSv]	0	0	0	0	4.40E-5	1.49E-5	1.15E-5	0
collect. worker [manSv]	0	0	0	0	3.54E-2	2.94E-3	3.52E-3	0
no. of workers [#]	0	0	0	0	159	87	93	0
total food above [kg]	7.49E+6	7.49E+6	3.95E+5	7.45E+6	3.69E+6	7.08E+6	7.39E+6	3.81E+5
food above yr-1 [kg]	1.94E+4	1.94E+4	0	1.94E+4	1.94E+4	1.94E+4	1.94E+4	0
size of aff. area [km²]	3.93E+2	3.93E+2	7.02E+1	3.93E+2	4.84E+1	3.93E+2	2.93E+2	7.02E+1

Table B.7: Decision Table – Part 1 – Scenario 7

	No Action	Disp	Proc	Stor	Rmov, T=0	Rmov, T>0	Rduc, T=0	AddS+ Proc
avoided ind. ad. [mSv]	0	1.66E+1	1.42E-2	1.36E-5	4.51E-3	7.10E-4	2.30E-4	2.83E+0
avoided ind. chi. [mSv]	0	1.66E+2	3.27E-2	2.44E-4	4.90E-2	6.48E-3	2.37E-3	5.41E+0
avoided collect. [manSv]	0	8.42E+4	4.63E+3	2.60E+2	1.15E+4	4.94E+2	2.74E+3	3.75E+4
collective dose [manSv]	8.49E+4	6.95E+2	8.03E+4	8.46E+4	7.34E+4	8.44E+4	8.22E+4	4.74E+4
max. ind. work. [mSv]	0	0	0	0	3.91E-3	3.03E-3	3.30E-3	0
collect. worker [manSv]	0	0	0	0	1.79E+0	3.98E-1	4.33E-1	0
no. of workers [#]	0	0	0	0	370	297	303	0
total food above [kg]	8.03E+8	8.03E+8	4.64E+7	8.03E+8	7.47E+8	7.75E+8	7.97E+8	3.95E+7
food above yr-1 [kg]	6.75E+5	6.75E+5	7.27E+4	5.62E+5	5.62E+5	5.62E+5	5.62E+5	6.28E+4
size of aff. area [km²]	3.97E+3	3.97E+3	2.19E+3	3.97E+3	1.68E+3	3.97E+3	3.96E+3	2.19E+3

Table B.8: Decision Table – Part 1 – Scenario 8

	No Action	Disp	Proc	Stor	Rmov, T=0	Rmov, T>0	Rduc, T=0	AddS+ Proc
avoided ind. ad. [mSv]	0	3.06E+0	1.26E-2	6.77E-5	1.15E-2	6.97E-4	2.28E-4	5.19E-1
avoided ind. chi. [mSv]	0	3.05E+1	2.80E-2	1.25E-3	1.61E-1	6.41E-3	2.37E-3	9.94E-1
avoided collect. [manSv]	0	2.24E+4	1.34E+3	6.96E+1	3.55E+3	3.85E+1	7.34E+2	9.71E+3
collective dose [manSv]	2.24E+4	5.13E+1	2.11E+4	2.24E+4	1.89E+4	2.24E+4	2.17E+4	1.27E+4
max. ind. work. [mSv]	0	0	0	0	6.83E-3	2.11E-4	2.32E-4	0
collect. worker [manSv]	0	0	0	0	1.21E+0	8.12E-2	9.10E-2	0
no. of workers [#]	0	0	0	0	218	120	130	0
total food above [kg]	1.12E+8	1.12E+8	1.49E+7	1.12E+8	9.43E+7	1.10E+8	1.12E+8	1.32E+7
food above yr-1 [kg]	1.86E+5	1.86E+5	2.60E+4	1.80E+5	1.80E+5	1.80E+5	1.80E+5	2.40E+4
size of aff. area [km²]	2.23E+3	2.23E+3	9.55E+2	2.23E+3	7.50E+2	2.20E+3	2.10E+3	9.55E+2

Table B.9: Decision Table – Part 1 – Scenario 9

	No Action	Disp	Proc	Stor	Rmov, T=0	Rmov, T>0	Rduc, T=0	AddS+ Proc
avoided ind. ad. [mSv]	0	1.59E+3	1.43E-2	2.51E-5	4.49E-3	5.86E-4	1.90E-4	6.82E+2
avoided ind. chi. [mSv]	0	1.59E+4	3.23E-2	4.37E-4	6.46E-2	5.20E-3	1.91E-3	1.30E+3
avoided collect. [manSv]	0	5.00E+6	1.49E+3	2.35E+1	5.25E+5	2.70E+1	1.31E+5	2.41E+6
collective dose [manSv]	5.00E+6	3.31E+1	4.99E+6	5.00E+6	4.47E+6	5.00E+6	4.87E+6	2.58E+6
max. ind. work. [mSv]	0	0	0	0	4.65E-3	6.34E-4	6.93E-4	0
collect. worker [manSv]	0	0	0	0	1.15E-1	1.05E-2	1.14E-2	0
no. of workers [#]	0	0	0	0	96	60	60	0
total food above [kg]	6.54E+9	6.54E+9	1.83E+9	6.54E+9	6.53E+9	6.54E+9	6.54E+9	1.77E+9
food above yr-1 [kg]	9.01E+5	9.01E+5	7.86E+5	8.90E+5	8.90E+5	8.90E+5	8.90E+5	6.24E+5
size of aff. area [km²]	3.33E+3	3.33E+3	3.10E+3	3.33E+3	3.09E+3	3.33E+3	3.33E+3	3.10E+3

Table B.10: Decision Table – Part 1 – Scenario 10

	No Action	Disp	Proc	Stor	Rmov, T=0	Rmov, T>0	Rduc, T=0	AddS+ Proc
avoided ind. ad. [mSv]	0	3.85E+0	1.40E-2	1.83E-5	8.22E-3	6.19E-4	2.00E-4	6.53E-1
avoided ind. chi. [mSv]	0	3.83E+1	3.20E-2	3.01E-4	1.15E-1	5.65E-3	2.08E-3	1.25E+0
avoided collect. [manSv]	0	2.21E+4	1.77E+3	1.60E+2	3.89E+3	1.82E+2	7.51E+2	9.88E+3
collective dose [manSv]	2.24E+4	2.46E+2	2.06E+4	2.22E+4	1.85E+4	2.22E+4	2.16E+4	1.25E+4
max. ind. work. [mSv]	0	0	0	0	4.61E-3	7.13E-4	7.77E-4	0
collect. worker [manSv]	0	0	0	0	1.99E+0	2.33E-1	2.52E-1	0
no. of workers [#]	0	0	0	0	407	304	308	0
total food above [kg]	1.72E+8	1.72E+8	1.42E+7	1.71E+8	1.27E+8	1.61E+8	1.69E+8	1.29E+7
food above yr-1 [kg]	3.03E+5	3.03E+5	1.64E+4	2.81E+5	2.81E+5	2.81E+5	2.81E+5	1.58E+4
size of aff. area [km^2]	2.57E+3	2.57E+3	9.17E+2	2.57E+3	8.25E+2	2.54E+3	2.39E+3	9.17E+2

B.2   A Statistical Test for the Data of the Case Study

The propagation of uncertainties through a complex model chain, such as in RODOS, is a challenging task in practice [O'Hagan and Oakley, 2004]. When describing the uncertainties by means of probability, the distributions of the high-dimensional input data are subject to a number of nonlinear transformations while being propagated through the model chain. In general, Monte Carlo simulation allows to consistently propagate uncertainties of the input data through large model chains but it is nevertheless hardly possible to make a statement about the probability distributions of the simulated consequences in the decision table (or rather the set of decision tables). Thus, a statistical procedure is described in the following: the W test introduced by Shapiro and Wilk [1965]. This procedure is suitable to analyse if the data in the set of decision tables presented in Section B.1 is normally distributed. It has been chosen instead of the often used χ^2 test [cf. e.g. Roussas, 1973; Büning, 1991] since it performs considerably better for small sample sizes [cf. R. B. D'Agostino and M. A. Stephens, 1986]. A major drawback concerning the W test of Shapiro and Wilk [1965] is its high computational effort but since the sample size in the case study is quite small, this drawback is negligible. While the procedure of the test is described in Section B.2.1, its application to the data of the case study is presented in Section B.2.2.

B.2.1   Procedure of the W Test

The W test consists in testing the *null hypothesis* that a vector of ordered random observations $y = (y_1, ..., y_\nu)$ is a sample from a normal distribution with unknown mean μ and unknown variance σ^2. For this, let $e = (e_1, ..., e_\nu)$ denote the vector of *expected values of standard normal order statistics* and let $V = (v_{kl})$ be the $\nu \times \nu$ covariance matrix corresponding to e. This means that, if $x_1 \leq ... \leq x_\nu$ denotes an ordered random sample of size ν from a standard normal distribution (with mean 0 and variance 1), the *expected values of standard normal order statistics* and the corresponding covariance matrix can be obtained as follows [Shapiro and Wilk, 1965]:

$$e_k = E(x_k) \quad (k = 1, ..., \nu), \tag{B.1}$$

$$v_{kl} = cov(x_k, x_l) \quad (k, l = 1, ..., \nu). \tag{B.2}$$

The test statistic W, testing the random observations y for normality, is then defined by

$$W = \frac{\left(\sum\limits_{k=1}^{\nu} a_k y_k\right)^2}{\sum\limits_{k=1}^{\nu} (y_k - \bar{y})^2}, \tag{B.3}$$

where $\bar{y}$ is the mean of the random observations $(y_1, ..., y_\nu)$ and the coefficients $a_1, ..., a_\nu$ are given by

$$(a_1, ..., a_\nu) = \frac{eV^{-1}}{(eV^{-1}V^{-1}e^T)^{\frac{1}{2}}}. \tag{B.4}$$

If y is normally distributed, the numerator and the denominator of W are both estimating the same value (up to a constant): σ^2. For non-normally distributed y, the numerator and the denominator would in general not be estimating the same quantity [Shapiro and Wilk, 1965].

It should be emphasised that the null hypothesis (that y is normally distributed) can be rejected but not corroborated by the W test: small values of W are significant (i.e. indicate non-normality) but large values do not indicate normality. However, for values of ν between 2 and 50, the coefficients a_i as well as different levels of significance are given in Shapiro and Wilk [1965].

B.2.2   Application of the W Test to the Data of the Case Study

In order to calculate the test statistic W for the case study, let now W_{ij} denote the test statistic corresponding to the consequence of the jth alternative ($1 \leq j \leq m$) with respect to the ith attribute ($1 \leq i \leq n$). The coefficients a_i for $\nu = 10$ are taken from Shapiro and Wilk [1965]. The results are compiled in Table B.11.

According to Shapiro and Wilk [1965], the rejection of the hypothesis of normally distributed data is significant at the 5 % level if $W_{ij} < 0.842$ (for $\nu = 10$). This means that, if $W_{ij} < 0.842$, the probability of an error of the first kind (i.e. the hypothesis of normally distributed data is rejected although it is true) is smaller than 5 %.

Table B.11 shows that the hypothesis of normality can be rejected for most of the consequences (at the 5 % level). Taking the logarithm of the case study data and subsequently applying the W test (i.e. investigating whether the data is log-normally distributed) leads to less rejections of the hypothesis but the hypothesis can still be rejected for many consequences. It can thus not be significantly concluded that the data in the set of decision tables are normally or log-normally distributed. For a large part of the simulated conse-

Table B.11: Results for the Test Statistics W_{ij} (All Values in the Table are Dimensionless)

W_{ij}	No Action	Disp	Proc	Stor	Rmov, T=0	Rmov, T>0	Rduc, T=0	AddS+ Proc
avoided ind. ad.	-	0.4643	0.7925	0.9112	0.8821	0.8083	0.8186	0.4609
avoided ind. chi.	-	0.4644	0.8307	0.9042	0.9200	0.8612	0.8564	0.4609
avoided collect.	-	0.5200	0.7195	0.8978	0.5382	0.7916	0.5370	0.5093
collective dose	0.5201	0.3060	0.5191	0.5201	0.5177	0.5201	0.5196	0.5289
max. ind. work.	-	-	-	-	0.5415	0.2331	0.2608	-
collect. worker	-	-	-	-	0.8204	0.7826	0.7996	-
no. of workers	-	-	-	-	0.9065	0.8694	0.8857	-
total food above	0.5828	0.5828	0.5281	0.5828	0.5802	0.5815	0.5825	0.5261
food above yr-1	0.8689	0.8689	0.5992	0.8315	0.8316	0.8313	0.8313	0.6020
size of aff. area	0.8815	0.8815	0.8473	0.8815	0.8099	0.8850	0.8841	0.8473

quences in the decision tables, it can actually be significantly concluded that the values are not normally or log-normally distributed.

Consequently, it is not advisable to apply methods presupposing normal or log-normal distributions of the data. In the context of the case study, methods based on discrete empirical distributions should be used instead, as demonstrated when calculating the expected utilities (cf. Section 4.5 and Section 4.6).